SARDINE

Simple, seasonal, southern French cooking

Alex Jackson

PAVILION

CONTENTS

DÚN LAOGHAIRE-RATHDOWN LIBRARIES

DLR27000054864	
BERTRAMS	09/12/2019
GP	02451672

SOUTHERN FRENCH COOKING

We opened Sardine in the summer of 2016 after spying a gap in London's restaurant market. Southern French cooking was underrepresented in the capital, so we decided to open a neighbourhood restaurant serving simple, homely food from Provence and the Languedoc. We've been lucky to have many kind words said about us, but one comment has stuck with me: that eating at Sardine was 'like meeting with an old friend, who you hadn't realised you missed as much as you did.' I am too young to remember the first Provençal love-in and, at first, I was oblivious to the fact that the 'old friend' had since been forgotten.

Peter Mayle's *A Year in Provence*, published in 1989, sold a million copies in the UK alone and brought a largely unknown region to the attention of hordes of red-trousered Englishmen keen to experience its rustic charms. Served at every nineties dinner party, Provençal food was suddenly the thing: pissaladière, stuffed vegetables, salade Niçoise, ratatouille, herbes de Provence with everything. All these dishes are classics, obviously, but have been done to death in a thousand botched efforts to impress.

All too soon the public ended their love affair with Provence and turned their attention to other climes. The publication of a certain *The River Cafe Cook Book* in 1995 coincided with, or perhaps began, our obsession with regional Italian cuisine. Simplicity, authenticity and attention to detail were the tenets to cook by and, above all, the most important thing was the quality and provenance of ingredients: a bottle of new season's extra virgin olive oil, a tin of salted anchovies, proper dried porcini, a tomato that actually tastes of something. And rightly so! But what we seem to have forgotten is that the food of Provence is, and always has been, very closely linked to the rustic cooking of rural Italy and Spain: one man's *soupe au pistou* is another's *minestrone con pesto*; Sardinian *bottarga*

is *poutarge* from the Camargue; the famous Ligurian *farinata* is the proud Niçois *socca*; and anyway, just how different, really, is *alioli* from *aïoli*?

Provence and the Languedoc are France's window onto the Mediterranean Sea and all that lies beyond. The culinary influences that converge there make for a cuisine that is varied, rich and deep. These regions stand apart from the rest of French cuisine. There is something altogether lighter, more exotic and, dare I say it, more Italian about the whole thing. In Lyon, the gastronomic capital of France, some 300km north of the Provençal coast, butter remains the cooking fat of choice while further into the south west, it's the land of duck fat. In Provence and the Languedoc, however, there's olive oil. The Greeks brought the olive tree to Provence over 8,000 years ago and it is, perhaps, the olive that anchors the region to the rest of the Mediterranean with olive oil remaining the basis, and sometimes even the focus, of its cooking.

My interest in southern French cooking started a long time ago. I'm from the distinctly unglamorous city of Birmingham – not considered to be one of the great food cities of the world – but luckily I grew up in the era of the nineties dinner party and my Mum owned a formidable cookbook collection. It was also the age of the summer holiday to the South of France – the Tarn region of the Languedoc, to be specific – and as a kid, it was the start of an appreciation of that part of France that has stayed with me. I remember our morning trips to the village *boulangerie* and what was, to a British sensibility, an intoxicating smell of a hundred baguettes fresh from the oven. I'd be made to order the bread in nervous French. (I suppose those were my first steps that led to studying French at university later on.) We enjoyed that children's favourite – and, let's admit it, adults' too – of steak haché, <u>pink</u> in the middle. And on some forgotten D-road, we discovered a now mythical roadside van serving an absolutely blinding steak, chips and mustard on a paper plate, which we ate at a plastic table next to the car.

Already a keen cook, as part of my French degree at university, I moved to Paris for a year. This was ostensibly to study, but in reality it was to drink rough red wine and attempt to chat up French girls. Our daily ritual was to decamp to the cheapest of the cafés, find a decent outward-facing table, order a coffee and watch the locals go by with their shopping.

In the 'Maison de Jambon', as it was called, hung legs of Parma's finest and, in the winter, a huge sign was pasted onto the window: LES TRUFFES BLANCHES D'ITALIE SONT ARRIVÉES'. We didn't have the money for white truffles, but once a week we'd go to the market on the Avenue de Saxe, the Eiffel Tower looming high at the end of the street, and walk up and down inspecting the produce. We'd buy a whole rabbit, because we'd never made *lapin à la moutarde*, to be cooked in a tiny electrical oven that hung off the wall of our apartment. We'd pick up a big bunch of spinach to go with some gnocchi, blue cheese and walnuts, to be eaten on a freezing cold night. Baby squid and fennel would accompany a plate of orecchiette with breadcrumbs and herbs. Oysters and Champagne would celebrate some occasional small victory or other. A ripe, raw milk Camembert would be stuck with garlic, soused with white wine and baked, gloriously drunk, in the oven.

From the odd casual meal out, it struck us how easy it was to eat very well in Paris for relatively little money and we were determined to profit from it. These meals were inevitably at a tiny restaurant with a one-man, everything-within-reach kitchen. After a free Kir while you waited to be seated, cold prawns and mayonnaise, then *gésiers en salade*, then duck confit with lentils, were washed down with a bottle of house red.

In retrospect, living in Paris during my early twenties served as an introduction to authentic, rustic French food. Soon enough I got the opportunity to practise the French country cooking I had only read about. Although I vowed to live in Paris again, I've yet to return. I moved to London and fell into my first restaurant job at Stevie Parle's Dock Kitchen. It's fair to say, Stevie took a punt on someone with bags of enthusiasm but absolutely no experience, and he was willing to put up with a split mayonnaise or two. At the start, there was a single cook at Dock Kitchen. He turned up late every day and wrote the menu on the spot. I would set up the restaurant with record speed so I had time to get involved in the cooking. I soon came to realise that I should give the chef thing a shot.

In the early days of Dock Kitchen, we cooked set menus for dinner that changed weekly. The themes of these menus ranged from a certain season to a specific ingredient or to a particular cuisine. The first set menu that I got to write was a Provençal-themed one. We cooked an artichoke salad with walnuts and cream, then a chickpea and sausage soup with aïoli, followed by roast quails with spinach and anchovy butter. Some sort of disastrous attempt at a sweetened fougasse was served for dessert. Three decent courses out of four still counts as a success, I think. Of the different cuisines we focused on, I found a certain romance in the cooking of the South of France. It may be that there is simply a wealth of fantastic writing on the subject: from the chapter in Elizabeth David's *French Provincial Cooking* to Leslie Forbe's gorgeously illustrated *A Table in Provence*, and anything and everything Chez Panisse. The seminal *Lulu's Provençal Table* by Richard Olney is a great source of inspiration, and on several occasions we cooked menus drawn from its pages. But as well as having this wonderful library of cookbooks, we were lucky to be able to make several trips to explore the food firsthand.

A visit to any market in the region confirms that the Provençal people really are a lucky bunch. I'm not too comfortable in the heat, but the vegetables love it. Here, the market stalls groan with sun-kissed produce. In Aix-en-Provence there's a market every day in the main square by the town hall, where olive oil producers, jam makers and cheesemongers jostle for space alongside no less than twenty fruit and vegetable stalls. There's the old chap (who's either deaf or indifferent to English-accented French) with a selection of home-grown produce: a jumble of perfect green beans, a stack of misshapen courgettes, a few jars of honey and a crate of jammy Reine Claude plums attracting the wasps. Elsewhere there are piles of herbs in flower – wild thyme, winter savory, rosemary, marjoram, chervil, parsley and basil – a fast-disappearing box of fresh Coco de Paimpol beans, and a bowl of proper pre-cooked chickpeas to sling into soups. There are farmhouse goats' cheeses topped with wild herbs, punnets of ruinously expensive black figs, and black truffle and wild boar sausages, cut with a bone-handled knife by a man wearing a beret. There are tight-headed lettuces, purslane, sweet white salad onions, gorgeous bunches of green sorrel. And the tomatoes! There are at least twelve different varieties of tomato to be found, all *ancienne et indigène Provençal*: huge yellow-tinged *Coeur de Boeuf*; deep, purplish-black *Noir de Crimée*; and the kilo-heavy, juice-laden, deep red *Catalane*. You get the idea.

The consistent supply of local fruit and vegetables has a huge influence on the cooking in these parts. Confronted with a basket of impeccable veg, a fistful of wild herbs and a bottle of good olive oil, the Provençal cook belongs to Club Med (no, not that one). There's no need for the overwrought, heavy, cream-laden sauces for which France is most famous, but instead a happy understanding of how to cook simply, with the seasons, and with respect for the ingredients at hand. In this way, I see a lot of similarities between southern French cooking and that of its neighbouring regions: Catalonia, Liguria, the Basque Country, Corsica and Piedmont, and further afield, to Tuscany, Sicily, Greece and beyond.

Sardine is a restaurant with a focus on the food of Provence, but acts as a prism for the sun-drenched cooking of the whole Mediterranean Sea and the common thread that runs through it.

I hope that in some ways Sardine is different. We cook food that was originally popularised decades ago, a cuisine that in many ways is considered passé. There are no 'small plates' (although there is, I concede, a communal table). One could level the criticism that the cooking at Sardine is old-fashioned, but I would take that as a compliment. Our food, I hope, is more farmhouse than fine dining and, in this respect, there shouldn't be anything within these pages that will worry the confident home cook. What I really would like to impress upon the reader is that cooking the food of the South of France is about simplicity, good ingredients and a generosity of spirit. Regardless of modern tastes, for me the appeal of Provençal cooking has always been obvious. The food is vibrant, colourful and exotic, and it has been incredibly rewarding to rediscover a forgotten classic.

HOW WE COOK

The cooking in our restaurant, Sardine, is really no different to home cooking. There are no water baths, Thermomixes or other niche gadgets. Our only specialist equipment is a barbecue. We don't do fancy presentation – by which I mean all those swooshes, towers and swirls – because I don't really know how to do that and, anyway, I think a plate of food looks better a little simpler and more (dare I say it) *rustique*. This might give further ammunition to the 'I could have made it at home' brigade – those who begrudge a simple approach from the restaurant cook and would rather we spent all day torturing birds into ballotines and the like, rather than just roasting the bloody thing – but phooey, I say it's far better to concentrate on some intelligent shopping and then to *faire simple*.

Seasonal vegetables, I would say, exert the biggest influence on what we decide to cook and when. Word of the first tomatoes from the Amalfi Coast or earliest proper English strawberries prompts the *à la carte* menu to pivot to incorporate the new season's must-haves. If an addition means something else on the menu must change to avoid repetition, then so be it. Thus we keep ourselves busy, constantly evolving and improvising dishes to suit the season, the weather and our mood. It's a great way to cook, and keeps our food full of energy and interest. I find our choice of meat or fish for the menu is often dictated first and foremost by whichever vegetables are eating well at that moment. Many of my favourite dishes have come about through happy coincidence. Last year, at the peak of tomato season, a sudden drop in the usually ludicrous price of wild sea bass coincided with one of hottest weeks of the year. The tomatoes were too good to warrant any complicated cooking, the fish was so tasty all it needed was to be grilled plain, then a blob of aïoli and a handful of basil seemed only sensible. A dish was born! Nothing new, nothing fancy, but delicious nonetheless.

One of the major frustrations for the homely cook turned professional is that some dishes just don't work in a restaurant. A whole leg of lamb, roasted slowly over a fire, serves around ten people. If I roast two legs and have eleven orders, well, that's a lot of leftover lamb to get through the next day. That large line-caught turbot can't be roasted whole as nature intended, but must be painstakingly portioned, carefully stored and cooked individually to order. What a faff. There's a certain satisfaction in cooking a set menu in a restaurant. It opens up many options – large format dishes, whole fish and joints of meat, more complicated processes, economies of scale and, above all, a feeling that, somehow, this is the way that eating is supposed to be.

In that spirit, once a month at Sardine we cook a *Grande Bouffe*, which loosely translates as 'Big Feast'. It's a chance to cook a set menu based around a certain theme, be it a cookbook we love, an irresistible ingredient, a particular point in the season or one of the famous French feasts. It's also an exercise in composition, a challenge to ensure that the menu reads beautifully, flows right and eats even better. Plus it's an opportunity to shoehorn the best ingredients of the moment into one evening's cooking. In those sections within this book, I have included notes on how these *Grande Bouffe* menus went down on the night in the restaurant, but these menus work very well, better even, at home. From *bouillabaisse* and *le grande aïoli* to *aligot* and *pot-au-feu*, most of these menus revolve around a central celebratory dish framed by several more courses. An evening would be slightly less work, but no less a success, if one were to cut a course or two.

ON AUTHENTICITY

Irving Davis's seminal *A Catalan Cookery Book* is subtitled 'A Collection of Impossible Recipes'. It's filled with terse instruction that barely conceals the author's contempt for anyone attempting a recipe. Fantastic! A taste of the truly authentic, the poetic, the romantic. But what constitutes romance in a recipe? We are allured, perhaps, by the unattainable. In this instance, this is surely bundled up in the sense of place, and Irving Davis's cynicism is born out of a respect for what is truly local to the recipes: an indigenous rockfish, an earthenware cooking pot, or a fire made from cuttings from the family vineyard. I'm sure he would hate the fact that I have cooked from his book. While I could never have hoped to achieve the absolute authenticity demanded on its pages, inspired by the ideal I cooked merrily away; transported, despite my efforts, to the coast of Catalonia. Best, I would contest, to happily ignore Mr. Davis's protestations. In this modern, globalised age, it is enough to recognise what true authenticity is: to learn one's lessons, and then, where appropriate, to disregard them.

What does this mean for the aspiring Provençal cook? I, for one, have been seduced by its charms, but it's important to note that, in reality, the Provence of Peter Mayle, Richard Olney and Robert Carrier exists mainly on the pages of their books. A visit to Provence, for all but the impossibly fortunate, is bound to frustrate: where can this perfectly rustic cooking be found? There's some excellent cooking to be found at the high end of the spectrum, and romance abounds for those who can afford it, but short of knocking on farmhouse doors, it's difficult to piece it all together. I've had some wonderful meals in Provence – some affordable, and some not – but I've had a few shockers too.

Better maybe to stick to the books in the first place. Unless one is lucky enough to bag an invite to Richard Olney's house for lunch, the reality is that the rustic cooking described by my favourite writers is hard to find. But this matters not. Authentic Provençal cooking is attainable anywhere. It requires only a basketful of proper ingredients, a light touch and a healthy pinch of enthusiasm.

SPRING

Winter in Britain is long and lingering – we pine for a glint of sunlight, a shimmer of something green and sweet to haul us out of hibernation. But spring arrives to the South of France at a proper time of year, and as those first tendrils reach their way across the Channel, there is, finally, relief for the long-suffering cook. While the British weather makes up its mind, we can pounce upon the first green podded pulses and we can gorge upon hop shoots, nettles, bitter weeds and sweet lettuces. It's a time of year for wild, strong-tasting ingredients – garlic from the woods, wild asparagus plucked from the hillsides, and the first morels and *mousserons* from the fields.

The spring produce arrives all at once, in a thrilling rush – there are even bloody courgettes (zucchini), for god's sake. Courgette flowers! It's all too much. Spring is a wonderful time of year, a moment of renewal, a chance to start over, afresh. For the Provençal cook it brings a first look at some of the ingredients that write its signature – the most expensive Gariguette strawberries, sitting pretty in their little *barquettes*; the finest asparagus, green, white and purple, to eat simply with salted butter; little peas and broad beans for soups, dandelions for salads and the first fragrant basil, a hint of the hot, long summer to come.

For the home cook it's a relief to move away from the slowly boiled and the braised, and towards the fresh, the simple, the quick, the delicious. It's less about elaborate recipes than careful shopping, and at this time of year there are simple menus that write themselves: deep-fried courgette flowers with fresh cheese; a salad of all sorts of wild and green leaves; some fish with grilled asparagus and olives, perhaps; and a bowl of strawberries with nothing on them. See, look, I just made that one up on the spot.

SOCCA WITH ARTICHOKES

Serves 4

200g/7oz/2¼ cups Italian chickpea
flour (farina di ceci)

1 tbsp olive oil, plus extra for frying

4 small artichokes

A sprig of rosemary, leaves picked

Parmesan cheese, to finish (optional)

Sea salt and freshly ground black
pepper

After *panisse*, *socca* is the most famous Niçois chickpea snack. A crispy crêpe made from chickpea flour and baked in special pans in a wood oven, socca is akin to the Ligurian *farinata* and very moreish. It's simple to make, even if you don't have a wood oven to hand. The batter always works best when made the night before. From time to time, I like to add ingredients to the socca batter: rosemary, thyme, artichokes, broad beans, cheese, or all of the above. Here's a version with artichokes and rosemary.

——————————

Sieve the chickpea flour into a large bowl and then slowly whisk in 360ml/ 12fl oz/1½ cups cold water, taking care to beat out any lumps. Whisk in the olive oil. The batter should now be the thickness of single (light) cream. Leave to stand, covered, in the refrigerator overnight.

Preheat an overhead grill (broiler).

To prepare the artichokes, remove the tough outer leaves by snapping them off with your thumb and forefinger. Remove more leaves until what is left seems paler and tender to the touch. Cut the top 1cm/½ inch off the artichoke, at the point where you see the artichoke changing colour from purple to yellow. You might need to cut off some of the stalk – usually anything more than 5cm/ 2 inches away from the head is too tough. Using a paring knife or a vegetable peeler, trim the stalk of any tough dark green bits. Cut the artichoke in half and remove the choke (the fuzzy centre). Slice lengthways into fine strips. Keep the prepared artichokes in lemon water until ready to use.

When ready to eat, drain the artichokes and season them with salt.

Place a non-stick frying pan (skillet) over a high heat until it is very hot. Add an even depth of around 1mm/¹⁄₃₂ inch of olive oil to cover the whole pan. As the oil begins to smoke, slowly pour in the chickpea batter. The layer of batter should be no more than 2mm/¹⁄₁₆ inch deep, like a thick crêpe. The oil will fizz up and start to make bubbles around the outside of the batter. Scatter the artichokes over the top of the socca along with the rosemary leaves. Cook for 1 minute over a medium heat to crisp up the bottom of the socca.

Remove the pan from the heat and place it under the hot grill. Grill the socca until golden brown and crispy on top, but still a bit soft inside. It may catch slightly in places, but this is to be encouraged.

Slice the socca into strips straight from the pan. Grate over some Parmesan, if desired, then sprinkle with flakes of salt and grind over black pepper. Eat hot.

GRILLED SARDINES WITH CUCUMBER SALAD & HARISSA

Serves 4

12 sardines, fresh, whole, scaled and
gutted – as many as you fancy, but
I recommend at least 3 per person

Olive oil

1 tsp fennel seeds, toasted slowly and
roughly ground

4 small cucumbers (Italian, Lebanese
or Turkish, for preference)

Lemon juice

A big handful of chopped mint

Sea salt and freshly ground black
pepper

Flatbreads, to serve (optional)

For the harissa (this makes too much
but it keeps well in the refrigerator):

4 fat garlic cloves, peeled

100g/3½oz medium red chillies,
deseeded and any white removed

150g/5¼oz tomatoes, halved

1 tsp cumin seeds

1 tsp caraway seeds

1 tsp red wine vinegar

2 tsp olive oil

Salt, to taste

This extremely simple recipe is a taste of North Africa, where they grill sardines probably better than anybody. Sometimes the fish are rubbed in a fragrant *chermoula* made with fresh coriander (cilantro), parsley, green chillies and garlic. I would not dissuade you from doing the same, although I would say that this assembly is very nice as it is. The sardines are grilled, the harissa is hot, the cucumber is cool. What's not to like? This makes a very satisfying lunch, perhaps with the addition of some grilled flatbreads to soak up the juices.

———————

First, make the harissa. Preheat the oven to 170°C fan/190°C/375°F/gas mark 5. Roast 3 of the garlic cloves, three-quarters of the chillies and all of the tomatoes in the oven for 25 minutes, or until soft and beginning to blacken.

Meanwhile, toast the spices slowly in a heavy-based pan until they release their aromas but are not bitter or burnt. Grind the toasted spices in a pestle and mortar. Add the remaining garlic clove and a pinch of salt to the ground spices, then crush to a fine paste.

When the garlic, chillies and tomatoes are roasted, put them in a blender with the spice paste and the remaining raw chillies. Blitz very well, add the vinegar and olive oil once smooth, then season with salt.

The harissa should be very spicy, but not so spicy that you can't actually eat it. On occasion, the heat of the chillies takes me by surprise. If this happens to you, add a little more tomato to cool things down. This recipe will likely make more harissa than you are going to need to accompany the sardines, but it keeps well when stored in the refrigerator.

When ready to eat, build a charcoal fire under a grill. Light the fire, then wait until the flames have died down but the embers are still white hot. Rub the sardines with olive oil and sprinkle with salt, pepper and the ground fennel seeds. Place the sardines over the hot charcoal and grill for a couple of minutes on each side. If serving with flatbreads, lightly grill them too.

Meanwhile, using a vegetable peeler, cut the cucumbers into long ribbons. Dress the cucumber ribbons with a good squeeze of lemon juice, some olive oil, the chopped mint and a pinch of salt.

Serve the grilled sardines with the cucumber salad, harissa and flatbreads, if preferred.

PISSALADIÈRE

Makes 1 large tart (enough for a party)

2 tbsp olive oil, plus extra for drizzling

500g/1lb 2oz white onions, thinly
    sliced

A nice thyme sprig, leaves picked

A small pinch of fine salt

8 salted anchovy fillets, sliced
    carefully in half lengthways

8–12 black olives, pitted (Provençal
    Nyons or Italian Taggiasche,
    for preference)

Freshly ground black pepper

For the pastry:

130g/4½oz/1 cup plain
    (all-purpose) flour

80g/2¾oz/5½ tbsp unsalted butter

A small pinch of fine salt

Pissaladière is much more than the sum of its parts. To call it 'onion tart with anchovies and olives' somehow underplays it. The sweet, white onions with the salty, fishy fillets work so well on top of buttery, flaky pastry. I have heard many arguments for the use of puff pastry for a pissaladière, and I have even tasted a few pizza-like numbers made with semolina flour, but for me a shortcrust does the job perfectly. I make mine very buttery. Shortcrust tends slightly to fall apart while you are eating it, but I think that rather adds to the fun.

This tart derives its name from the Niçois *pissalat*, a concoction of salted anchovies, cloves, thyme, bay and pepper, left to marinate to a mulch – almost like a Roman *garum* or Thai fish sauce – then topped with olive oil. The *pissalat* would be brushed over the top of a freshly baked tart to add a whack of fishy funk. I haven't – yet – gone so far as to make my own *pissalat*, partly because it might stink out my home, but I make do nicely with some good-quality salted anchovy fillets criss-crossed on top.

The best onions for a pissaladière are expensive small white onions from Italy and France, not a spring onion, but sweet and delicate nonetheless. When cooked very slowly in olive oil, they are remarkably mild, even sweeter and strangely delicious for something so simple. These are sometimes hard to find in Britain, but I have substituted large yellow Spanish onions with great success. It strikes me that this tart would be just as wonderful when the anchovies and olives are replaced by some cheese – a little crumbled Cantal, Cheddar, Gruyère, Lancashire, or the like.

———

First, cook the onions. Heat the olive oil in a heavy-based pan over a low heat and add the sliced onions along with the thyme leaves. Add a small pinch of fine salt to help the onions cook, but don't overdo it or the tart will be too salty with the addition of the anchovies and olives. Put a tight-fitting lid on the pan and sweat the onions very slowly and gently over a low heat for at least an hour and a half, until they are very sweet and soft to the point of collapse. It's very important that the onions are cooked slowly and take on absolutely no colour at this stage, otherwise they will burn when the tart is baked. Tip the onions out of the pan, spread them over a flat tray, and allow them to cool completely.

To make the pastry, sift the flour into a large bowl. With your hands, rub in the butter until the mixture resembles fine breadcrumbs, although a few larger lumps of butter are fine. Add a pinch of fine salt and then sprinkle over 1 tbsp cold water, or just enough to bring the pastry together. Knead the dough briefly until it is smooth and incorporated. Mould the pastry dough roughly into a rectangular block; this will make it easier to roll out later. Wrap the pastry in clingfilm (plastic wrap) and chill in the refrigerator for at least 1 hour.

Preheat the oven to 180°C fan/200°C/400°F/gas mark 6.

Once the pastry has rested, roll it out on parchment paper to a rectangle 2mm/ ¹⁄₁₆ inch thick. I find it is easiest to roll out the pastry between two sheets of parchment paper; this way requires little to no extra flour and gives a mess-free, even result. While rolling, peel back and flip over the parchment paper from time to time to avoid it sticking. It's good to flip both the pastry and the paper in contact with it on a regular basis. If it seems to be getting too warm, return the rolled-out pastry to the refrigerator on the parchment paper. The colder the pastry is before baking, the flakier the result will be.

Drain the onions of any excess liquid to avoid soggy pastry. Leaving a 2-cm/1-inch border all the way round the edge, spread the onions in a thin but comprehensive layer over the pastry. Arrange the anchovies in a criss-cross pattern over the onions and then place a pitted olive in the centre of each resultant diamond. Use the tines of a fork to press a pattern into the pastry border. Drizzle the whole tart lightly with olive oil.

Meanwhile, place a heavy flat baking tray in the oven to preheat for 5 minutes. Slide the tart, still on its parchment paper, onto the hot tray. Return to the oven and bake the tart for 15–20 minutes, or until the onions have started to colour and the pastry looks golden brown underneath when lifted with a spatula.

Slide the cooked tart onto a chopping board, grind over a little black pepper, and allow to cool. Serve the pissaladière just warm or at room temperature.

NETTLE SPAGHETTI
WITH NETTLES & CREAM

Serves 2

A plastic bag crammed full of nettle
tips, picked and washed well,
weighing approximately 250g/
8¾oz (but who takes their scales
along when foraging?)

1 whole egg

2 egg yolks

150g/5¼oz/1 cup Italian 00 flour

150g/5¼oz/1 cup semolina flour,
plus extra for dusting

50g/1¾oz/½ stick unsalted butter

25g/1oz Parmesan cheese

1 tbsp crème fraîche

Extra virgin olive oil

Freshly ground black pepper

Herbaceous, foraged, young nettle tips are both delicious and free: the
ultimate pick-your-own spring ingredient. Making green pasta is very
satisfying and easier than you might think. This recipe includes eggs for
richness, but also semolina flour for bite. I have bought a chitarra pasta
cutter online, for making straight spaghetti at home. I recommend it as the
noodles have a rough texture that's hard to replicate. Alternatively make
thin noodles like tagliatelle or, better still, tagliolini with a pasta maker.

───────────

Bring a pan of salted water to the boil. Fill a bowl with iced water and place it
next to the stove. Blanch the nettle tips in the boiling water for 5 seconds, then
transfer to the iced water. When thoroughly chilled, remove the nettles from the
water and squeeze to remove excess moisture. Set aside a quarter of the nettles.

Place the rest of the nettles in a blender with the egg and egg yolks, then blitz
to a smooth paste. Transfer to a bowl, add both flours and work into a smooth
dough. Wrap the dough in clingfilm (plastic wrap) and refrigerate for 30 minutes.

When ready to make the pasta, remove the dough from the refrigerator. Using a
pasta maker, roll out the dough into thin sheets and then push them through the
chitarra. Alternatively, cut the noodles by stacking a few pasta sheets, dusting
generously with semolina flour between each one to stop them sticking, roll up
lengthways into tight coils and slice through the coils. Dust the noodles with
more semolina flour to stop them sticking, then twist them into nests.

Bring a large pan of water to the boil and salt well. Add the pasta and boil for a
few minutes until the noodles are cooked al dente. Drain the pasta, but reserve
the cooking water.

Meanwhile, put the unsalted butter into a pan with 4 tbsp of the pasta cooking
water. Heat slowly to form a thin emulsion. Transfer the cooked pasta to the pan
with the emulsion. Roughly chop the reserved nettles and add them too. Swirl
and toss everything together, and simmer for a minute or two until the sauce
begins to thicken. Remove the pan from the heat and grate in the Parmesan
cheese. Continue to toss the pasta until the cheese has melted into the sauce.
The pasta should be well coated but not too dry – add a few splashes of the
pasta cooking water to moisten. If there's too much sauce, continue to simmer
slowly, if the pasta is still underdone, or grate in some more Parmesan to
thicken. Finally, off the heat, stir in the crème fraîche.

To serve, transfer the pasta to a plate, grind over some black pepper and drizzle
over a little extra virgin olive oil – a nice grassy note to cut through the butter.

CRUDITÉS & ANCHOÏADE

Makes enough for 4–6 people

For the anchoïade:

50g/1¾oz salted anchovy fillets in oil (tinned ones are fine)

¼ garlic clove, peeled and crushed to a paste with salt

1 thyme sprig, leaves picked

1 tbsp lemon juice

100ml/3½fl oz/½ cup olive oil (extra virgin, as it always should be!)

1 tbsp red wine vinegar

Freshly ground black pepper

No one really needs a recipe instructing them how to cut up sticks of celery, so think of this more as a reminder that crudités were once considered elegant, rather than naff. Just make sure the vegetables are fresh, crisp and delicious. After all, no one likes a floppy carrot stick. Serve a selection of seasonal vegetables, washed, peeled if necessary, and cut into batons for easy dipping: radishes, cucumber, tomatoes, chicories, carrots, celery, raw artichoke, lettuce hearts and so on. Anchoïade is right up there as one the best things to dip raw vegetables into, and if made right, it's rather less fishy than you might think. Anchoïade is also delicious on toast.

———————

Pat the anchovies dry, then blitz them in a food processor to a fine paste. The fineness of this anchovy paste is the key to achieving a perfect emulsion.

Add the crushed garlic and thyme leaves to the paste and then blitz again.

With the motor of the food processor running, slowly trickle in the lemon juice, followed by the olive oil until the anchoïade has emulsified, like a mayonnaise. Add a touch of water if it's getting too thick. Once all the olive oil has been incorporated, add the vinegar. The anchoïade should have the consistency of a loose, wobbly mayonnaise, and taste salty and sour in equal measures. Sometimes an extra splash of water is necessary when the sauce is a little too strong – if its saltiness or acidity makes you wince, it just needs reining in a little.

Arrange the crudités on a serving plate around the anchoïade dip. Grind over some black pepper to finish.

GRILLED YOUNG LEEKS (OR GREEN GARLIC) WITH HAM

Serves 4

1 bunch of young, thin leeks or
    fresh green garlic shoots

Olive oil

4 thin slices of prosciutto
    (the thinnest possible)

Sea salt

During the spring months, sometimes you can find shoots of fresh or 'green' garlic. Harvested when very young, green garlic is like a spring onion but with a thin, white, fresh bulb of garlic at the end. It's not always possible to find green garlic, however, young, thin leeks are much more available and, luckily, just as delicious (although a little sweeter).

Whether green garlic or young leeks, the first impulse is to grill them, just like spring onions (scallions). This is best done over a hot wood fire, until the shoots start to blacken and smoke. Just as the grilled alliums come off the fire, drape thin slices of ham over them. A few additions are possible: toasted, crushed hazelnuts; a little thyme; a scattering of diced fresh red chilli; a drizzle of chestnut honey and so on. The ham could be replaced by thin slivers of hard cheese. A sweet and nutty sheep's milk, such as Ossau Iraty, would be delicious here.

———————

Light a wood fire under a grill, then wait for the flames to die down. Wash the leeks or green garlic, rub with olive oil and scatter with salt. While the embers are still white hot, place the leeks or garlic over the fire and grill on all sides until blackened and soft.

To serve, arrange the charred leeks or garlic a serving plate and drape the slices of prosciutto over the top. Serve immediately with lots of chilled wine.

SQUID & BROAD BEANS EN PAPILLOTE

Serves 4

4 small squid, with tentacles, cleaned, weighing approximately 500g/1lb 2oz

4 handfuls of podded broad (fava) beans or peas, weighing approximately 200g/7oz

A few small glugs of olive oil

½ bunch of monk's beard (agretti) or other greens, picked and washed well, weighing approximately 100g/3½oz

2 tbsp mixed chopped herbs (fennel herb, parsley, chervil)

A big pinch of dried red chilli

1 tsp grated zest and the juice of ½ orange (blood orange, if still available)

A few splashes of white wine

4 tbsp butter

Sea salt and freshly ground black pepper

Baguette, to mop up the juices

Cooking in a paper parcel, or *en papillote*, is a delicate method that sits somewhere between steaming and roasting. It has the added benefit of a flamboyant and aromatic rush of steam when the parcel is opened at the table. Cooking *en papillote* suits ingredients that are quick to cook and require just a little butter and white wine to bring them together. Seafood and spring vegetables fit the bill perfectly. The squid cooks in just a few minutes. I've included some monk's beard (agretti), a marsh grass from Italy, which adds a lovely minerality, but feel free to improvise with samphire, baby spinach, finely sliced chard leaves and so on. Yes, there's a lot of herbs and plenty of butter – but that's the way you want it. The orange zest, fennel herb and dried chilli lend a satisfying southern accent.

Preheat the oven to 200°C fan/220°C/425°F/gas mark 7.

Prepare the squid. If they need further cleaning, cut off the tentacles, remove the eyes and mouth, slip out the bone and rinse well. Cut into 5-mm/³⁄₁₆-inch tubes or strips. Cut the tentacles in half, if they are large.

If the broad beans are tough, remove their outer skins. Bring a pan of water to the boil and add salt. Fill a bowl with iced water and place it next to the hob. Plunge the broad beans into the boiling water for 1 minute, then transfer immediately to the iced water to stop them cooking. Drain and set aside.

Cut four 60-cm x 35-cm/14-inch x 16-inch pieces of parchment paper and fold each in half to double the thickness. Leaving a border of 5cm/2 inches on all sides to make a good seal, drizzle the top of the paper lightly with olive oil.

First lay the monk's beard (or other greens) onto one half of the oiled paper. If using monk's beard or samphire, there's no need to season. For other greens, add a little salt. Season the squid and arrange on top. Scatter over the blanched broad beans (or peas), chopped herbs, chilli and grated orange zest. Splash a glug of wine and a squeeze of orange juice over each parcel. Nestle the butter in with the other ingredients and then lightly drizzle with more olive oil.

Bring the paper over the fish and roll up the unsealed edge to form a pouch. Fold over and crease the edges three times, by 1–2cm/½–¾ inch, on all sides. Press down to seal well, but not so that the ingredients get squashed inside.

Place the parcels on a tray. Bake for 8 minutes in the oven. Transfer the parcels to individual plates. Encourage your guests to (tentatively) tear open and dive in.

SPRING VEGETABLE, COUS-COUS & HERB SALAD

Serves 4

300g/10½oz Jersey Royals or other baby waxy potatoes, washed well

1 bunch of green asparagus, tough woody ends of stalks snapped off and chopped into 1-cm/⅓-inch lengths

50g/1¾oz green beans, topped, tailed and chopped into 1-cm/⅓-inch lengths

50g/1¾oz podded broad (fava) beans

1 tsp caraway seeds, gently toasted in a dry pan and cracked in a pestle and mortar

25g/1oz/2 tbsp salted butter

1 tbsp olive oil, plus extra for drizzling

Juice of 1 lemon

½ small firm cucumber, finely diced (1 tbsp when finely chopped)

4 cherry plum tomatoes on the vine or 1 medium tomato, finely diced

1 spring onion (scallion), finely diced

50g/1¾oz pea shoots or rocket (arugula), roughly chopped

¼ bunch of mint, roughly chopped

¼ bunch of coriander (cilantro), roughly chopped

Aleppo chilli flakes (optional)

1 packet of courgette (zucchini) flowers (optional)

Sea salt and freshly ground black pepper

For the cous-cous:

100g/3½oz dry cous-cous

1 tsp olive oil

Sea salt

'Cous-cous salad' is a phrase that strikes fear in many hearts, conjuring images of a soggy, raisin-strewn yellow mess that comes in square plastic pots. But fear not! When used sparingly in a salad like this, cous-cous is a good base to bring a few ingredients together. The grain itself should by no means be the bulk of the dish, but used wisely it adds a lovely nubbly texture and helps to soak up buttery juices. I originally made this dish on a crisp, sunny April afternoon, as the first of the British asparagus and tiny Jersey Royals appeared in the shops. A little yogurt thinned and seasoned with cumin or caraway seeds is a delicious accompaniment, and a blob of harissa on the side is optional but advised. Incidentally, if you omit the butter then this dish is vegan, and not much poorer for it at all.

Boil the potatoes in salted water for approximately 15 minutes. Towards the end of cooking time, add the chopped asparagus, chopped green beans and broad beans to the pan and continue to boil for a further 2 minutes.

For the best results when cooking cous-cous, follow the steaming method on page 109. However, if you are pressed for time, do it this way. Put the kettle on to boil. Place the cous-cous in a shallow bowl, season lightly with salt and add the olive oil. Rub the cous-cous together with your hands until you think that all the grains are thinly coated in oil. Pour over boiling water from the kettle, just enough to cover the grains, then wrap the bowl tightly in clingfilm (plastic wrap). Leave to stand for 5 minutes or until the grains have plumped up and lost their bite. Remove the clingfilm and fluff the grains carefully with a fork. Discard any that have clumped together in a layer at the bottom.

When the potatoes, asparagus and beans are all cooked, drain and then toss them with the toasted caraway seeds, butter, 1 tbsp olive oil and the juice of half of the lemon. Season to taste with salt and black pepper.

Combine the diced cucumber, tomatoes and spring onion in a mixing bowl with the roughly chopped pea shoots or rocket and herbs. Season lightly with salt, more olive oil and the juice of the remaining half of the lemon.

To serve, divide the warm buttery vegetables between four plates. Spoon over a little of the cooked cous-cous. There should be far less cous-cous than vegetables, around a 1:4 ratio. Arrange the herb salad in one corner of the plate. Try not to mix everything too much: part of the joy of this salad is to build each mouthful as you eat. Sprinkle with Aleppo chilli flakes and tear over the courgette flowers, if using, and drizzle with a little extra olive oil.

PETITE FRITURE (FRITTO MISTO)

Makes one large platter (enough for 4 people as a light starter or 6 people as a snack)

1 bunch of asparagus or 2 small firm courgettes (zucchini)

100g/3½oz monk's beard (agretti) or samphire

A small handful of fresh oregano or rosemary or sage, picked

½ unwaxed lemon, finely sliced into thin half moons

200g/7oz small prawns, head and shell on

250g/8¾oz mussels

½ glass of white wine

2 salted anchovy fillets

1 tbsp olive oil

Clean (unused) sunflower oil, for frying

1 tsp dried red chilli flakes

Sea salt and freshly ground black pepper

For the batter:

100g/3½oz/¾ cup plain (all-purpose) flour

100ml/3½fl oz/½ cup chilled sparkling water

The Italians, it seems, have worked out that the more *misto* the *fritto* the better. I tend to agree. A mixed fry is a fantastic way to get a few nicely complementing flavours on the same plate, which can be easily customised according to ingredient availability and whim. The result, when done right, is a remarkably clean-tasting plate of whatever is in season. As such, I like to vary it throughout the year: in spring, a light assembly of monk's beard, mussels, herbs and new season's asparagus; in summer, aubergines (eggplants), courgettes (zucchini) and their flowers stuffed with soft herbs and fresh cheese; and in autumn, chunky pieces of wild mushrooms, sage leaves and a few choice cuts of meats (for those in the know).

Here's one *petite friture* combination I enjoyed this spring. Small, fresh prawns with their heads and shells on add some extra crunch. Otherwise, brown shrimp are a bit different but just as nice. The fresh oregano is delicious here; the leaves are hardy enough that they withstand a quick dip in the hot oil. I steamed open the mussels before shelling and frying. If you steam them in a little white wine, when combined with a little anchovy and some oil, it makes a quick, tasty sauce to drizzle over at the end for extra punch.

The key to a *petite friture* is using clean oil at the correct temperature, as well as making the batter to the right consistency: too thin and the oil will seep in and saturate your food, too thick and there will be too much fatty crunch and not enough flavour.

───────────

Snap off the tough woody ends of the asparagus stalks. Slice the asparagus (or courgettes) on an angle into pieces around 5mm/³⁄₁₆ inch thick, but as long as you like. Remove any tough stalks on the monk's beard (or samphire), and wash well. Pick the oregano (or rosemary or sage) from the tough central stalk, but leave some stem attached. Press the lemon slices against a chopping board to remove some of the juice, otherwise they tend to burst through the coating of batter and take on a lot of oil.

Rinse the prawns and mussels under cold running water. Remove the beards from the mussels and place in a hot pan, then swiftly pour in the white wine and cover with a tight-fitting lid. Cook, covered, on a medium heat for a few minutes, until the mussels have just opened. Discard any that do not open, remove the pan from the heat and allow the mussels to cool before removing them from their shells. Strain the cooking liquid into a jug and set aside.

Once the ingredients for frying have been prepared, make the batter. Place the flour in a bowl. Make a space to one side of the bowl and pour in the same volume of very cold sparkling water. Working lightly but quickly, whisk the flour into the water to make a smooth batter. Keep going, adding more water if necessary, until the batter is free of any lumps and has the consistency of thin cream. Dip a clean fingernail into the batter – if the batter clings but you can just make out the shape of your nail then the consistency is about right. You can always check the consistency of your batter by test-frying one piece of food: if you think it needs thickening or thinning, adjust accordingly with more flour or water. Keep the batter chilled until needed.

Pour the reserved cooking liquid from the mussels back into a pan and reduce it to around 2 tbsp. Keeping the heat very low, whisk in the anchovies, olive oil and a few good grinds of pepper. Remove from the heat and set aside.

In a deep-fat fryer or heavy-based deep pan, heat the oil to 175°C/350°F.

One-by-one, drag the prepared ingredients through the chilled batter and smoothly and swiftly drop them into the hot oil. Try to keep each ingredient separate so that they don't fuse together in the pan. Using a skimmer or slotted spoon, gently stir the ingredients around in the hot oil as they fry. After one minute, turn each ingredient over and continue to fry for a further one minute. When everything has turned an appetising golden brown, remove from the oil and drain on paper towels.

Arrange the petite friture attractively on your best large serving platter or plate. Sprinkle lightly with salt and drizzle over the sauce that you made earlier. Don't add too much sauce, however, or you risk everything becoming soggy. Finally, dust the petite friture with a pinch of dried chilli flakes.

PROVENÇAL GARLIC SOUP
WITH SAFFRON, SAGE, SORREL & EGG

Serves 4

3 litres/5¼ pints water (if I have some good, light, homemade chicken stock to hand, I sometimes make this soup with stock instead of water)

2 heads of garlic, cloves separated and 1 small garlic clove reserved

4 sage leaves

A small pinch of saffron

4 eggs

4 thin pieces of bread, sourdough or similar

A handful of sorrel or chard leaves (100g/3½oz), finely shredded

40g/1½oz Parmesan or other hard cheese

Sea salt and freshly ground black pepper

Garlic soup is a dish that pushes 'French country cooking' as far as it will go. It's rustic to the point of rough: simple, severe, Spartan. The Provençal classic *aigo boulido* translates literally as 'boiled water', which tells you exactly what it can taste like when made without care. It's a restorative broth made from water, garlic and sage: a dish traditionally for the very young, the very old or the sick. In the right hands, however, an *aigo boulido* can be strangely satisfying, in a nourishing kind of way.

There's real appeal in making something so delicious out of only three ingredients. This traditional soup is certainly more than the sum of its parts. In his fantastic *Feasts of Provence*, Robert Carrier recommends a couple of embellishments to the broth: a little saffron or a few sorrel leaves. It's down this route I head when I want something less simple.

———————

Pour the water (or stock) into a pan and add the garlic, sage leaves and a pinch of salt. Place over a high heat and bring to the boil, then turn down to a simmer for 20 minutes, or until the garlic is soft and the broth tastes full and delicious. Mash the garlic cloves into the soup to extract all of their garlicky goodness, then strain the broth through a sieve (strainer) and discard the mashed garlic and sage. Add the pinch of saffron and a little black pepper, then return to the heat and simmer gently for a further few minutes.

One at a time, crack each egg into a small bowl and slide it into the broth. Simmer gently for around 2 minutes, or until the eggs are soft-poached. Using a slotted spoon, remove the eggs carefully from the broth, place them in individual serving bowls and set aside.

Next, toast the bread. Rub each slice with the reserved raw garlic and drizzle with olive oil. Place one slice of toast in each serving bowl next to the egg.

You can strain the broth again to remove any straggly egg whites, if they bother you. If you do so, you'll lose the saffron, which is a shame. Bring the broth back to a simmer, taste for seasoning – last chance! – and throw in the shredded sorrel or chard leaves. The sorrel brings a much-needed acidity to the soup, but if using only chard, I would add a little squeeze of lemon. Cook the leaves for no more than 10 seconds or they will discolour and go a little sludgy.

To serve, pour the broth into the bowls over the eggs and toast. Grate the Parmesan (or other hard) cheese over the soup and eat while hot.

LAUTREC-STYLE
NEW SEASON'S GARLIC SOUP

Serves 4

3 litres/5¼ pints homemade chicken stock or water

2 heads of new season's garlic, Lautrec Pink Garlic if possible

1 thyme sprig

1 bay leaf

50g/1¾oz vermicelli pasta, broken into short pieces, or any other soup pasta

Sea salt and freshly ground black pepper

For the mayonnaise:

2 egg yolks

2 tbsp Dijon mustard

100ml/3½fl oz/½ cup olive oil

1 tsp lemon juice

1 tsp cold water

Sea salt

Over now to Languedoc, where the annual garlic festival in Lautrec is a hoot – ceremonial robes, marching bands, garlic sculptures and grumpy-looking men with big hands braiding garlic. It's a celebration of the arrival of the new season's Lautrec Pink Garlic. Competition plays a serious part in proceedings, which are taken, typically, a little too seriously. The centrepiece contest is for the best *tarte* à *l'ail rose de Lautrec*, an absolutely honking quiche of slow-roasted garlic, pine nuts and cheese, which was not to my taste at the time. All things considered, it's a good day out. We took souvenirs home: plaits of pink garlic heads that hung reassuringly next to the oven, seeing us through to next year's festival.

I remember vividly the plastic bowls of soup being passed around, and the heated arguments as ladies from rival villages spat at each other over the inclusions or exclusions that amounted to heresy. The 'official' version served at the festival was delicious: a heady broth made with fresh Lautrec Pink Garlic, broken vermicelli for body and a mustardy mayonnaise stirred through for richness. This one is best made with chicken stock.

Pour the chicken stock or water into a pan and add the garlic, herbs and a pinch of salt. Place over a high heat and bring to the boil, then turn down to a simmer for 20 minutes, or until the garlic is soft and the broth tastes delicious. Mash the garlic into the soup to extract all of their garlicky goodness, then strain the broth through a sieve (strainer). Discard the mashed garlic and herbs.

Meanwhile, make the mayonnaise. Beat the egg yolks in a bowl, blender or pestle and mortar with the mustard and a pinch of salt. Slowly drizzle in the olive oil, drop by drop at first and then in an increasingly steady stream, whisking continually. Thin the mayonnaise with the lemon juice and 1 tsp cold water. Check the seasoning and add more salt if needed.

Add the broken vermicelli to the broth, stir well, return to the heat and simmer for 5 minutes, or until the pasta is soft. Season with black pepper and any additional salt if necessary.

Gradually add a ladleful of the hot broth to the mayonnaise, whisking as you pour. When you have a smooth but thin emulsion, whisk the mayonnaise back into the soup – and I mean whisk. To serve, heat the soup again, stirring all the while, but do not allow it to boil as the emulsion will split. Ladle into bowls and eat while hot.

SALT COD BRANDADE

Serves 4

400g/14oz salted cod fillet,
  soaked overnight

1 tsp black peppercorns

2 bay leaves

Milk, to cover

4 tbsp olive oil

2 garlic cloves, peeled and crushed

200g/7oz floury potatoes, peeled and
  roughly cut into chunks

Salt cod has been a staple of the Provençal larder since Roman times. Old cookbooks are full of recipes for it. *Brandade de morue*, said to originate in Nîmes, combines mashed potatoes with a purée of milk-poached salt cod, garlic and olive oil to make a satisfying, pungent thing.

Brandade has many applications. Smear it on top of a croûton to make a simple canapé or, for a party piece, fry triangles of bread in olive oil to stick into a mound of it, like some delicious fishy hedgehog, and then scatter with black olives or truffles. Brandade is also delicious hot. Serve with a little toast, a soft-boiled egg and some chopped parsley. Most of all, I like to use brandade to stuff vegetables. The possibilities are endless: courgette (zucchini) flowers, roast courgettes, tomatoes, artichokes, scooped-out baked potatoes…

Salt cod is a strong flavour – all the more so when combined with garlic – and so I find it's best when balanced with a bit of greenery. In the restaurant we salt our own cod, which is very easy to do. Simply cover the fish in salt and then leave it in refrigerator. The fish will be cured after a few days, but can be left in the salt for a long time. It'll need soaking overnight before use. If you buy ready-cured salt cod, remember that it will need at least 48 hours, if not 72 hours, of soaking with repeated changes of water. It's actually easier to make your own, I think.

─────────

To make the salt cod, take a cod fillet and pin-bone it. Leaving the skin on, salt the fish heavily with coarse rock salt. A few peppercorns and some thyme in the mix never go amiss. Place in a plastic storage container, cover with a lid and leave in the refrigerator overnight. The next day, pour off any liquid that has appeared and repack the fish with more salt. Leave in the refrigerator, again covered with a lid, for a few days or up to a week. When ready to use, wash off the salt and leave the fish to soak in clean cold water overnight or longer. Change the water once or twice to help with the de-salting process.

To make the brandade, place the salt cod, peppercorns and bay leaves in a pan. Add enough milk just to cover the fish. Place the pan over a low heat and bring very slowly to a simmer, then turn off the heat. Leave the cod to poach in the hot milk for 5 minutes, then carefully remove the fish from the milk. Discard the peppercorns and bay leaves, and set aside the milk left in the pan.

Take the skin off the cod and slip out any bones that you can see.

Heat the olive oil gently in a pan with the crushed garlic. Slowly deep fry the garlic for 5–10 minutes, until the oil takes on all the flavour. Set aside.

Add the potatoes to the fishy milk in the pan and boil until soft. Taste the milk to see whether any salt is required – the answer is usually an emphatic no. Drain and mash or rice the potatoes. Reserve the milk.

Flake the cod into a blender and add 1 tbsp of the reserved milk. Blitz until you have a smooth(ish) purée. Add the mashed or riced potatoes, garlic oil and another 1 tbsp of the milk. Blitz again until it is all amalgamated.

Loosen the brandade with a little more of the reserved milk should it need it. The brandade should taste strong but not overly salty, with a good hit of garlic and a lot of olive oil.

A ROUGH GUIDE TO STUFFING VEGETABLES WITH BRANDADE

Artichokes: Take a small artichoke, peel off the worst of the outside layers and any green bits from the base. Cut off the top and scoop out the choke, if there is one. Cook slowly in lightly salted water with thyme and olive oil. Allow to cool. Season the brandade with chopped parsley and some grated unwaxed lemon zest. Stuff the cavity in the centre of the artichoke with the brandade up to the brim. Fry the stuffed artichoke, brandade side down, in hot olive oil in a heavy ovenproof pan. The brandade will fry to a crispy golden crust. Serve with some salad, a few capers and a sprinkle of cayenne pepper.

Courgette flowers: Season the brandade as for the artichokes. Stuff the insides of the courgette flowers and fold them carefully to seal. Make a quick tempura batter (see page 26), then dip and deep fry the courgette flowers. Alternatively, drizzle them with olive oil and bake in the oven. Serve with lemon.

Peppers: Brandade-stuffed peppers is a very Mediterranean-tasting dish.Take a small red or green pepper – nothing too spicy, but certainly not a tasteless Dutch bell pepper – deseed and then roast with a pinch of salt and a drizzle of olive oil in a medium oven until soft. Allow the pepper to cool, stuff with the brandade, then return to a slightly hotter oven to heat through and colour a little.

Potatoes: Bake small floury potatoes with some salt. Scoop out the flesh and use this baked potato to make the brandade. Stuff the finished brandade into the hollowed-out potato skins and return them to the oven to warm through before serving. Rather nice with some spiced tomato sauce, this one.

LAMB SWEETBREADS, BROAD BEANS & MORELS ON TOAST

Serves 4

250g/8¾oz lamb sweetbreads, washed well

1 thyme sprig

1 tbsp chopped parsley leaves, stalks reserved

Black peppercorns

200g/7oz podded broad (fava) beans

1 tbsp olive oil

150g/5¼oz fresh morels, St. George's mushrooms or any other preferred variety of mushrooms, cleaned and halved, if large

½ glass of dry white wine

1 tbsp chicken stock

50g/1¾oz/½ stick butter

A squeeze of lemon juice

4 slices of hot buttered toast

Sea salt and freshly ground black pepper

Sweetbreads are the most unchallenging of offals, with a lovely delicate flavour. They are usually available all year round but are at their best during spring. At this time of year I love to cook them with fresh broad (fava) beans, which makes for a delightful spring lunch. Fresh morels are elusive and expensive, but are completely delicious. St George's mushrooms, also in season during spring, have a milder flavour but work just as well. Feel free to substitute any fungi you prefer, including soaked dried ceps. For me, a good-quality chicken stock is necessary here as it really helps to tie everything together.

———————

Soak the sweetbreads in cold water for 30 minutes to remove a little of the blood. Remove the sweetbreads from the water, give them a quick rinse under cold running water, then place them in a pan with the thyme sprig, a couple of parsley stalks and a few black peppercorns. Cover with fresh cold water and bring to the boil over a medium–high heat. Once boiling, remove the pan from the heat. The sweetbreads should have a little spring to them but still be quite soft. Scoop out the sweetbreads and, while still warm, painstakingly peel away the membranes and set aside. If the sweetbreads are allowed to cool, this arduous peeling task will take even longer, so work fast.

If the broad beans are on the larger side, you can peel off their outer skins. I never bother to do this unless I am sure that they will be very tough if the skins are left on. Blanch the broad beans for 1 minute in boiling salted water, then set aside.

Season the sweetbreads with salt. Heat the olive oil in a frying pan (skillet) over a high heat. When the oil starts to smoke, add the sweetbreads and colour them on all sides until an even golden brown. Lower the heat to medium and throw in the mushrooms. Cook, stirring, until they begin to soften. Lower the heat still further and add the broad beans, followed by the white wine. When the wine has reduced slightly, add the chicken stock.

Simmer everything together gently until the liquid in the pan begins to thicken. Add the butter and swirl it around the pan to make an emulsion. Check the seasoning and add more salt if needed. Finish with a squeeze of lemon juice, a grind or two of black pepper and a scattering of chopped parsley. Serve the sweetbreads on the slices of hot buttered toast.

SEAFOOD & CAMARGUE RICE SALAD

Serves 4, as a light lunch

200g/7oz Camargue red rice
or 'wild rice' mixture

250g/8¾oz squid, cut into fine strips
or thin tubes

200g/7oz firm white fish (such as
hake, cod or monkfish), cut into
bite-size pieces

3 tbsp olive oil

1 garlic clove, peeled and sliced finely
lengthways

1 tsp fennel seeds

250g/8¾oz clams or mussels, or even
better a mixture of both

2 tbsp fresh peas, broad (fava)
beans or asparagus (chopped into
1-cm/½-inch pieces)

A glass of white wine

100g/3½oz brown shrimp

A nice big handful of picked mixed
herbs (parsley, tarragon, chervil,
fennel herb)

1 tsp salted capers, soaked in cold
water and drained

1 tsp black olives, pitted

1 tsp red wine vinegar

1 tsp lemon juice

A handful of rocket (arugula) or other
peppery green salad leaves, roughly
chopped if large

Sea salt and freshly ground black
pepper

Seafood salad is another naff-sounding dish that has suffered from poorly executed efforts over the years. Rubbery, overcooked squid rings, a couple of tough prawns, floppy salad leaves and dodgy mayo… well, you know what I mean. I can assure you that this dish is quite different. The Camargue red rice adds a nutty bite to an otherwise very light assembly, absorbing some of the flavourful juices from the shellfish (in the same way linguine soaks up the cooking liquor when you make pasta with clams). Feel free to improvise on the theme.

Red rice is a famous export of the Camargue and it's seen quite commonly in south east France. It has a wonderful nutty flavour and, when cooked, a texture that is perhaps more akin to farro than a fluffy rice like basmati. Red rice isn't always widely available. Health shops are quite a good bet. If not, you could easily use one of those 'wild rice' mixes that you can often find in the supermarkets.

First, cook the rice. Boil the rice in lightly salted water for 30 minutes, or until the rice has cracked a bit and softened, but retains a slight bite. Drain and keep warm.

Cook the seafood to coincide with the rice being ready. Season the squid and the fish lightly with salt and pepper. Gently heat 1 tbsp of the olive oil in a heavy pan with a lid. Put in the garlic and the fennel seeds and fry slowly for one minute. Increase the heat to medium, then add the shellfish, squid, chunks of fish, spring vegetables and lastly the white wine. Cover with a lid and cook at a simmer for a few minutes until the fish is cooked through and the shellfish have opened. Add the brown shrimp at the last second so that they warm through but not cook. Remove the seafood and spring vegetables from the pan and set aside, then slowly simmer the juices left in the pan to reduce them slightly while you assemble the salad.

Combine the rice, seafood, spring vegetables, chopped herbs, capers and olives in a serving bowl. When the juices in the pan have reduced to around 2 tbsp left, turn off the heat. Add the remaining 2 tbsp of olive oil, the vinegar and lemon juice, then swirl in the pan. Dress the rice and seafood salad with the resultant sauce. Add the rocket (or green salad) leaves, fold everything gently together, and serve.

PIG'S HEAD SALADE LYONNAISE

Serves 6–8 or more, with the possibility of leftovers

For the pig's head:

½ pig's head

500g/1lb 2oz rock salt

2kg/4lb 8oz duck fat, or enough to submerge the pig's head

A 2.5-cm/1-inch thick slice of sourdough bread, cut lengthways so it is large enough to sit the pig's head on top

For the vinaigrette:

A little scrap of peeled garlic

1 tbsp mustard

1 tbsp white wine vinegar

A squeeze of lemon juice

50ml/1⅔fl oz/2¾ tbsp olive oil

Sea salt and freshly ground black pepper

For the salad:

A mixture of salad leaves (feel free to use the traditional frisée with beetroot, mustard and young spinach leaves, but particularly nice are lettuces with dandelion leaves)

A handful of fresh peas or broad (fava) beans, blanched in salted water and refreshed in iced water (optional)

About 8 radishes, halved or quartered and leaves chopped

1 tbsp chopped parsley leaves

1 tbsp tarragon leaves

1 tsp salted capers or 1 tsp chopped cornichons, soaked in cold water and then drained

½ shallot, very finely sliced, soaked in cold water and then drained

A *salade Lyonnaise* at its most basic is frisée, lardons, croûtons and a poached egg, dressed with vinaigrette. This version takes that idea and runs with it a little. A pig's head holds many flavourful, textural delights and is certainly not something to be scared of. When prepared in this way, it is mostly meaty and delicious.

Here, a split pig's head is cooked slowly in duck fat, then the whole thing is roasted atop a thick slice of bread. The pig's head crisps up nicely and its fat renders into the bread underneath, transforming it into one large tasty croûton. The pig and toast, now bonded as one with sticky fat, are removed from the oven and chopped enthusiastically with a big knife, ready to be tossed with the rest of the salad. Although untraditional, I like to work a few spring vegetables into this dish whenever possible – radishes, ribbons of raw asparagus, just-cooked peas and broad (fava) beans, roast young beetroots and so on – and I love a bit of tarragon and dandelion in the salad. This is also one of the only recipes in which I'll encourage the use of chives.

───────────

The day before you want to confit the pig's head, sprinkle the pig's head heavily with the rock salt and leave it to sit overnight in the refrigerator.

The next day, wash the pig's head well to rinse off the salt and pat dry with paper towels. Preheat the oven to 130°C fan/150°C/300°F/gas mark 2.

Melt the duck fat in a deep cooking pot or ovenproof dish and then carefully slide in the pig's head. Make sure the pig's head is fully submerged in the melted fat. Place the pot or dish in the preheated oven and slow cook for 3–4 hours, or until the meat slips off the bones. Remove the pig's head from the fat and allow both to cool.

While the pig's head is still warm, slip the meat off the bones. Remove and discard the eyes and any other inedible parts (watch out for teeth). If storing the meat for use later, place the meat in a refrigerator-friendly container, pour over the fat to leave a good layer on top to prevent any air getting in, then allow to cool.

Turn the oven up to 180°C fan/200°C/400°F/gas mark 6.

To serve:

1 soft-poached egg per person

A glug of olive oil

1 tsp finely chopped chives

Sea salt and freshly ground black
  pepper

Lay the confit pig's head meat on top of the thick slice of sourdough bread. Roast in the hot oven for 30 minutes, or until the skin is crisp. Transfer to a chopping board and cut the meat and bread into 2.5-cm/1-inch cubes. At this stage, the pig's head can be stored in the refrigerator if needed.

Return the cubed meat and bread to the oven for a further 5 minutes to crisp up and warm through.

To make the vinaigrette, crush the garlic with a pinch of salt to a fine paste. Whisk in the rest of the ingredients in order along with 2 tsp cold water.

To serve, toss the warm pig's head on crispy toast with the rest of the salad ingredients and dress with the mustardy vinaigrette. Arrange the salad on serving plates and nestle into each nest of leaves one warm soft-poached egg. Drizzle the poached eggs with a little olive oil and then sprinkle them with salt, pepper and a touch of chopped chives.

GURNARD, LENTILS, PEAS & LARDO

Serves 4

2 small handfuls (100g/3½oz) green
  lentils, French or Italian, such as
  Puy or Spello

1 bay leaf

1 small ripe tomato, fresh or from
  a can

A few glugs of olive oil

A splash of red wine vinegar

200g/7oz shelled fresh peas

2 thyme sprigs

2 garlic cloves, unpeeled

A piece of unwaxed lemon peel

4 gurnard fillets (150g/5¼oz each),
  pin-boned

A glass of white wine

1 tbsp chopped mixed soft herbs
  (parsley and tarragon, for
  preference)

4 thin slices of lardo di colonnata

Sea salt and freshly ground black
  pepper

Gurnard is a great fish to pair with pork. It's robust and earthy, with a
flavour that can hold its own. Feel free to substitute any other fish, but
I would advise nothing too delicate for this recipe. I love this dish with
brill, turbot and monkfish, although these are all more expensive than
gurnard. Some clams would be very delicious thrown into the roasting
pan here too. The combination of sweet fresh peas with cured pork fat
is a particularly nice one. Place the lardo on top of the hot fish at the last
minute and it will drape, droop and melt seductively onto it.

———————

In a pot, put the lentils, a bay leaf, the tomato and a glug of olive oil. Pour over
enough cold water to cover well and bring to the boil over a high heat. Turn
the heat down to a simmer and cook slowly for around 30 minutes, or until the
lentils are soft to the bite but not mushy. You want them to still be covered with
water when cooked. Do not drain. Add more olive oil, the red wine vinegar and
salt to taste. Set aside and keep warm.

Preheat the oven to as hot as it will go.

Boil the peas in a pan of salted water with a sprig of thyme, the 2 unpeeled
garlic cloves and the lemon peel. They will only take 1 minute to cook. Drain
and dress well with olive oil.

Season the gurnard with salt and pepper. Heat some olive oil in a heavy-based
ovenproof pan. When it starts to smoke, add the gurnard, skin side down.
Cook until the skin is golden brown, then turn over. Reduce the heat a touch,
and throw in the second sprig of thyme. Pour in the white wine and a splash
of cold water. Drizzle with olive oil and put the pan in the hot oven. Cook for
around 5 minutes depending on the thickness of the fish. To test that the fish is
cooked, insert a skewer into the thickest part of the fish. If it goes through the
flesh without any resistance, the fish is ready.

Once the fish is cooked, the wine and oil will have reduced to make a delicious
sauce. Add a splash more water if the sauce is threatening to reduce to nothing
and catch on the base of the pan. If it's too watery, remove the fish while you
bubble the sauce down to a better consistency.

Reheat the peas and throw in the chopped herbs. Arrange the lentils and peas
attractively on individual plates. Put a cooked gurnard fillet on top and pour over
the juices from the pan. Finally, drape slices of lardo sensually over each fish.

BROAD BEANS
SLOW-COOKED IN THEIR PODS

Serves 4, as a side or as part of
a spread

1kg/2lb 4oz young broad (fava) beans
in their pods

4 ripe tomatoes, peeled and roughly
chopped (or 4 peeled plum
tomatoes from a can, rinsed of their
juice)

1 tbsp olive oil

25g/1oz pancetta, bacon, guanciale,
or cured ham, cut into thin little
matchsticks (optional)

2 garlic cloves, peeled, green sprout
removed, sliced thinly lengthways

A sprig of thyme

1 glass of white wine

A small handful of chopped parsley
and/or tarragon

1 tbsp crème fraîche (optional)

Salt and freshly ground black pepper

This is an excellent and thrifty way with normally expensive young broad (fava) beans at the start of the season. When the pods are young and tender, they are not only edible but delicious. A little judicious trimming is all that is required, then the pods can be sliced through, beans and all, ready for the pot. This will not work well at all with floppy, rubbery, stringy old pods – they will be tough and the dish inedible. You have been warned!

I like to cook young broad beans in tomato sauce with a bit of white wine and some herbs. A few thin matchsticks of pancetta, guanciale or cured ham would be very welcome too. These broad beans are lovely as part of a spread; I often serve them as a side for some roast pork (without the optional bacon), a grilled, spatchcocked chicken, or some robust white fish such as monkfish (in which case the optional bacon is encouraged).

———————

Top and tail the whole broad beans in their pods and trim carefully of any discoloured, black or heavily spotted parts, as well as any other parts you think may be tough. Slice the pods on a diagonal into thin strips, ideally no thicker than 1cm/½ inch.

Peel the tomatoes by making a criss-cross on their base with a sharp knife. Blanch them in boiling water for 30 seconds, then remove to iced water, and the skins will slip off.

Heat 1 tbsp olive oil in a suitable pot. If using, add the bacon or ham, then the sliced garlic and the sprig of thyme. Fry until all is a light golden brown, then add the tomatoes. Season well with salt and pepper.

Bring to the boil and then simmer gently for 10 minutes, crushing the tomatoes with a spoon from time to time as they cook. Add the sliced broad beans, stir, and throw in the wine. Bring to the boil again, then turn down and simmer, covered, for around 40 minutes, or until the broad beans are soft and the sauce has thickened.

Check the seasoning again and add the chopped herbs. It's sometimes nice to add a small spoon of crème fraîche at the end, but it depends what you're eating it with, and whether you like tomatoes with cream or not. (I do.)

PEAS SLOW-COOKED
WITH SHALLOTS, WHITE WINE & HERBS

Serves 4, as a side dish

100g/3½oz/1 stick unsalted butter

4 small shallots, or 2 banana shallots, finely diced

2 garlic cloves, peeled, halved, green sprout removed, sliced finely lengthways

1 thyme sprig

4 nice handfuls shelled fresh peas (200g/7oz)

½ glass of dry white wine

1 tbsp chopped parsley

1 tbsp chopped tarragon

Sea salt and freshly ground black pepper

This is a rustic, grandma-style way with fresh peas. The colour might fade but the peas will sing sweetly. Ideal with roast pigeons, quail, chicken, grilled calf's liver, pork chops, veal chops, legs of spring lamb cooked *à la ficelle*... I could go on.

———————

Melt the butter in a wide heavy pan. Put in the shallots, garlic and thyme, and season with salt. Sweat the shallots and garlic over a low heat for at least 15 minutes, or until the shallot is soft and sweet. Add the shelled peas, stir well, then throw in the half glass of wine. (You can always drink the other half).

Half-cover the pan with a lid and cook over a low heat for a further 30 minutes, stirring occasionally, until the peas are soft. Season with salt and pepper. Stir in the chopped soft herbs before serving.

BOURRIDE

Serves 4

For the stew:

1 medium onion, roughly chopped

2 celery stalks, roughly chopped

1 small head of fennel, roughly chopped

1 small leek roughly chopped into rounds

6 garlic cloves, peeled

Olive oil

A few parsley stalks

1 thyme sprig

1 bay leaf

2 strips of orange peel (use a vegetable peeler)

1 tsp black peppercorns

1 tsp fennel seeds

A pinch of saffron

2 fresh tomatoes, blanched, peeled and roughly chopped

1kg/2lb 4oz fish heads and bones, gills removed, washed well (gurnard and red mullet bones make the most delicious stews)

A glass of dry white wine

200g/7oz waxy potatoes, peeled and cut into chunks

Salt

A cousin of bouillabaisse, bourride is a rich, saffron-spiked fish stew thickened with aïoli. It's somehow less riotous than bouillabaisse, but no less flavourful, and the saffron/aïoli combination is rich and deeply satisfying. Some recipes call for a dice of vegetables, or chunks of carrots or leeks floating around in the stew, but I prefer to roughly chop everything and then strain it at the end. We add a little orange peel to the base, and a good pinch of hot cayenne pepper on top.

A bourride needs its accoutrements. Croûtons, spread with extra aïoli, make useful vehicles for excessive amounts of garlic, and are fun to float around on top of the stew, soaking up the sauce. Waxy potatoes cooked in the broth offer some respite from the richness.

The choice of fish, I think, is not as important as some make out, but monkfish is delicious here. Red mullet is also great, and we usually try to mix it with some cheaper things like gurnard, grey mullet, hake or bream. Mussels add a great depth of flavour.

Fry the roughly chopped vegetables and the whole garlic cloves slowly in olive oil, with a good pinch of salt, until they are soft. This should take at least 30 minutes.

Throw the herbs into the pan, then add the orange peel, peppercorns, fennel seeds and saffron. Cook, stirring, on a low heat to bring out the flavours of the spices.

When all is soft, sweet and aromatic, add the chopped tomatoes. Cook for 5 minutes over a medium–low heat, then add the fish bones, followed by the white wine. Cover with water.

Bring to the boil, reduce to a simmer, and cook for around 30 minutes, or until the bones have given up their flavour. As the fish cooks, skim off any scum that gathers on the surface of the stew.

Strain the stew into a clean pan, discarding the vegetables, herbs and fish bones to leave the liquid only. Next, cook the potatoes in the strained stew. Remove the potatoes, taste for salt, adjust with more salt if necessary and set aside.

For the aïoli:

1 fat or 2 small garlic cloves, peeled
  and green sprout removed

1 tsp fine salt

2 egg yolks

200ml/7fl oz/1⅓ cup extra virgin olive
  oil

Juice of ½ lemon

For the croûtons:

Some stale baguette

Olive oil

For the bourride:

150g/5¼oz monkfish, filleted weight

150g/5¼oz red mullet, filleted weight

150g/5¼oz gurnard, filleted weight

150g/5¼oz hake, filleted weight

200g/7oz mussels

A handful of parsley, chopped

A pinch of cayenne pepper

Sea salt and freshly ground black
  pepper

For the aïoli:

Make an aïoli (see page 173), but add an extra egg yolk at the beginning of the process. This helps to enrich the soup and makes it less likely to split. Add a little less lemon than usual.

For the croûtons:

Cut a stale baguette into thin rounds, rub with olive oil, and toast gently in a low oven until crunchy.

For the bourride:

Fillet and pin-bone the fish if it hasn't been already done by your fishmonger. Cut each fish into four equal pieces and season with salt. Clean the mussels, washing well in cold water, scraping well, and discarding any that remain open when tapped.

Season the fish with salt and poach very gently in the hot stew, covered with a lid. If some pieces are thicker than others, add the thickest bits first, and the thinnest bits last. Just before the fish is cooked, add the mussels and the cooked potatoes. Test to see if the fish is cooked: insert a thin skewer into the thickest piece of fish. If the skewer passes through with no resistance, the fish is cooked. Make sure the mussels are open, discard any that remain closed.

Carefully scoop out all of the fish, shellfish and potatoes from the pan and divide between individual bowls or, better still, place on one large serving platter. Keep warm while you finish the stew.

Take some aïoli, about a tablespoon per person, and put it in a decent-sized bowl. Slowly whisk in a ladleful of the stock, until you have a thick aïoli soup. Off the heat, pour this tempered aïoli back into the hot fish soup, whisking furiously as you go. Return to a very low heat or a bain marie over some simmering water. Bring the bourride up to eating temperature slowly.
Take extreme care not to boil the soup at this stage or the emulsion will split. You are looking for a smooth, velvety finish to the soup. If the worst happens, whisk in a little more aïoli using the same method, and this should smooth things over.

Pour the bourride over the fish and potatoes, and sprinkle with chopped parsley and some cayenne pepper. Serve with the croûtons and bowls of extra aïoli.

GRILLED RED MULLET WRAPPED IN VINE LEAVES

Serves 4 or any number of people but adjust accordingly

Whole red mullets, 1 medium or 2 small per person, scaled and gutted, but the liver left inside

Vine leaves in brine, 2 per person

A bunch of fennel herb (or tarragon)

Juice of lemons and sharp oranges, if available, to serve

Olive oil

I'm not sure if this counts as a full recipe; it's maybe more of a handy guide. Grilling in vine leaves imparts an instant taste of the Mediterranean: a salty, mineral twang, a hint of smoke, a glimpse of somewhere over the sea. The vine leaves, rubbed with olive oil, blister and char over the fire, while the fish stays moist and protected from the harsh heat. Red mullet lends itself particularly well to grilling over charcoal and wood, and has a perfect affinity with vine leaves. A little fennel herb tucked in between the fish and its wrapper will lend an aniseed hit to cut through the smoke. Leave the livers inside the gutted fish if possible – red mullet is the 'woodcock of the sea'.

────────────

On a clear late spring evening, light a charcoal and/or wood fire under a grill. Wait until the flames have died down but the embers are still quite hot.

Season the fish lightly with salt: remember the vine leaves are themselves salty.

Lay a sprig of fennel herb on each side of the fish, and drizzle lightly with olive oil. Wrap the fish tightly in the vine leaves, leaving the fish heads and tails poking out.

Rub the wrapped fish with more olive oil and grill over the hot fire. Try not to move the fish more than once when turning. When the fish is cooked (around 5 minutes for a medium fish), transfer to a serving dish.

Squeeze over some lemon and orange juice. Drizzle again with olive oil and eat while hot, ideally with a green salad, some bread and a glass of chilled white wine.

GRANDE BOUFFE

BOUILLABAISSE

Three Toasts: Tomatoes, Tapenade or Anchoïade, Smashed Peas & Ricotta

–

La Bouillabaisse (served in two parts):
Fish Broth with Croûtons & Rouille
Fish from Cornish Day Boat Fisherman (Red Mullet, John Dory, Octopus, Mussels, Crab,
Hake, Bream, Gurnard & Monkfish) with Potatoes Cooked in Broth

–

Plum Galette

Bouillabaisse is the Grande Dame of fish stews. It's a riot of many fish, shellfish, ripe tomatoes, wild fennel and saffron, served in two parts. First comes the rich broth, served with croûtons and rouille, the spicy, garlicky, saffron-spiked mayonnaise. Next is the fish stew and potatoes cooked in the stock.

There's an awful lot of hot air blown by the Marseillais, who insist loudly that a true bouillabaisse should contain only three, perhaps four at a stretch, local fish, which must be fished only from the bay of Marseille. This is all very well and good – milking tourists to the tune of €50 for a bowl is a nice bit of business, after all – but I say take no notice of the Marseillais and their fierce fish criteria. All other inhabitants of the coastline of the Var make bouillabaisse however they jolly well want, and it is in that spirit that I propose a bouillabaisse made with fish from the Atlantic can be just as good as one made in the sea of its origin. The key, of course, is good fish: a wide, carefully chosen selection of sparkling fresh specimens. As with all the best things, we adapted our recipe from one by everyone's favourite Provençale grandma, Lulu Peyraud of Domaine Tempier near Bandol, via *Lulu's Provençal Table* by Richard Olney.

Bouillabaisse is a proper feast. Anything too substantial beforehand will leave you groaning and unable to eat any cheese before dessert: a disastrous state of affairs. I propose to start this meal with a few toasts topped with neatly selected friends: anchoïade or tapenade, some ripe tomatoes and a rub of garlic, fresh cheese with smashed green peas. If this seems too much of a stretch, a simple green salad will do nicely. We made a delicious plum galette to finish, which seemed just right.

Three Toasts

Make enough toast for everyone. The slices should be thin and the toast chopped into pieces of an appropriate size depending on the style of your meal. Stack the toast into three separate piles.

Attack the first pile with a peeled clove of garlic, and top with slightly squished thin slices of ripe tomatoes. Season with salt, pepper and red wine vinegar, then drizzle liberally with your good olive oil.

To the next pile of toast introduce a generous smear of tapenade (see page 61) or indeed anchoïade (see page 20), should the mood take you.

Lastly, smash some raw fresh peas in a pestle and mortar with a touch of garlic. Keep smashing until you have a fairly smooth, muted green paste. Add grated Parmesan, salt, pepper and lemon juice to taste, then drizzle in olive oil until you are happy with the consistency. Spread the smashed peas on the toasts, then top with a blob of highest quality fresh ricotta. Season the ricotta with salt and pepper.

Serve the three different toasts on big platters for everyone to help themselves.

La Bouillabaisse
Makes enough for 8 people

This recipe is simpler than it might look at first glance, but it does take a while. Due to the variety of fish required, I recommend making it for a minimum of eight people. If you are only going to use the bones of one or two fish, I enthusiastically recommend gurnard and red mullet, as these by far make the best broth.

The fish and shellfish listed here is what we used the last time we made a bouillabaisse at the restaurant, but you should buy whatever is available and good. I would say gurnard and red mullet are musts, as are octopus and mussels, but the other fish and shellfish can be varied according to what is around.

1 small crab (this will be smashed up so buy cheap crippled crabs, if possible)
1 each of gurnard, red mullet, John Dory, bream, all weighing approximately 500g/1lb 2oz, filleted, head and bones reserved, gills removed and washed
1 octopus, washed
1 monkfish tail fillet, approximate weight 500g/1lb 2oz
1 hake fillet, approximate weight 500g/1lb 2oz
1kg/2lb 4oz mussels, cleaned

To marinate the fish:
1 small pinch of good-quality saffron
½ garlic clove, peeled
1 tbsp parsley
1 tbsp olive oil

For the broth:
4 tbsp olive oil
2 onions, roughly chopped
½ head of celery, roughly chopped
1 head of garlic, smashed up a bit
1 Florence fennel bulb, roughly chopped
1 handful of wild fennel stalks, if available, roughly chopped
4 bay leaves
4 thyme sprigs
1 tsp black peppercorns
1 tbsp fennel seeds
Peel of ½ orange, ideally dried, but fresh is fine
1 dried Spanish chilli, stalk and seeds removed
1 tsp good-quality saffron
1kg/2lb 4oz ripe tomatoes, roughly chopped
½ bottle dry white wine
A big glug of brandy
A big glug of pastis
Sea salt and freshly ground black pepper

For the potatoes and croûtons:
1kg/2lb 4oz waxy red potatoes (such as Desiree), peeled, cut into chunks
½ day-old crusty baguette, thinly sliced

CRAB IN BITS

crab, shell, juices and all, to the pan. Fry the crab with the vegetables over a medium heat for about 5 minutes, stirring often, until the rich shell flavour starts to make itself known. Add the tomatoes to the pan and stir well to mix. Cook for a few minutes while you gather the fish bones.

Add the cleaned, gilled fish heads and bones to the pan. Smash them up in the pan until you have a delicious mulch of bones, tomatoes, saffron and oil. To this mulch add the white wine, brandy and pastis, then pour over cold water to top it up. You need enough water so that there is plenty of broth, but remember the more water you add here, the less powerful the broth will be, so it's a fine balance.

Bring the bouillabaisse to the boil, then turn down to a fast simmer and cook for about 45 minutes. Skim the surface of the broth to remove any impurities. Add half the mussels to the pan. They will boil and overcook, but will sacrifice their tasty juices and enrich the broth nicely. Taste the broth. It should be full, rounded and approaching delicious. If not, continue to cook and reduce slightly until you are happy that a good flavour is simmering under the surface.

Strain the broth into a bowl. Squish the mulch left in the pan with something sturdy to encourage it to release all the liquid and strain again. Rinse out the pan if there are any nasty bits left inside, then return the strained broth to the pan. Put the cleaned octopus into the broth and

For the rouille:
2 tbsp fresh bread, crust removed
1 fat or 2 small garlic cloves, peeled and green sprout removed
2 salted anchovy fillets
A small pinch of good-quality saffron
2 egg yolks
½ tsp cayenne pepper
100ml/3½fl oz/½ cup olive oil
1 tbsp lemon juice
1 tsp red wine vinegar

To make the broth:
Heat the oil in a large pan and add the onion, celery, garlic, fennel, fennel stalks (if using), bay leaves and thyme. Season with a big pinch of salt. Fry the vegetables over a medium heat, stirring often, for 10 minutes, or until they begin to soften. Add all the peppercorns, fennel seeds, orange peel and chilli, lower the heat to medium—low and continue to cook for another 20 minutes, or until everything is quite soft, has taken on only a little colour and is smelling excellent. Add the saffron, stir well, and cook over a low heat for another 5 minutes.

If not dead already, kill the crab by spiking the hole under the flap on the underneath of its body. Smash up the crab with a pestle or a heavy rolling pin. Add the smashed

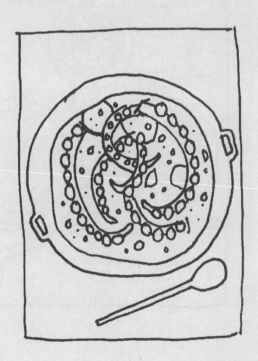

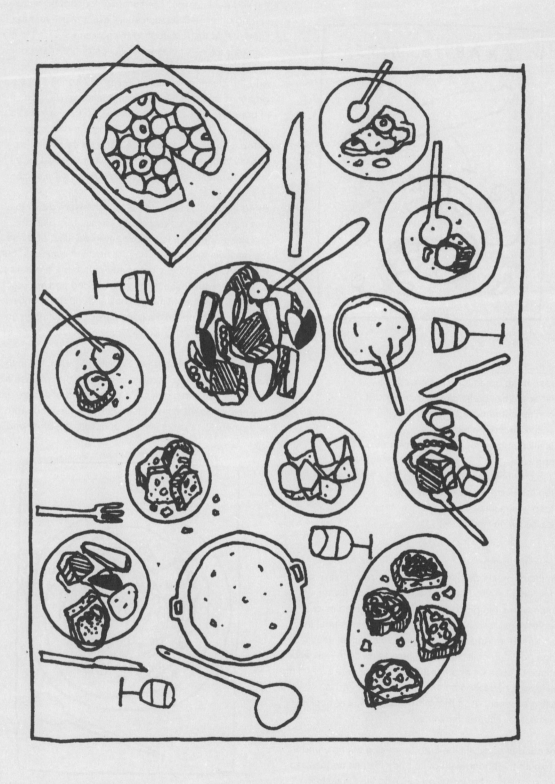

bring everything slowly to the boil. Simmer the octopus for around 30 minutes, or until cooked but not mushy. Remove the octopus, chop it into appropriate-sized pieces and set aside. Taste the broth carefully for seasoning; by now it should be utterly delicious. Set the broth aside until needed – this can happily be made a day ahead.

To marinate the fish:

Cut the filleted fish into bite-size pieces. Aim for one nicely sized piece of each fish per person. Crush the garlic to a paste with a small pinch of salt with a pestle in a mortar. Throw in the parsley and the saffron and pound until you have a smooth, aromatic paste. Stir well and set aside.

To make the rouille:

Completely soak the bread in a little of the hot bouillabaisse broth, then allow to cool.

Crush the garlic, with a little salt, to a fine white paste in the pestle and mortar. Add the anchovy fillets, saffron and broth-soaked bread, then pound to a thick paste. Add the egg yolks and cayenne pepper, and emulsify as best you can. Start to add the olive oil very slowly – at first, drop by drop and then in a slow, steady stream. As the emulsion starts to thicken, add a few drops of lemon juice or vinegar, plus a few of water, then continue with the oil. It's important to add the lemon, vinegar and water gradually as this will prevent the rouille from splitting. When all the oil is used up, taste the rouille for salt and acid, and try to find a nice balance. A rouille stabilised with bread and anchovy is harder to split than an aïoli, but I have managed it.

For the potatoes:

Pour off some of the broth into a smaller pan. Add the the potatoes to this broth and bring to the boil. For those worried about not having enough broth, a little half broth– half water arrangement is fine. Try not to overcook the potatoes: they should be soft but not falling apart.

For the croûtons:

Lay the thinly sliced baguette on a tray and drizzle lightly with olive oil. Bake at 130°C fan/150°C/300°F/gas mark 2 for 10 minutes, or until golden brown and crunchy.

To cook the fish and serve:

Season the marinated fish with salt. Poach the fish in the broth at a gentle simmer for around 5 minutes, turning once if necessary. Add the remaining mussels and octopus pieces towards the end of the cooking time – they need only a minute or two to cook and heat through. If you are worried about crushing the fish or the pan being overcrowded, poach the fish in batches according to size

of morsel, species and firmness: monkfish or gurnard, for example, will hold their shape more readily than other species, and could be cooked first and kept warm. Remove the fish from the broth and keep warm.

Bring the broth briefly to a fast, rolling boil, then pour into serving bowls while still piping hot. Serve the hot broth first, with bowls of rouille and croûtons to float on top.

As your guest coo over the broth, bring over the cooked fish and shellfish arranged artfully by species on a huge platter. The cooked fish should be moistened with broth to keep it warm and juicy. Also bring out the warm potatoes to complete the picture. There should be plenty of hot broth in reserve for top-ups.

Plum Galette
Makes enough for 8 people

   1 quantity of galette pastry (see page 249)
   1kg/2lb 4oz plums, stoned and halved
   4 thyme sprigs
   1 egg yolk
   1 tsp double (heavy) cream
   2 tbsp demerara sugar
   1 tbsp runny honey
   Crème fraîche, to serve

Preheat the oven to 220°C fan/240°C/450°F/gas mark 8. Place a heavy baking tray in the oven to heat up.

On a sheet of parchment paper, roll out the galette pastry in a circle to a thickness of 3mm/⅛ inch.

Arrange the plums and thyme sprigs in the centre of the pastry disc, leaving a 5-cm/2-inch border on all sides. Fold the edges of the pastry over the fruit, crimping together slightly where it overlaps. Beat the egg yolk and cream together and brush over the pastry border, then sprinkle it with the sugar.

Slide the galette, still on the parchment paper, onto the hot baking tray and bake for 15 minutes before turning the oven down to 160°C fan/180°C/350°F/gas mark 4. Cook for a further 30 minutes until the plums are soft and bubbling and the pastry is an even golden brown. Remove from the oven, glaze the plums with the honey and cool.

When ready to serve, slice the galette into pieces and eat with crème fraîche.

COQ AU VIN

Wild Garlic & Cantal Tart

–

Christina's Salad, Walnut Oil & Crème Fraîche Dressing

–

Coq au Vin, Buttered Noodles

–

Tomme de Savoie

–

Poached Pears & Honey Ice Cream

My Uncle Tim, something of a gourmand, used to cook a very good coq au vin. It's quintessential French country cooking and, in the right hands, can be something wonderful. Debate rages fiercely over every aspect of the recipe, even what kind of coq to use. An old, tough boiling rooster, a younger, more tender specimen, or even (gasp) a hen? To marinade in wine overnight or not? And what wine? The questions go on. What I would say is that the quality of both coq and vin are paramount.

We were especially pleased with the balance and simple feel of this menu. We cooked this Grand Bouffe in very early spring, when the days were still crisp and the nights lengthening: a gentle nudge from one season to another. The Tomme de Savoie was delicious here, a cheese course to bridge the gap nicely between the earthy and the milky sweet.

The argument over which region of France coq au vin originated in is possibly as old as the dish itself. We based our version around a recipe found in the excellent Mourjou by Peter Graham, an authentic account of the cooking traditions of an Auvergne village. Instead of a scrawny old *coq*, we used a delicious plump chicken. I advise you to do the same. The most important thing is that the chicken has good flavour. While I would never advocate spending £20 or $25 dollars on a bottle of wine to cook with, the better the wine you use, the better the dish will be. Note that the carrot and celery in the marinade are not cooked with the stew. I find that they collapse into a mulch and also add an unwelcome sweetness.

Wild Garlic & Cantal Tart
Serves 4 as a little snack or 2 as a light lunch

For the pastry:
125g/4½oz/1 cup plain (all-purpose) flour
A pinch of salt
75g/2½oz/5 tsbp unsalted butter
2 tbsp milk
1 egg, beaten

For the filling:
2 shallots, peeled, halved lengthways, and sliced
into half moons
2 tbsp unsalted butter
1 thyme sprig
25g/1oz wild garlic leaves, washed
2 whole eggs
3 egg yolks
185ml/6¼fl oz/¾ cup double (heavy) cream
75g/2½oz Cantal cheese (if you can't find Cantal then
Cheddar or Lancashire would both work here)
A few gratings of nutmeg
Sea salt and freshly ground black pepper

Preheat the oven to 180°C fan/200°C/400°F/gas mark 6.

To make the pastry, sift the flour and salt into a large
bowl. With your hands, rub in the butter until the mixture
resembles fine breadcrumbs. Sprinkle over 1 tbsp of the
milk, or just enough to bring the dough together. Wrap the
pastry in clingfilm (plastic wrap) and refrigerate for at least
30 minutes.

Once the dough has rested, roll it out to a rectangle
2mm/¹⁄₁₆ inch thick. Lay the rolled-out pastry in a
rectangular baking dish, ideally around 4cm/1½ inches
deep. Line the pastry with ceramic baking beans or dried
pulses and blind bake the tart case for around 10 minutes,
or until a light golden brown.

Remove the tart case from the oven, empty out the baking
beans or dried pulses and then brush the pastry with the
beaten egg. Return to the oven for 1 minute to firm up the
egg wash. Remove from the oven and allow to cool.

Lower the oven temperature to 170°C fan/190°C/375°F/
gas mark 5.

To make the tart filling, fry the sliced shallots slowly in the

butter with the thyme sprig, a pinch of salt and a grind
of pepper. When the shallots are soft, discard the thyme
sprig and set aside to cool.

Blanch the wild garlic leaves briefly in boiling salted water,
only for a second. Refresh in iced water. Set aside half of
the leaves. In a blender or smoothie maker, blitz the other
half of the leaves to make a smooth purée. Add a little of
the cooking water, if necessary.

In a bowl, beat the eggs, egg yolks and cream together
well. Season to taste with salt and pepper. Mix in the
softened shallots, wild garlic purée and reserved wild
garlic leaves.

Pour the filling mixture into the pre-baked tart shell.
Coarsely grate the cheese evenly into the filling, then finish
with a few grates of nutmeg.

Place in the preheated oven and bake for about 15
minutes, or until golden green and with a slight wobble.

Remove the tart from the oven and allow to cool slightly.

This is delicious served just warm from the oven, cut into
small squares.

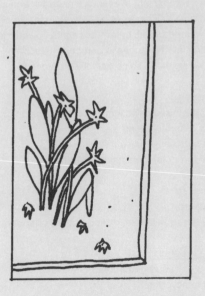

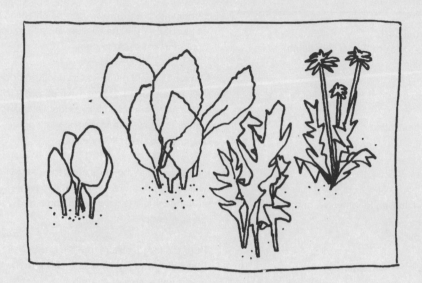

Christina's Salad, Walnut Oil & Crème Fraîche Dressing
Serves 4

Christina is a lovely lady who grows produce for us in south east London. A mainstay of our regular order is her mixed salad, which is the finest I've tasted anywhere. For this dinner I convinced her to deliver slightly earlier than usual, so that the salad was only a few hours out of the ground… it was the best ever. We paired it with a walnut oil and crème fraîche dressing, which tastes wonderfully full and rounded. Both cream and walnut oil are delicious with young, fresh lettuces in particular. I seem to remember we made some garlicky croûtons too.

For the salad:
50g/1¾oz mixed salad leaves per person, ideally a mixture of the following:
Young soft leaf lettuces
Rocket (arugula), domestic rather than wild
Dandelion
Mustard leaves
Baby chard
1 tbsp tarragon leaves, picked but not chopped

For the croûtons:
100g/3½oz sourdough bread (stale is best), crusts removed
1 tbsp olive oil
4 garlic cloves, peeled and roughly crushed
1 thyme sprig

For the dressing:
A tiny scrap of peeled garlic
½ tsp mustard
1 tbsp red wine vinegar
4 tbsp olive oil
1 tbsp crème fraîche
A pinch of salt
A grind of black pepper

Preheat the oven to 160°C fan/180°C/350°F/gas mark 4.

To make the croûtons, chop the bread into small 1-cm/½-inch cubes. Toss in the olive oil, garlic and thyme. Lay the cubes of bread on a roasting tray and then toast in the preheated oven until crunchy and golden brown. Remove from the oven and discard the garlic and thyme.

For the dressing, crush the scrap of garlic with a pinch of salt to a fine paste. Put the garlic paste into a bowl and, one by one, whisk in all the other ingredients in the order listed above. Pause before you whisk in the crème fraîche: try to emulsify the vinaigrette before you add it in. Season to taste with salt and pepper.

To assemble the salad, wash and dry the salad leaves well. Tear any larger leaves into smaller pieces. Toss the salad and tarragon leaves in the dressing, then top with the croûtons.

Combine all the marinade ingredients in a bowl or pot. Place the jointed chicken pieces in the marinade, making sure that they are all submerged. Leave in the refrigerator overnight.

The next day, preheat the oven to 170°C fan/190°C/ 375°F/gas mark 5. Remove the chicken from the marinade. Reserve the marinade and set aside. Pat the chicken pieces dry with paper towels, season well with salt and pepper, then dredge lightly with the flour.

In a deep, spacious, heavy-bottomed pot with a lid, fry the lardons in a little olive oil over a medium heat. When the fat has rendered and the lardons are golden brown, remove with a slotted spoon, leaving the fat in the pot.

Add a touch more olive oil to the fat, and fry the floured chicken pieces until a rich, deep golden brown on all sides. Remove the chicken from the pot and set aside.

Coq au Vin
Serves 4

1 plump chicken, weighing around 2kg/4lb 8oz, jointed, with the liver reserved and cleaned of any sinew (optional)
2 tbsp plain (all-purpose) flour, to dredge
100g/3½oz pancetta, cut into chunky lardons around 1cm/½ inch thickness
Olive oil
150g/5¼oz button mushrooms
10g/⅓oz dried ceps, soaked in hot water
15 small pickling onions, or small round shallots, peeled
6 garlic cloves, peeled and very lightly crushed
Sea salt and freshly ground black pepper
A small bunch of chopped parsley
Buttered boiled potatoes or buttered tagliatelle, to serve

For the marinade:
1 bottle of full-bodied red wine, such as Corbières or Cahors (but anything good will do)
A good glug of brandy
1 carrot, cut into 4 pieces
1 celery stalk, cut into 4 pieces
2 garlic cloves, peeled and lightly crushed
2 cloves
6 black peppercorns
A pinch of salt
A bouquet garni made from thyme, bay leaves, parsley stalks and winter savory (if available)

Add the mushrooms, the onions or shallots and the garlic. Stir them around in the fat to coat and then fry slowly for a few minutes until they have taken on some flavour and started to soften. Season with salt.

Put the chicken pieces and bacon lardons back in the pot along with the mushrooms, onions and garlic.

Strain the reserved marinade and discard the carrot, celery and garlic. Return the strained marinade, along with the spices and bouquet garni, to the pot with the chicken.

Bring the liquid to a rapid simmer, skim once, then reduce the heat to a low simmer (one bubble every second or so). If the chicken pieces are not submerged, add a little water. Cover the pot with the lid and place in the preheated oven. Cook for around an hour and half, or until the chicken is tender but not falling off the bone. Remove the pot from the oven. The chicken should be cooked, the mushrooms and shallots whole but yielding, and there should be plenty of liquid still to play with.

From here there are two possible routes to take: to thicken the sauce with butter or to thicken the sauce with the chicken's liver. The liver adds a gamey finish, but does leave the sauce ever so slightly grainy. Here's how: blitz the trimmed liver in a blender, then slowly whisk in a ladleful of the sauce from the pot. Return this mixture to the rest of the sauce in the pot and warm through without boiling. Otherwise, or as well, whisk in a few lumps of cold unsalted butter to thicken the sauce and add a gloss. Taste the sauce carefully and season with salt and pepper, if needed. The texture of the sauce is important; it should be neither too thick nor too thin. Adjust by simmering to thicken, or add water to thin.

Serve with a little chopped parsley, some buttered boiled potatoes or some plain buttered noodles (tagliatelle). We made our own fresh pasta for this meal, but decent pasta from a packet is just fine.

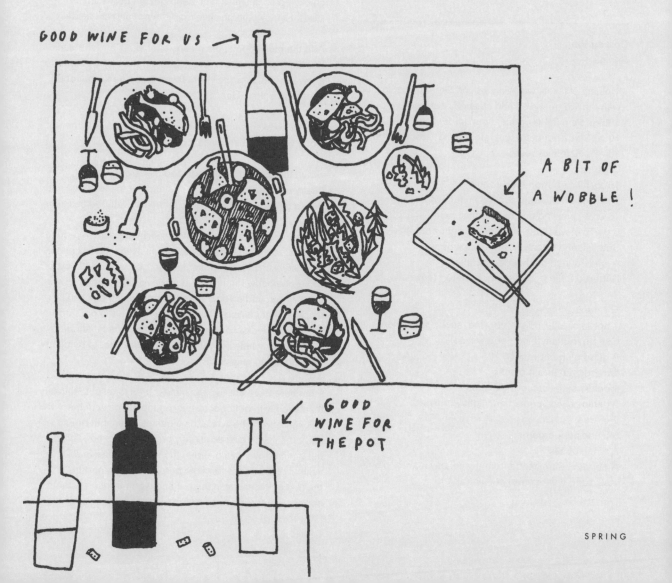

GOOD WINE FOR US →

A BIT OF A WOBBLE!

← GOOD WINE FOR THE POT

Poached Pears & Honey Ice Cream
Serves 4

Sometimes I like to add a little thyme when cooking
poached pears. If you think that's weird, then just leave it
out. This dessert was definitely on the sweet side, but it
worked well within this menu.

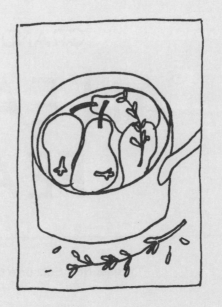

For the pears:
100g/3½oz/½ cup caster (superfine) sugar
200ml/7fl oz/1 cup water
2 fat pears, peeled, halved and cored
2 cloves
1 thyme sprig (optional)

For the ice cream:
8 egg yolks
75g/2½oz honey
500ml/18fl oz/2 cups whole milk
500ml/18fl oz/2 cups double (heavy) cream
Dried lavender buds (optional)

To make the ice cream, whisk the egg yolks well in a bowl
with the honey.

Combine the milk and cream in a pan and bring to scalding
point over a high heat.

Pour the milk and cream very slowly onto the egg yolk
mixture, whisking continually as you go. Continue, pouring
gradually faster, until all the milk and cream has been
added to the bowl.

Transfer the lot back to the pan and cook stirring over
a medium–low heat for around 5 minutes, or until the
custard reaches 82°C/180°F.

Strain the mixture through a fine sieve (strainer) into a tray.
Refrigerate until cold, then churn in an ice-cream maker.

To poach the pears:
Dissolve the sugar in the water, add the pears, cloves and
thyme, then simmer for 10–12 minutes or until soft.

To serve:
Heat the pears and place one half in each serving bowl.
Add a scoop of ice cream to each bowl so that the heat
from the pear starts to melt the ice cream and their juices
start to mingle. For an optional floral flourish, place a
singular dried lavender bud on each ball of ice cream.

GRANDE BOUFFE

AN EASTER FEAST

Roast New Season's Garlic & Tapenade Toasts

–

Asparagus, Crème Fraîche, Bottarga & Herbs

–

Whole Chicken Baked in Salt, Spring Vegetables, Spinach & Mayonnaise

–

Provençal Goats' Cheeses

–

Rhubarb & Strawberry Millefeuille

This is a slightly unconventional Easter feast. Easter is a time for tradition, but it also often occurs at the point in spring when the new seasonal produce starts to arrive – tender asparagus, wet garlic, fresh Provençal goats' milk cheeses and the first strawberries.

Whole chicken baked in salt is a showstopper. Cooked in this way, a chicken will taste as though it has been roasted but will eat almost like it has been poached – ideal when served with some baby spring vegetables and a proper mayonnaise.

At this time of year, the goats' cheese producers in Provence restart production after winter. The maturing caves are filled with fresh little cheeses, wrapped in sweet chestnut leaves, topped with sprigs of mountain herbs and generally tasting of spring: now's the time to pounce.

Forced rhubarb and strawberries are a fantastic winter–spring crossover combination. The sweet, fresh berries work well with the astringent cooked rhubarb.

Roast New Season's Garlic & Tapenade Toasts
Serves 4

For the garlic:
2 heads of new season's wet garlic
2 tsp olive oil
2 tsp unsalted butter
2 thyme sprigs
Salt and pepper, to taste

For the tapenade:
100g/3½oz black olives, drained of any brine or oil and pitted (I prefer to use Nyons olives, which make the best tapenade, but any soft black olives work well)
⅛ garlic clove, peeled and crushed to a fine paste
½ tsp picked thyme
1 salted anchovy fillet, washed and patted dry
1 tsp salted capers, soaked well, rinsed and drained
1 tsp brandy
4 tsp olive oil
1 tsp red wine vinegar

To serve:
Slices of toast

Preheat the oven to 170°C fan/190°C/375°F/gas mark 5.

Slice the heads of garlic in half horizontally through the cloves. Arrange them cut-side up, so that the cut cloves are exposed, drizzle with olive oil, dot with the butter and scatter the thyme on top. Season with salt and pepper.

Cover the garlic loosely with foil and roast in the hot oven for around 40 minutes or until soft and sweet. Towards the end of the cooking time, remove the foil to give the garlic a nice golden brown colour.

Meanwhile, make the tapenade. Put all the dry ingredients in a blender. Blitz well. Add the wet ingredients and blitz further until everything is fully incorporated. The tapenade should be very smooth.

Serve the roasted garlic with slices of toast and a blob of tapenade. Encourage your guests to mush the garlic onto the toast, adding the tapenade as they go for a more spirited Provençal bite.

Asparagus, Crème Fraîche, Bottarga & Herbs
Serves 4

Asparagus is very nice with cream and fish roe. The secret here is to use loads of bottarga. If you can't find bottarga, use caviar.

12 green asparagus spears, tough stalk snapped off
A good glug of olive oil
1 tsp lemon juice
4 tbsp good-quality, full-fat crème fraîche
20g/¾oz bottarga
1 tbsp chopped mixed herbs (parsley, chervil, tarragon and mint)
4 radishes, thinly sliced on a mandoline or with a sharp knife
Coarse sea salt, to taste

Boil or grill the asparagus, as preferred, until cooked to your liking. Place the asparagus in a bowl and season lightly with olive oil, lemon juice and sea salt.

Divide the dressed asparagus between four serving plates. Dollop a tablespoonful of the crème fraîche onto each plate, then finely grate the bottarga over the crème fraîche so that the surface of the cream is covered. Scatter over the herbs and the sliced radishes. Finally, drizzle with a little more olive oil.

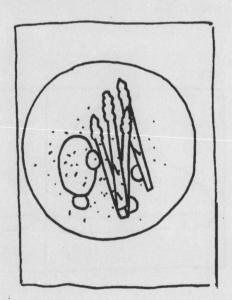

Whole Chicken Baked in Salt, Spring Vegetables, Spinach & Mayonnaise
Serves 4

For the chicken:
1 chicken (weighing approximately 1.8kg/4lb)
1.5kg/3lb 5oz rock salt
500g/1lb 2oz fine salt

For the 'gravy':
Giblets and wing tips of the chicken
Chicken stock, if you have any to hand
1 shallot, cut in half
1 tarragon sprig
A few parsley stalks
10 black peppercorns
A good glug of brandy, Armagnac or Calvados
1 tbsp cold butter, cut into little cubes

For the vegetables:
200g/7oz spinach
100g/3½oz podded broad (fava) beans
100g/3½oz podded peas
100g/3½oz asparagus, cut into 1-cm/½-inch lengths
A good glug of olive oil
Juice of 1–2 lemons
Salt

For the mayonnaise:
2 egg yolks
200ml/7fl oz/1 cup olive oil
2 tsp lemon juice
2 tsp cold water
Salt

Prepare and roast the chicken following the instructions given on page 156 for Salt-Baked Guinea Fowl. A chicken that is 1.8kg/4lb in weight should take 45 minutes to cook, plus a little extra time to rest: allow 1 hour cooking and resting time in total.

For the vegetables, blanch the spinach for 10 seconds (or 5 seconds if using baby spinach) in a pan of boiling, salted water. Remove the spinach with a slotted spoon and squeeze well to remove any excess water. Keep warm. To the same pan of boiling water, add the broad beans, peas and asparagus, and cook for 1 minute. Drain, then combine with the spinach and season the mixture with olive oil, lemon juice and salt, if needed.

To make the mayonnaise, whisk the egg yolks in a bowl with a pinch of salt until slightly thickened. Very slowly drizzle in the olive oil, drop by drop at first, until you have a thick emulsion. Continue to add the oil until you have a thick, glossy, wobbly mayonnaise, thinning the mayonnaise with a teaspoon of lemon juice or water as you go. Season with salt and taste for lemon juice.

To serve, pluck the salty crust from the chicken, scraping off any excess salt from the meat, and portion the chicken on the bone. Serve with the dressed vegetables and a spoonful of mayonnaise. Some chopped herbs (chervil, parsley or tarragon) would go very nicely here, but aren't strictly necessary.

Serve with the juices.

Provençal Goats' Cheeses
Serves 4

In general, I am opposed to any kind of Anglicised chutney business with cheese, but Provençal goats' milk cheese pairs well with good-quality honey and some rye crackers.

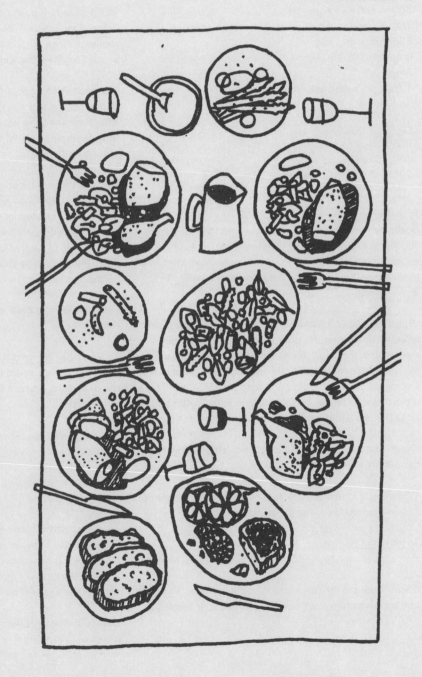

Rhubarb & Strawberry Millefeuille
Serves 4

1 block (250g/8¾oz) of puff pastry – the better the quality, the better the millefeuille!
A handful of delicious strawberries (Gariguette are very good at this time of year)

For the pastry cream:
500ml/18fl oz/2 cups milk
1 vanilla pod, scraped out, or 1tsp vanilla essence
55g/2oz/⅓ cup flour
90g/3½oz/½ cup sugar
6 egg yolks
1 tsp cold butter, cut into small cubes

For the rhubarb:
250g/8¾oz rhubarb
100g/3½oz/½ cup sugar
200ml/7fl oz/1 cup water

To make the pastry cream:
Scald the milk and whisk in the vanilla. Mix the flour and sugar well in a pot. Whisk the hot milk into the flour and sugar mixture, taking care to avoid lumps. Cook this mixture over a medium heat, whisking all the while, for 2–3 minutes.

Whisk the egg yolks briefly to thicken slightly. Very slowly, while whisking furiously, pour some of the gloopy milk mixture onto the egg yolks. Continue until all is mixed together. Transfer back into the pot and cook, stirring, until the mixture thickens slightly and reaches 75°C/167°F (use a thermometer for best results). Whisk in the butter and pass through a fine sieve (strainer) into a tray.

Cover with clingfilm (plastic wrap) and refrigerate until thoroughly cooled, at least 2 hours.

When ready to use, transfer to a piping bag. Take care not to overwork the cream as it may thin out.

To make the rhubarb:
Preheat the oven to 160°C fan/180°C/350°F/gas mark 4.

If the rhubarb is very thick, cut in half lengthways. Cut the lengths of rhubarb into pieces as wide as your millefeuille will be – I suggest 5cm/2 inches. Bring the sugar and water to the boil, then pour into a deep tray. Put in the rhubarb. Cover with foil and bake in the oven for 10 minutes, or until the rhubarb is soft but not frayed or falling apart. Remove from the oven and cool thoroughly before placing in the refrigerator.

To make the pastry:
Preheat the oven to 180°C fan/200°C/400°F/gas mark 6.

Roll out the puff pastry to a rectangle approximately 2mm/¹⁄₁₆ inch thick. Trim the sides to make a perfect rectangle, then cut this pastry into three or four strips about 5cm/2 inches wide.

Arrange the strips on a flat tray lined with parchment paper. Put the tray into the oven and bake for 8 minutes. After 8 minutes, the pastry will have partially risen. At this stage, place a light tray on top of the pastry to stop it puffing further. Bake for a further 8 minutes.

Remove the tray, reduce the heat of the oven to 150°C fan/170°C/325°F/gas mark 3, and continue to cook for a further 40 minutes, or until the pastry is a deep golden brown and extremely crisp. You should be able to lift one of the strips of pastry from one end and have it stay intact. If you feel the pastry could cook for longer, add another 10 minutes cooking time.

Remove from the oven and dust lightly with icing sugar. Allow to cool.

To assemble the millefeuille:
Take the cooked, crisp, puff pastry, the cooked rhubarb, the pastry cream and a handful of delicious sweet strawberries.

Cut the pastry into rectangles as long as you want the millefeuille to be – around 10cm/4 inches should do it.

Cut these lengths carefully in half along the edge to make two thinner pieces.

Find your flattest piece of pastry and put it on a plate. Pipe over the pastry cream – I go for the messy method. Don't get too carried away – you'll be making two layers. Arrange the strips of rhubarb over the top, then top with another rectangle of pastry.

Repeat the pastry cream layer, but this time top with some slices of strawberry. Top with the third bit of pastry. Dust with icing sugar and serve.

LEG OF LAMB À LA FICELLE (ON A STRING)

Serves 6–8

1 whole leg of lamb (2kg/4lb 8oz), H-bone removed, but otherwise intact, particularly the tendon at the end

Butcher's string

A meat hook (where appropriate, but not always strictly necessary)

An open wood fire

Something to hang the lamb from (the branch of a tree, a sturdy clothesline, a purpose-built frame)

For the basting brine and herb brush:

200ml/7fl oz/1 cup water

50g/1¾oz fine salt

1 tbsp cayenne pepper

6 garlic cloves, unpeeled and crushed

Juice of 1 lemon

3 tbsp olive oil

1 large woody sprig each of rosemary, bay, thyme, lavender (the more herbs the merrier)

First, inherit an ancient stone farmhouse lost somewhere in the hills of the Luberon, then string up a leg of young lamb, hang over a smoky wood fire in the fireplace and let it spin slowly as it roasts. Baste it using a bundle of woody herbs gathered from the nearby hillsides… Yes, I know, me neither.

While I've not been lucky enough to cook a leg of lamb à la ficelle in Provence, my friends and I have made a pretty good show of it on a wet Bonfire Night somewhere on Hackney Marshes in East London. Our substitute farmhouse was a willow tree with a tarpaulin draped over its branches, and what we lacked in a stone fireplace we made up for with a wonky campfire. We hung the leg of lamb from a tree branch. Many hours later, with our motley crew slightly merry and well and truly smoked out, the leg was cut down and carved into. The meat was sweet, smoky, salty, slightly too pink perhaps, but we cared not. The end result was no less authentic, romantic or delicious than the sun-drenched idyll.

This recipe is one to be attempted only when you have a few people coming round and a bit of time on your hands. Cooking a large piece of meat like this over a wood fire is so satisfying, and the result so spectacular, that it's worth investing the time and the effort. With a lot of practice, at the restaurant we have come to understand the process a little better, so here I offer a few tips for success:

– Build a wood fire next to the hanging leg of lamb as high as possible. At the same time, hang the lamb as low as you can adjacent to the fire, around 30–50cm/12–20 inches away – but this will depend on how hot your fire is. Do not place the fire directly beneath the lamb as the bottom of the leg will overcook while the top part will remain raw.

– Make a fire using seasoned oak logs. As the whole cooking process will take a few hours at least, keep the fire topped with more logs.

– The tying of the lamb doesn't need to be complicated. Wrap the string around the leg of lamb until you're satisfied that it's sufficiently sturdy, then pass it through the 'hoop' where the tendon is on the shank. The weight of the leg means the lamb should spin naturally while hung.

– Baste the lamb periodically with a brush made from a bunch of hard herbs – rosemary, sage, thyme and so on. Dip the herb brush into a mixture of heavily salted water, olive oil, lemon, crushed fennel seeds and cayenne pepper.

– Invest in a digital temperature probe. Take the lamb off the heat when it reaches 50°C/120°F. Allow time for the lamb to rest after cooking.

– Position a tray of baked potato slices or bowl of slow-cooked white beans beneath the roasting leg to catch the juices. This is delicious, of course, but be aware that much of the fat from the lamb will render into it, so skim the fat off the vegetables before serving. Alternatively, catch the fat and juices in an empty bowl – add a few splashes of water to stop the fat from frying and you're left with an intense sauce of sorts.

———————

Well before building your fire, remove the leg of lamb from the refrigerator and allow to come to room temperature.

Build a wood fire in an appropriate spot in your garden. You'll need something to hang the leg of lamb from – the branch of a tree is ideal. The lamb should hang about 30–50cm/12–20 inches from the fire depending on how hot it is. You can always unhook or untie the lamb and re-tie it in a better position. When the fire is hot and the flames have mostly died down, it's time to cook.

Trim any excess fat from the leg of lamb – leaving too much will lead to flare-ups on the fire. Season with salt and pepper, rub with olive oil and string up the lamb as described opposite. Hang the lamb near the fire and give it a spin. The string will slowly wind up and then unwind again, and should keep the lamb turning like a vertical spit. When the lamb stops spinning, give it another twirl.

To make the brine, bring the water and the salt to the boil with the garlic. Add the cayenne pepper, lemon juice and olive oil and whisk to combine. Make the basting brush by tying the woody herbs together tightly with string. Dip the herb brush into the brine and periodically baste the leg of lamb – every 30 minutes or so. This will help to form a delicious salty crust.

Cook the lamb over the fire for 2–3 hours depending on the size of the leg of lamb, the intensity of the fire, the prevailing wind conditions, and so on. Using a digitial temperature probe to check, take the lamb to an internal temperature of 50°C/120°F – this will be a very pink. Take the lamb down from the fire and allow to rest in a warm spot for 30 minutes, during which time the temperature of the lamb should rise to around 60°C/140°F, and the cooking should be spot on.

The lamb is best carved thinly. Serve in bread, smeared with tapenade or anchoïade (see page 20), or with cooked white beans, roast potatoes, a green sauce with lots of anchovies, capers and mint, or anything else that's good with roast lamb.

GRILLED VEAL CHOP
& WILD GARLIC BUTTER

Serves 2

For the wild garlic butter (this makes far too much for one veal chop, but it is far too delicious to only use for one meal at a time. It keeps for a while in the refrigerator and freezes well too, enjoy!):

A big handful of wild garlic, washed and dried

4 anchovy fillets

1 x 250-g/9-oz pack of unsalted butter, at room temperature

Lemon juice

A splash of brandy

Sea salt and freshly ground black pepper

For the veal chop (enough for 2):

1 rose veal T-bone chop (approximate weight 500g/1lb 2oz or more)

Sea salt and freshly ground black pepper

The arrival of the wild garlic in the spring is a happy time in the kitchen. During the month-long window after it arrives, and before we are wholly sick of the sight of the stuff, we manage to cram it into as many dishes as possible. One recipe that we keep coming back to is this wild garlic butter. It's more herbal, and much more green, than your normal *beurre maître d'hôtel*, and works well with a nice thick-cut veal chop cooked on the grill. Try to get your hands on a nice veal T-bone chop. It's important that it weighs at least 500g/1lb 2oz or it will be a bit thin. Make sure it's rose veal. It will cost a fortune but it will be worth it.

———————————

Whizz the wild garlic in a food processor to a fine paste. Add the anchovies, whizz again, then add the butter. Blitz again until all the ingredients are completely amalgamated, then season with a little salt, a lot of pepper and a squeeze of lemon juice. Splash in the brandy, then mix and taste.

Transfer the butter mixture onto a piece of parchment paper and roll up into a cylinder. Twist the ends well and tie with string. The wild garlic butter keeps well in the refrigerator for at least two weeks, or in the freezer for longer.

Season the veal chop heavily with salt and pepper. Grill over a hot charcoal or wood fire until encrusted but still pink inside, about 5 minutes on each side. Leave the chop to rest.

While the veal chop is resting, cut two circles of the wild garlic butter and place on each side of the T-bone to melt.

Serve the veal chop with some spinach and perhaps some potatoes. It's also good with sautéed morels and snails, but that's another story.

GRILLED RABBIT
IN GARLIC & HARD HERBS

Makes enough for 4 people

1 whole farmed French rabbit or,
  failing that, 4 rabbit legs
Salt and freshly ground black pepper

For the marinade:

1 fat head of garlic or 2 smaller ones

A selection of hard herbs, such as
  savory, thyme, myrtle, hyssop or
  rosemary, leaves picked

2 tsp fennel seeds, lightly crushed

1 dried chilli, roughly crushed

Grated zest of 1 orange and juice of
  ½ the orange

2 egg yolks

1 tsp Dijon mustard

4 tbsp olive oil

2 tbsp dry white wine

Sea salt

At the weekly market in Lourmarin, a village nestled in the hills of the Luberon, there are stands selling roasted meats. On the trailer-mounted rotisserie behind the butcher, various cuts turn slowly over flames: three types of chicken, including the prized birds from Bresse, quails, farmed pigeons, fatty ham hocks, pork loins stuffed with herbs and chopped offal and – sometimes – whole roast rabbits at a humble €20 a pop.

Cooked on a spit mounted over a wood fire, rabbit tastes magical. Failing that, a charcoal barbecue is a pretty decent second best. This is incredibly garlicky and utterly delicious. Serve with some boiled and dressed greens, maybe a bit of dandelion and borage in there, and a touch of crème fraîche stirred through to cool things down a bits. And come to think about it, what about some chips?

———————

First make the marinade. Peel the garlic cloves and smash to a fine paste with a little salt in a pestle and mortar. Throw in your herbs of choice and smash again to a paste, then add the fennel seeds, dried chilli and orange zest.

Put the egg yolks in a bowl with the mustard, add a pinch of salt, then whisk to thicken. Add the garlic and herb smash to the egg yolks, then whisk in the olive oil slowly as if making a mayonnaise. Thin the marinade with the orange juice and white wine. The result should be a fiercely garlicky, thin emulsion, with a consistency a little like a thick vinaigrette.

If you are cooking over a charcoal barbecue, joint the rabbit so that you have two hind legs, two front legs and two pieces of loin. Season the pieces of rabbit well with salt and pepper. Reserve a little of the marinade for basting during cooking, then smear the rest of the marinade over the rabbit and leave for at least 30 minutes, but the longer the better.

Grill the rabbit over a medium hot charcoal or wood fire. If you have a spit mounted over a wood fire (lucky you!), then put the rabbit on it whole. It is also possible to cook the rabbit under the grill (broiler) of a domestic oven, although a lot of the smokiness and a little of the magic will be lost. Grill the rabbit slowly and baste regularly. For extra points, use a bunch of whichever herbs you are using as a brush to baste the rabbit with the marinade.

After 25–30 minutes the rabbit should be cooked through but still juicy. Rest it for 5 minutes in a warm place before serving.

CHOUX À LA CRÈME

Makes enough for 8 people

For the choux buns:

250ml/8fl oz/1 cup cold water

100g/3½oz/½ cup cold unsalted butter, cubed

8g/⅓oz caster (superfine) sugar

A pinch of salt

140g/5oz/1⅛ cups plain (all-purpose) flour, sifted

5 whole eggs, or 4 if large

For the honey crème patissière:

500ml/18fl oz/2 cups milk

3 tbsp honey

50g/1¾oz/⅓ cup plain (all-purpose) flour

3 tbsp caster (superfine) sugar

6 egg yolks

2 tsp cold unsalted butter, cut into small cubes

For the almonds:

100g/3½oz/7 tbsp unsalted butter

25g/1oz/⅛ cup whole almonds (skinless)

10g/⅓oz/⅛ cup icing (confectioners') sugar

A big pinch of salt

For the caramel sauce:

25g/1oz/⅛ cup caster (superfine) sugar

Cold water, to cover

1 tsp cold unsalted butter, cubed

1 tbsp single (light) cream, warmed

This plate is all cream and gold: a joy. There are a lot of steps for one dessert, but bear with me, as all are simple things to make.

———————————

To make the honey crème patissière, scald the milk and whisk in the honey. Mix the flour and sugar well in a pan. Whisk the hot milk into the flour and sugar mixture, taking care to avoid lumps. Cook this mixture over a medium heat, whisking continually, for 2–3 minutes. Whisk the egg yolks briefly. Then, whisking furiously, slowly pour some of the milk mixture onto the egg yolks. Continue until combined. Transfer back to the pan and cook, stirring, until the mixture thickens slightly and reaches 75°C/165°F on a thermometer. Whisk in the butter and pass through a fine sieve (strainer) into a tray. Cover with clingfilm (plastic wrap) and chill in the refrigerator for at least 2 hours.

To make the choux buns, put the water, butter, salt and sugar in a pan and bring to the boil while whisking. Cook for 2 minutes, whisking continuously, then add the flour all at once. Reduce the heat to low and stir with a wooden spoon until the mixture comes together. Cook, stirring, until the mixture comes away from the pan and is stiff enough to stand your spoon up in it. Transfer the mixture to a stand mixer or bowl and slowly beat in the eggs one by one, until it is almost at room temperature. Transfer to a piping bag and allow to cool. Preheat the oven to 180°C fan/200°C/400°F/gas mark 6. When cool, pipe the pastry into rounds the size of a golf ball on a baking tray lined with parchment paper. Put the tray in the hot oven and bake for 35–40 minutes, or until light golden brown, puffed and crisp. Don't open the oven door for at least 30 minutes. When done, the choux buns should sound hollow when tapped on the bottom. Pierce each bun with a toothpick so that any excess steam can escape. Allow to cool.

To make the almonds, melt the butter in a pan. Add the almonds and cook slowly, submerged, until a deep brown. Drain and sprinkle with the sugar and salt. Allow to cool, then slice lengthways as thinly as you can be bothered.

For the caramel sauce, put the sugar in a small pan and pour in enough cold water just to cover the sugar. Place over a low–medium heat and wait until the sugar dissolves and the syrup turns into a light caramel. At this stage, remove the pan from the heat and whisk in the cold butter and the cream. The sauce should be of a drizzle-able consistency: add a dash more cream if it is too thick.

To serve, transfer the cooled honey crème patissière to a piping bag and fill the choux buns from the bottom. If you don't have a piping bag, no problem. Simply cut the buns in half and spoon in the cream. Drizzle the buns with warm caramel sauce and top with the almonds.

APRICOT & BROWN BUTTER TART

Makes a 28-cm/11-inch tart

For the pastry:

235g/8oz/1¾ cups plain (all-purpose) flour

65g/2½oz/½ cup icing (confectioners') sugar

A pinch of salt

150g/5½oz/1¼ sticks cold unsalted butter, cubed

2 egg yolks

For the filling:

115g/4oz/1 stick unsalted butter

Juice of ½ lemon

2 eggs

170g/6oz/1¾ cups caster (superfine) sugar

A pinch of salt

½ vanilla pod or 1 tsp vanilla extract (optional)

2 tsp brandy (or plum brandy, kirsch or grappa)

4 tsp double (heavy) cream

4 tsp plain (all-purpose) flour

10 ripe apricots or plums (about 450g/1lb), halved and stoned

This airy, light, fudgy tart filling is adapted from a Chez Panisse recipe. It's a little tricky to get right, but even if the texture varies slightly, it always tastes delicious. Resist the temptation to put too much flour in the filling as it ruins the silky texture that you are aiming for. This works with many different fruits. The original recipe uses plums (I love this with greengages), but you can use any soft fruit: a brandy-soaked prunes, macerated rhubarb, mixed berries or, like here, apricots. The pastry for this tart is fantastic and can be made well in advance. It keeps well in the freezer and blind-bakes (from frozen) without the need for baking beans.

Put the flour, icing sugar and salt in an electric mixer and blitz until thoroughly mixed. Add the butter, then pulse blitz until the mixture resembles fine breadcrumbs. Add the egg yolks, one by one, pulsing as you go, until the pastry starts to come together. Take care not to overwork the dough.

When the pastry has come together, remove from the machine and, using your hands, knead the dough briefly to smooth and to even out the pastry, but no more.

Press the pastry into a rough circle, wrap in clingfilm (plastic wrap), and freeze.

When ready to use, unwrap from the clingfilm, grate with a coarse grater into a 28-cm/11-inch fluted tart tin, ideally one of those with a loose base for easy removal. Press with your fingers into shape. Try not to overwork the pastry, if possible. Press to an even thickness of 2mm/¹⁄₁₆ inch over the base. Take care not to leave any fat bits where the base meets the sides.

Return the pastry lined tart tin to the freezer, for about 30 minutes, or until it hardens. (A lined tart shell, when wrapped in clingfilm or otherwise covered to protect from frost, can be kept in the freezer well in advance – simply remove, blind bake, and you're in business!)

Preheat the oven to 170°C fan/190°C/375°F/gas mark 5.

First, blind-bake the tart shell. If you've followed the above method, there's no need for baking beans and so on. Just remove from the freezer and place straight into the preheated oven. Cook for 12 minutes or until a golden, biscuity brown.

Remove the tart shell from the oven and allow to cool while you make the filling.

Melt the butter in a heavy-based pan. Bring the butter to a fast simmer and cook until the solids begin to brown. When the butter has turned golden brown and smells deliciously nutty, squeeze in the lemon juice to stop the cooking. Pour the brown butter out of the pan and allow to cool to room temperature.

Meanwhile, using a machine with a whisk attachment, beat the eggs with the sugar and a good pinch of salt. The salt added at this is vitally important to the texture of the tart, although don't ask me why. If using the vanilla pod, scrape in the seeds at this stage.

While the eggs are whisking, halve the apricots and remove the stones.

When the eggs have almost tripled in size and fall in thick ribbons from the beater, reduce the speed to the slowest setting, and slowly drizzle in the cooled butter, followed by the brandy and the cream. Lastly, fold in the flour. Pour into the tart shell. Be aware that the mixture will rise a bit so don't fill it right to the top. Arrange the apricots on top any way you like.

Bake at 170°C fan/190°C/375°F/gas mark 5 for 35–40 minutes. Remove from the oven and allow to cool fully.

Serve with some high-quality crème fraîche, naturally.

SUMMER

For many, this author included, Provence will always be associated with summer, when the sunlight shimmers on the Mediterranean, the lavender flowers open themselves up to the bees, and the weekly markets burst with life: taut aubergines (eggplants) of a dark, rich purple; bright courgettes (zucchini) that break with a snap and a teardrop of sweet juice; a knee-high pile of the finest green and yellow beans; the perfume of a melon heavy with nectar. The tomatoes, as big as your hand, smell not just of the green of their vines but of a real *terra cotta*. On the plate, it's time for *salade Niçoise*, for *soupe au pistou*, for *ratatouille*, those most quintessential of Provençal dishes. These are all simple things, but when done well and when there's a scrap of sunlight to enjoy them in, they sing loudly of summers and suppers beyond the sea.

British summer, as short as it usually is, is a lot of fun. Barbecues are dusted off, picnic blankets shaken out and the country's mood is lifted. Tally ho! Cucumber sandwiches on the lawn. But, looking overseas, I sometimes feel a twang of envy. 'Over there' opportunities to enjoy the weather come easily, and a summer day's cooking does not necessarily involve a link of sausages grilled in the garden, but rather a carefully curated basket of vegetables in fine health and full season. It seems somehow much easier to cook simply when the produce is so good: lunch can be some goats' cheeses, a tomato salad and grilled peppers with basil, then ripe peaches for pudding.

So where do these two summers meet? As much as I would love to shop in sunny village markets, buying direct from the farmers off their beat-up Citroën van, I can't. It's not like I have time, either, to shop only at the farmers' markets. I'm at work most Saturdays anyway. Where I live, in Hackney in East London, the best bet is the Turkish greengrocers, who seem to have a solid grasp of what is actually in season, and quality across the board is much better as a result. It is, of course, harder to buy really good vegetables in Britain, but by no means impossible: happily, we no longer live in times when olive oil must be procured from the chemist.

It's worth remembering that simple summer cooking only really shines when the cook makes the effort to seek out the best ingredients available. A dish as simple as a salad of tomatoes and figs stands or falls on whether the former are red, ripe and flavourful, while the latter are black, sticky and smell of the sun. All with a certain *je ne sais quoi*. Without this magic in the ingredients, your simple cooking may well lack sparkle.

PAN BAGNAT

Serves 4 as part of a picnic (or one hungry tourist who's walked around Nice all day)

1 large crusted white roll or crusty baguette

1 garlic clove, peeled

3 tbsp extra virgin olive oil

2 tbsp red wine vinegar

1 fat, ripe bull's heart tomato

2 tbsp tuna or 4 anchovy fillets

A few black olives, pitted

½ jar of artichokes, in oil

1 celery heart, finely sliced

1 handful of basil, torn

1 handful of rocket (arugula), roughly chopped

1 hard-boiled egg, sliced (optional)

Sea salt and freshly ground black pepper

This squished Niçois sandwich is ideal for a summer picnic. *Pan bagnat* means 'bathed bread' and here the bread is soaked in oil and vinegar before being lightly pressed. Originally this was a way to use up day-old bread and started life as a vinegar-soaked stale bread salad similar to the Tuscan *panzanella*, so remember this recipe next time you have a loaf going stale. It's not quite 'a *salade Niçoise* in a sandwich', but it really isn't that far off. There are, of course, different traditional ways to make this dish and, as with salade Niçoise, first choose whether you fancy anchovy or tuna. In Nice, the quality of pan bagnat varies wildly depending on how much of a tourist you look: the bad ones have a grey boiled egg and a bit of floppy lettuce, but the good ones are big, round, crisp-crusted and jam-packed with good tomatoes, artichokes and proper Provençal black olives.

———————

Slice the roll or baguette in half, cutting all the way through, and then rub enthusiastically on all sides with the garlic clove. Drizzle the olive oil and vinegar over the cut surfaces of the bread and leave to absorb for 15 minutes or longer.

Slice the tomato and season well with salt and pepper. Fill the bread with the tomato slices and all of the other ingredients. With the top on the sandwich, wrap the whole thing in clingfilm (plastic wrap) and press under a heavy weight, such as a heavy book or a big tin of olive oil, for an hour or more. This will squish even more of the juices into the bread.

When ready to eat, unwrap the sandwich; the outside of the bread should be still crusty, while the inside will be sodden with olive oil and bursting with flavour. Slice the sandwich into wedges to share at a picnic, or just cram the entire thing into your mouth and enjoy the dribbles of olive oil and vinegar that will run down your chin.

TUNA, POTATO, EGG & FRIED PEPPER SANDWICH

Makes 1 sandwich

1 small green pepper or
  2 Padrón peppers

A glug or two of olive oil

1 medium waxy potato, peeled

1 egg

¼ crusty baguette, sourdough
  if possible

½ tsp harissa, homemade (see page
  15) or Cap Bon

2 tbsp tuna (ideally an expensive
  Spanish one in olive oil, but use
  whatever you think is best quality)

1 tsp black olives, pitted

1 tbsp roughly chopped parsley
  or coriander (cilantro)

A squeeze of lemon juice

Flaky sea salt

The Noailles market in Marseille is full of North African bakeries selling semolina bread, sweet pastries and myriad snacks, among them this brilliant sandwich. Tuna, potato, egg and olives are a classic and extremely delicious filling on the other side of the Mediterranean, as substantial as it is tasty. It mirrors the Niçois *pan bagnat*, with an added shimmer of the exotic. A little harissa, if you are so inclined, helps things hum along nicely. If you don't want to make your own just for this, a tube of fiery Cap Bon harissa will be just the ticket.

First, fry the pepper in a little olive oil until the skin is blistered and soft, then sprinkle with sea salt and set aside.

Cut the potato into thick slices and boil in lightly salted water until soft. It's no bother if the potato slices fall apart a bit. Drain and leave to cool.

Cook the egg for 9 minutes in a pan of boiling salted water, then remove from the pan and place under running cold water to stop the cooking. Remove the shell, quarter the boiled egg and sprinkle with salt.

Split the baguette, drizzle with a good glug of olive oil, smear with harissa and stuff with the cooked potato, boiled egg, tuna, olives and parsley (or coriander). Squeeze over a little lemon juice and drizzle with a drop of olive oil.

Top with the fried pepper and eat.

SALT COD BRANDADE
BEIGNETS & RED PEPPER SAUCE

Makes approximately 15 beignets

For the dough:
125ml/4fl oz/³⁄₄ cup olive oil

125ml/4fl oz/¹⁄₂ cup dry white wine

2 egg yolks

375g/13oz/3 cups plain (all-purpose)
    flour

A pinch of salt

For the filling:
¹⁄₂ quantity of salt cod brandade
    (see page 32)

Zest of 1 unwaxed lemon and
    1 orange

2 tbsp very finely chopped parsley
    or chervil

For the sauce:
1 red bell pepper

2 garlic cloves, peeled

1 dried Spanish chilli

1 thyme sprig, leaves picked

2 tbsp olive oil

1 tbsp red wine vinegar

1 tsp sweet paprika

Sea salt

These beignets are effectively empañadas stuffed with a perked-up salt cod brandade and then deep-fried until puffed up, blistered and lightly crisp. Serve with a blob of harissa or, even better, a smooth, vinegary red pepper sauce.

———————

To make the dough, whisk the wet ingredients in a large mixing bowl and stir in the flour and salt. Knead briefly to make a smooth, oily dough. The dough is ready to use straight away, but is easier to work with if wrapped in clingfilm (plastic wrap) and refrigerated for 1 hour.

To make the sauce, heat an overhead grill (broiler). Rub the bell pepper and garlic with olive oil. Grill the pepper, turning occasionally, until the skin is blackened and blistered. About half way through the cooking time, add the garlic and grill until blistered and softened. While the pepper is cooking, put the dried chilli in a bowl, pour over boiling water to cover and leave to rehydrate.

Put the pepper in a bowl and cover tightly with clingfilm. Allow to steam for 15 minutes, then peel off the blackened skin. Don't worry if some of the skin adheres to the flesh. Scoop out the stalk and discard the seeds. In a blender, blitz the grilled pepper and garlic with the picked thyme until very smooth. Add the olive oil, red wine vinegar, sweet paprika and salt to taste. The sauce should be smoky, sharp and rounded in flavour.

To make the filling, mix all the filling ingredients together in a bowl. Check the season and adjust to taste, adding more salt if necessary.

To make the beignets, roll out the dough on a dry surface to a 1-mm/¹⁄₃₂-inch thickness. Using a 8-cm/3-inch cutter, cut the dough into rounds. Any excess dough can be rolled out without problem. Place a heaped teaspoon of the brandade in the middle of one half of each round, then fold over the other half to make a half moon. Rub the edges lightly with water to help the dough to stick. Press the edges to ensure a tight seal. Either crimp by hand or use the tines of a fork to make a pretty pattern. Lay the beignets on parchment paper or a lightly floured surface to stop them sticking.

Heat 5cm/2 inches of vegetable oil in a deep pan to 170°C/340°F, or until a small piece of bread fizzes and floats. Alternatively, heat 2.5cm/1 inch of olive oil in a deep wide pan. Fry the beignets in batches until a rich golden brown all over. This will take only 3–4 minutes, so keep a close eye on them.

Drain the beignets on paper towels, then serve with the sauce on the side. Cold beers, please!

TOMATO & TAPENADE TART

Makes 1 large tart (enough for 4 people for lunch or lots of small squares for a party)

For the tart:

4 bull's heart tomatoes

1 x 500-g/1lb 2-oz block of pre-rolled puff pastry

A handful of small Italian plum tomatoes, red and yellow if possible

Olive oil

1 bunch of basil

Sea salt and freshly ground black pepper

For the tapenade:

100g/3½oz black olives, drained of any brine or oil and pitted

⅛ garlic clove, peeled and crushed to a fine paste

½ tsp picked thyme leaves

1 salted anchovy fillet, washed and patted dry

1 tsp salted capers, soaked well, washed and drained

1 tsp brandy

4 tsp olive oil

1 tsp red wine vinegar

This tart is extremely simple. Given the right tomatoes, it's a highlight of the summer table. At Sardine, we wait until the heavy, deep-coloured Amalfi bull's heart tomatoes are in season and throw over some datterini or small plum tomatoes to fill in the gaps. A sprinkling of fragrant basil at the end is essential, as well as a drizzle of your best olive oil. Nyons olives make amazing tapenade, but any soft black olives will do nicely.

First, slice the bull's heart tomatoes into thick 1-cm/½-inch rounds. Transfer to a sieve (strainer) suspended over a bowl and season well with salt. Leave the tomatoes for a good half hour to allow the juices to drip into the bowl. This will prevent your pastry becoming soggy if the tomatoes hold a lot of juice.

To make the tapenade, put all the dry ingredients in a blender. Blitz well. Add the wet ingredients and blitz further until everything is fully incorporated. The tapenade should be very smooth.

Preheat the oven to 180°C fan/200°C/400°F/gas mark 6.

Next, roll out – or simply unfurl, if pre-rolled – the pastry to a rectangle to fit your largest, flat, heavy-based baking tray. Cut a rectangle of parchment paper to the same size, then place the pastry on top. Score a 2-cm/¾-inch border all around the edges of the pastry. This pastry border will puff up around the filling.

Put the baking tray in the oven to pre-heat for 10 minutes.

To assemble the tart, top the pastry inside the scored border with a generous smearing of tapenade. Arrange the sliced tomatoes in a single layer over the tapenade. Halve the small tomatoes, season with salt, and use them to fill any gaps. Drizzle the tart filling with olive oil and grind over some black pepper.

Remove the hot tray from the oven, slide in the tart on the parchment paper and return the tray to the oven. Bake the tart for 30 minutes, or until the pastry borders are puffed and crisp, the base is a light golden brown (lift the tart tentatively with a spatula to check) and the tomatoes are soft, squidgy and just started to take on a little colour.

Remove the tart from the oven, season lightly with a little flaky sea salt and black pepper, and scatter over the torn basil leaves. Allow the tart to cool on its tray, then slice into squares while still just warm. Drizzle with your best olive oil before serving.

FOUGASSE
WITH COURGETTES & OLIVES

Makes 3 breads, enough for
   4–6 people

1½ tsp dried yeast or 1 tbsp
   fresh yeast

450g/1lb/3¼ cups strong white bread
   flour mixed with 50g/1¾oz/5 tbsp
   rye flour (or 500g/1lb 2oz/4 cups
   strong white bread flour)

350ml/12fl oz/1½ cups
   lukewarm water

2 tbsp olive oil

2 tsp fine salt

1 tbsp semolina, for dusting

1 courgette (zucchini), sliced into
   very thin rounds

2 tbsp black olives, pitted

1 tbsp fresh oregano

1 water spray bottle, for spritzing
   the oven

Fougasse is traditionally a flatbread baked on the bottom of the oven, used by bakers to test the temperature before the main bake. This was well before the time of thermometers, of course. In contrast to its Ligurian cousin foccacia, fougasse contains much less olive oil and has more of a chewy crust. It's cut to resemble a sheaf of wheat, which is immensely satisfying to do and the results look stunning. Fougasse is a very simple bread; with a few practices, yours should turn out well. I like to jazz mine up by adding an extra ingredient. Plump olives, crushed walnuts, tasty lardons or (shudder) sun-dried tomato are all traditional. I say add whatever you have and is in season: asparagus and pine nuts in spring, courgettes (zucchini) and oregano in summer, wild mushrooms in autumn, and cheese – something with a bit of character – for the winter.

In a small bowl, mix the yeast with 50g/1¾oz of the flour and 50ml/1²⁄₃fl oz/ 2¾ tbsp of the lukewarm water. Mix well, cover with clingfilm (plastic wrap) and leave in a warm place to ferment for around 20 minutes. When the yeast mixture has started to expand and bubble, mix the rest of the flour in a large bowl with the rest of the water, olive oil and salt.

Add the yeast mixture to the rest of the dough. Mix thoroughly and knead for 5 minutes, stretching and folding the dough over itself. Cover the bowl with clingfilm or a clean dish towel, and leave to prove in a warm place for around an hour to an hour and a half.

Tip the dough out of the bowl onto a lightly floured surface. Try not to knock it around and deflate it too much. Cut the dough into three pieces using a dough scraper, bench scraper or blunt knife.

Put the sliced courgettes in a bowl, lightly season with salt and drizzle with olive oil. Add the olives and oregano.

Take one piece of the dough, sprinkle over a third of the courgettes and olives, then fold the dough back over itself so that the ingredients are incorporated into the dough. Repeat with the other pieces, or feel free to flavour them with different ingredients for variety. Use your hands to pull the dough this way and that to shape the bread. You want them to be roughly 1cm/½ inch thick and roughly oval shaped. I think fougasse look best when one end is slightly squarer than the other, a bit like a (birch) leaf.

Preheat the oven as hot as it will go (220°C fan/250°C/475°F/gas mark 9 for most domestic ovens). If you have a baking stone, then use it, otherwise place a heavy black tray into the oven to preheat. This will mimic the hearth and will make for a nice crust.

Cover the dough with a slightly damp, clean dish towel and allow to prove for another half an hour, until slightly puffed up by around 1cm/½ inch. Dust a heavy baking tray (or two) lightly with semolina, and transfer the pieces of dough to
the tray: if you can't fit all of them then either use a second tray or, they don't take long to cook, leave one to bake later.

Using a dough scraper, bench scraper, palette knife or (yes!) credit card, cut the dough down the middle, all the way through to the work surface, but not all the way to the edge of the bread. At 45-degree angles, cut three smaller lateral cuts in a similar fashion, so that the cuts make a pattern like a sheaf of wheat or a leaf. Use your fingers to slightly stretch out the bread around the cuts and make the holes bigger.

For a crispier crust, just before you bake the fougasse, spray the oven with a fine mist of water or put a small oven-proof container with a few ice cubes on the base of the oven. Put the fougasse onto the stone or tray in the hot oven and bake for 10–12 minutes or until golden brown. The courgettes should have roasted nicely inside and outside the bread. Remove from the oven and allow to cool slightly before ripping into fougasse, dunking pieces in your best olive oil.

Olive oil is a very fine accompaniment to still-warm fougasse, especially if you have chosen a tasty filling, but as with any crusty flatbread, fougasse does sometimes cry out for something savoury to dip it into. These simple combinations don't warrant a full recipe, but here are some suggestions: the smoky, garlicky aubergine dip that the French call 'caviar d'aubergines'; smoked cod's roe blitzed with bread, lemon and oil; a 'cervelle de canut' of seasoned fromage frais, chopped herbs, chives and shallots; smashed white beans or chickpeas (garbanzo beans) with vinegar; or some high-quality crème fraîche sprinkled with bottarga.

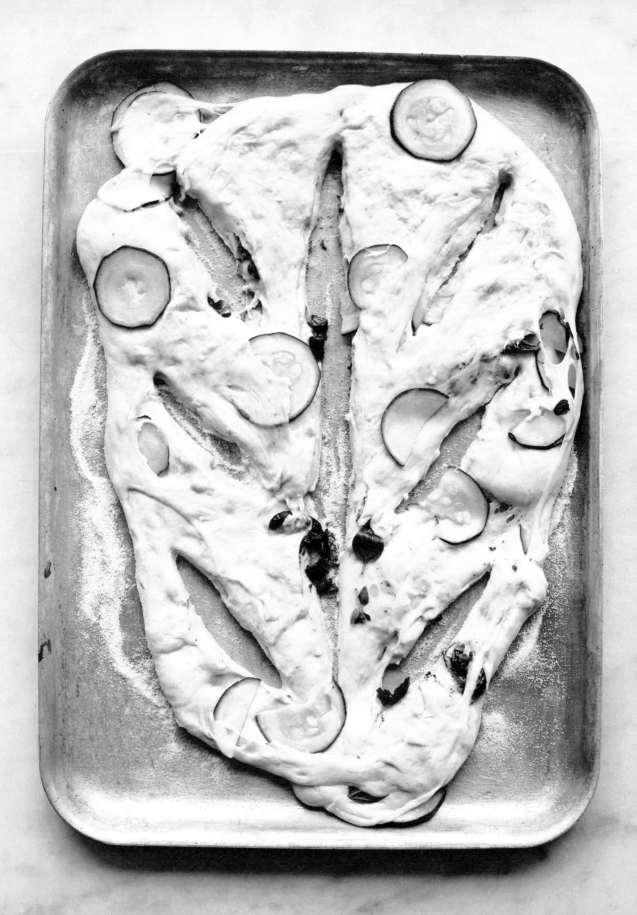

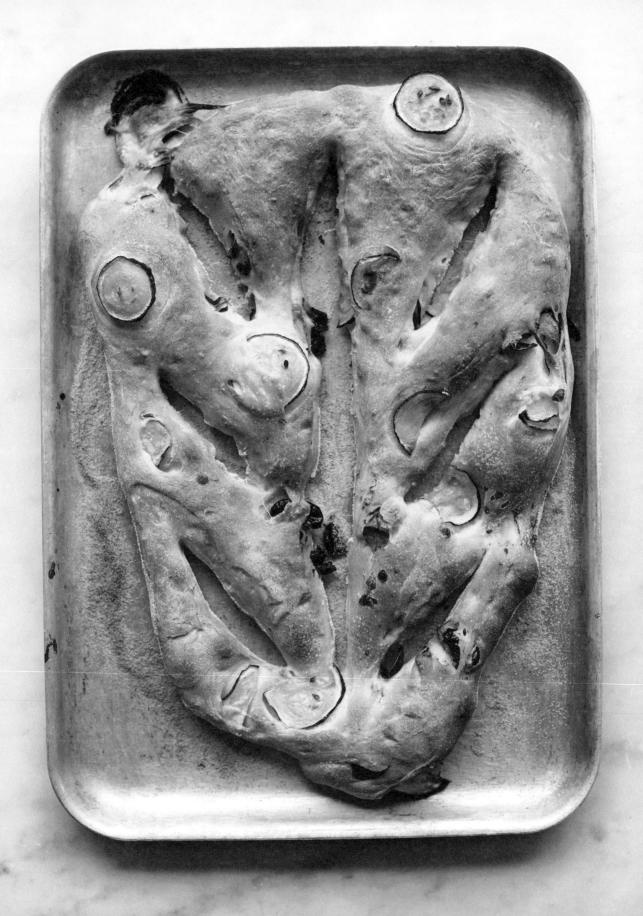

COLD ALMOND, MELON & PASTIS SOUP (WITH BITS OF CRISPY HAM)

Serves 4

250g/8¾oz ground almonds (almond flour)

½ garlic clove, peeled and crushed to a fine paste with salt

325ml/11fl oz/1⅓ cups cold water

2 tbsp olive oil

2 tbsp sherry vinegar

1 tbsp pastis

1 ripe melon (Charentais if possible), chilled

2 thin slices cured ham (prosciutto, serrano or bayonne ham if possible)

Sea salt

This is based on the famous Andalucian chilled almond soup, *ajo blanco*. The pastis gives this Moorish classic a lovely aniseed note. The sherry vinegar really is important here; its dark, deep character brings everything together very nicely, while a little lemon juice brings a brighter acidity to balance the pastis. Melon is my go-to addition to this dish on hot summer's days, curled with a spoon, dripping pale orange juices into the white pool of very cold soup. And the crispy ham is delicious with it because… well, it's crispy ham. I have always found that using almond flour rather than grinding whole almonds makes for a smoother result. Alternatively, you can pass the soup through a sieve (strainer) before adding your bits, but I detest passing things through sieves with a passion, and will go to any lengths to avoid it.

Place the almonds and crushed garlic in a blender and blitz until extremely smooth. The paste will reach a stage where it won't get any smoother without the addition of a little water, so add just enough water to facilitate this. If you add the water too quickly, the paste will thin out before it has had the chance to be cut thinner, and your soup won't be smooth. Continue, slowly, to blend while adding water until you are happy that the almond paste is suitably smooth.

When all the water has been added and the almond soup is the consistency of pouring cream, drizzle in the olive oil. (You can always add more water if the soup is too thick.) Add the sherry vinegar and pastis, then season with salt to taste. Chill the soup thoroughly in the refrigerator. (The chilling process can be sped up slightly by adding ice to the almond paste instead of water when the soup is almost ready).

While you wait for the soup to chill, crisp up the slices of ham by frying them gently in a pan or skillet, or by baking them in a low oven. Crumble the ham into shards and set aside.

When ready to serve, spoon out curls of cold melon and place in serving bowls. Pour over the almond soup, then drizzle with olive oil and top with the crispy ham. Serve very cold, with an extra ice cube in the bowl, if necessary.

GRILLED AUBERGINE VINAIGRETTE

Serves 4, as part of lunch

2 long black aubergines (eggplants),
or 1 large violet Italian one

Olive oil

2 tbsp mixed aromatic herbs
(marjoram, fennel herb, tarragon,
chervil), roughly chopped

1 medium mild red chilli, halved,
seeds removed and roughly
chopped

Flaky sea salt

For the vinaigrette:

¼ garlic clove, or ⅛ if the clove is
a large one, peeled

1 tsp mustard

1 tsp honey

1 tbsp red wine vinegar

3 tbsp olive oil

1 tbsp water

Sea salt and freshly ground black
pepper

An aubergine (eggplant) fizzing quietly over a wood fire is a lovely sight, heavy with olive oil, full of promise. A tart vinaigrette with a lick of honey is the perfect sauce for something so rich. A scattering of herbs completes the picture.

———————

Build a wood or charcoal fire under a grill. Light the fire, then wait until the flames have died down but the embers are still white hot. Rub the aubergines lightly with olive oil and prick all over with a sharp knife to avoid unwanted explosions. Place the aubergines over the fire and grill slowly on all sides, for about half an hour, until the skins are totally black and the flesh underneath is soft through, but take care to stop the cooking before the aubergine falls apart completely.

If you happen to have one of those large violet Italian aubergines, well done you. With this variety, I prefer to slice them thickly, drench them with olive oil and salt, then grill them over the fire until golden brown and charred.

Meanwhile, make the vinaigrette: crush the garlic to a fine, pale paste with a little salt. Put the garlic in a bowl. Add the mustard, honey and vinegar, and whisk well together. Add the olive oil slowly, whisking continually to make an emulsion. Thin the vinaigrette with the water; it should be more or less the consistency of thin pouring cream. Season with salt and pepper.

Carefully remove the blackened skins from the aubergines. It can be tricky to remove all the skin, but don't worry – it only improves things if small flecks of black cling to the flesh.

Cut the aubergines in half lengthways. Arrange them 'skin' side down on a serving dish, and sprinkle with flaky sea salt. Drizzle the aubergines, artfully or not, with the vinaigrette, then scatter the chopped herbs and red chilli on top.

MIXED BEAN SALAD WITH ANCHOVIES, TARRAGON & EGG

Serves 4

400g/14oz fresh Coco de Paimpol or borlotti beans, shelled

1 bay leaf

1 thyme sprig

2 tbsp white wine

3 tbsp olive oil

1 medium ripe tomato

2 tbsp red wine vinegar

100g/3½oz baby new potatoes, washed well

300g/10½oz fine green and yellow beans, topped and tailed, or flat beans or runner beans

1 bunch of summer purslane, leaves picked, or domestic rocket (arugula) or watercress

1 bunch of tarragon, leaves picked

8 salted anchovy fillets

2 eggs, hard-boiled for 7 minutes, shelled and halved

Sea salt and freshly ground black pepper

When made with care and proper fresh beans, this can be a true highlight of the summer. I first made this in Aix-en-Provence, where I was admittedly spoiled for choice at the market. I returned with two types of beans in my basket: fresh, buttery white Coco de Paimpol and fine, long yellow and green. The Coco de Paimpol are a wonderful thing; like a white version of borlotti, they require careful, delicate poaching. I added a bit of bulk to the salad with some tiny new potatoes and, also at the market, there was summer purslane, bursting with sour, succulent flavour. If you can find summer purslane, buy it immediately.

———————————

To cook the Coco de Paimpol or borlotti beans, put them in a pan with the herbs, white wine, olive oil and some water. Do not add salt at this stage as sometimes it can mean that the skins stay a little tough: it's best to season at the end of the cooking time. Squish and tear the tomato into rough pieces with your hands and add them to the beans. Using your hands to do this is important as the skin and flesh will break down more easily and imbue the beans with a needed bit of acidity. Bring to the boil, skim the surface of the water if necessary, then turn down the heat to a gentle simmer, cover with a lid, and cook the beans for around 45 minutes. Top up the water if the level threatens to go below the beans. Depending on the size and age of your beans, the cooking time might be slightly shorter or longer – taste the beans regularly until you are happy that they are completely soft but show no signs of falling apart.

Drain away some of the cooking liquid – keep the beans just covered, but not by too much, as the water will be seasoned as well as the beans. Season with salt, then add 1 tbsp of the red wine vinegar and a glug more olive oil. Taste the beans carefully: they should be full, rounded and have a pleasing balance of salt to vinegar. Keep warm.

Meanwhile, boil the potatoes in salted water for 15 minutes. Towards the end of the cooking time, add the fine beans. When all is soft, drain and keep warm.

When ready to serve, place the warm potatoes and fine beans in a large serving bowl. Spoon over the warm Coco de Paimpol with some of their cooking liquid. Dress the beans and potatoes with 2 tbsp olive oil, 1 tbsp red wine vinegar, more salt, if needed, and a grind of black pepper.

Stir to combine without breaking up the vegetables. Throw in the purslane and tarragon, mix briefly, then lay over the anchovy fillets and top with the halved boiled eggs.

MOZZARELLA, PEACHES & HAM

Serves 4

4 x 125-g/4½-oz balls of buffalo
    mozzarella

2 peaches (the most amazing ones
    you can find)

Olive oil

Lemon juice

12 basil leaves

4 slices cured ham (prosciutto
    if possible)

Sea salt and freshly ground black
    pepper

Although hardly a recipe, more of an assembly, this is summer 'cooking' at its simplest. As the success of this dish hinges on the quality of the ingredients, wait until the peaches are perfectly ripe and sweet. I prefer buffalo mozzarella from Campania, the fresher the better, but this would also be nice with fresh ricotta. You could also substitute nectarines in place of the peaches.

Tear the mozzarella with your hands into large pieces and scatter over a large plate or serving dish.

Halve, stone and slice the peaches into sixths or thick slices. Dress the peaches lightly with a tiny splash of olive oil and just enough lemon juice to balance out the sweetness of the peaches. Season with salt and black pepper.

Toss the basil gently and briefly with the dressed peaches, then arrange on the serving plate with the mozzarella. Drizzle the cheese with your best olive oil. Finally, drape the ham lovingly over the top.

SALT-BAKED TURBOT

Serves 6

1 x 2kg/4lb 8oz wild turbot, or wild sea
  bass, grey mullet, salmon or sea
  trout, gutted

1 bunch of tarragon

½ unwaxed lemon, sliced into rounds

1kg/2lb 4oz rock salt

500g/1lb 2oz fine salt

A spectacular dish if there ever was one. Salt-baking fish is a more
delicate process than it might seem: when exposed to the heat of the
oven, the rock salt forms a crust and the fish steams in its own juices.
While the resultant flavour has a little of the roasted about it, the texture
will be up there with the finest, juiciest and most delicate poached fish.

The king of the sea, a wild turbot is not – and never will be – a cheap
fish. Invest in a large, firm, glistening specimen. As you might imagine
with any salt-baked dish, the thicker the fish, the less likely the salt is to
overwhelm it. As the saying goes, in for a penny, in for a pound. A turbot
approaching 2kg/4lb 8oz will happily feed six hungry mouths, and there
might even be enough left over to make a salad.

———

Preheat the oven to 220°C fan/240°C/475°F/gas mark 9 or as hot as your oven
will go.

Rinse the cavity of the fish to remove any blood or guts. Sometimes there is a thin
membrane covering a bloody tract, which can be punctured to get at the bitter,
blackish stuff beneath. Pack the cavity with tarragon stalks and lemon slices.

Select a deep roasting tray or dish large enough to hold the fish. Line the tray
or dish with parchment paper.

Combine the rock and fine salts in a large bowl. Sprinkle over a little water and
mix the salts together until the mixture feels packable, like wet sand. Cover the
base of the lined tray or dish with the salt to a depth of around 1cm/½ inch.
Place the fish on the layer of salt and then completely cover it with the rest of
the salt. Pack the salt around the fish's body, but you can leave the head, tail
fin and flappy bits uncovered. In fact, leaving those parts uncovered will make
the dish look all the more impressive when it comes out of the oven. The salt
should form an even coating: it doesn't have to be thick, just remember that
the aim here is to form an airtight crust. No skin should be visible through any
cracks that might appear.

Put the tray into the hot oven and bake the fish for 20 minutes. The salt crust
should harden and the uncovered extremities of the fish crisp up. Check the
fish for doneness with a hardy skewer; puncture the salt where the fish's
head meets its body, leave the skewer in the flesh for 10 seconds, then test
the temperature of the skewer against your arm or top lip. It should be warm,
bordering on slightly too hot.

Remove the fish from the oven and allow it to steam inside its salty cocoon while you assemble the rest of the meal.

As far as accompaniments are concerned, take your pick. Some buttered new potatoes, a few boiled fine green beans with crème fraîche and marjoram, an olive-oil mayonnaise or aïoli, braised flat beans with basil, a tomato salad with black pepper and red wine vinegar, young lettuces and herbs in a light vinaigrette, some steamed spinach dressed with lemon and olive oil, good crusty bread… the list goes on and on.

When the troops are seated and it's time to eat, bring the fish to the table – hopefully to much applause. Crack open the crust and remove the salt in big chunks. When the fish is exposed and the excess salt has been brushed away, peel back the skin (which will be too salty to eat) and prise the flesh away from the bone. Lay the fish onto plates, then drizzle with your very best olive oil.

TURBOT SALAD, SHREDDED BEANS & WALNUT VINAIGRETTE

Serves 2, as a lunch

200g/7oz Italian flat beans or runner beans, topped, tailed and string removed

100g/3½oz leftover salt-baked turbot or 1 skate wing, weighing approximately 300g/10½oz, poached in a court-bouillon for 10 minutes and allowed to cool in the cooking liquid

1 tbsp chopped roasted walnuts

Sea salt and black pepper

For the vinaigrette:

A tiny sliver of garlic, approximately ¹⁄₁₀ of a clove, peeled

1 tsp white wine vinegar

1 tsp lemon juice

50ml/1⅔fl oz/2¾ tbsp walnut oil

1 tbsp each finely chopped parsley and tarragon leaves

1 tbsp crème fraîche

Sea salt

This salad is an excellent way to use up any leftover salt-baked turbot, a fine fish to use in this way as the salt-baking leaves the flesh moist. Any juicy firm fish, particularly when cooked on the bone, will do nicely. I have tried this dish with skate with excellent results. The flesh of the fish shreds neatly into delicate ribbons to tumble through the beans, served raw here; as such, they should be of the finest quality and not too large.

To make the vinaigrette, using the flat of a knife, crush the garlic with a little salt on a chopping board until the paste is very smooth and has turned pale in colour. Transfer the garlic to a bowl and add the vinegar and lemon juice. Gradually whisk in the walnut oil until you have a thick emulsified vinaigrette. Taste for balance: it should be only slightly garlicky and the acid should balance with the salt. Add the chopped herbs and the crème fraîche, then whisk together. The vinaigrette shouldn't be too thick – think the consistency of single (light) cream rather than double (heavy). Thin with a little water, if you need to.

Using a very sharp knife, shred the beans as finely as possible. You want the strips to be at least 7cm/2½ inches long. Take your time as a finer cut bean means a finer salad. Put the beans into a serving bowl and season lightly with salt. Leave for 5 minutes to get their juices going and soften slightly. Dress the salted beans with the vinaigrette and mix well.

If using skate, slip the fish off the bones. It's nicer if the fish is still warm. Add the cooked fish to the bowl and fold it delicately into the beans. Finally, scatter the salad with the chopped walnuts.

SOUPE AU PISTOU

Serves 4

To pre-cook the beans:

150g/5¼oz white beans, soaked overnight (if dried)

1 garlic clove, peeled

1 bay leaf

For the soup:

2 tbsp olive oil

2 medium white onions, diced finely

2 garlic cloves, peeled and sliced

1 bay leaf

1 thyme sprig

2 courgettes (zucchini), quartered lengthways and cut into rough 5-mm/¼-inch pieces

50g/1¾oz red waxy potatoes, peeled, cut into 5-mm/¼-inch dice

1 peeled tomato, fresh or from a jar

100g/3½oz green beans, topped and tailed, cut into 5-mm/¼-inch lengths

25g/1oz dried pasta (penne, ditalini, spaghetti or vermicelli)

Sea salt and freshly ground black pepper

For the pistou:

⅛ garlic clove, peeled

½ bunch of basil, leaves picked

50ml/1⅔fl oz/2¾ tbsp olive oil

15g/½oz Parmesan cheese, grated

Sea salt

This quintessential Provençal summer soup is almost identical in makeup to the Ligurian favourite *minestrone con pesto*. It's one example of the close ties between the cooking of the two regions. For sticklers: *pesto alla Genovese* contains pine nuts, Provençal *pistou* does not. Sometimes the French like to smash a little tomato into the garlic, cheese and basil. And why not? We're amongst friends here, after all. The best version of this soup is made with firm, ridged Italian courgettes (zucchini), fine summer green beans, and, most luxuriously, fresh white shelling beans. If you can get your hands on fresh Coco de Paimpol beans, in season in high summer, you're off to a very good start.

———

To make the pistou, smash the garlic with a small pinch of salt in a pestle and mortar. Add the basil leaves and pound to a fine paste. Drizzle in 1 tsp of the olive oil to facilitate this, if you feel the paste needs it. Stir in the Parmesan cheese and the rest of the olive oil. Season with salt to taste.

To make the soup, first cook the beans. If using dried beans, soak them overnight. If using fresh shelled beans, don't. Put the beans in a pan with the garlic, bay leaf and a glug of olive oil. Pour over enough water to cover the beans. Don't add any salt at this stage. Bring to the boil, skim the surface of the water, then cook at a simmer for about an hour or until the beans are soft but not falling apart. Once cooked, don't drain away the cooking water – there should still be enough left to cover the beans. Season with salt to taste and set aside.

Meanwhile, in a nice big pot, fry the diced onions and the sliced garlic slowly in the olive oil with the bay leaf, the thyme and a good pinch of salt. This will take at least half an hour until the onions are sweet and very soft. Add the diced courgettes and potatoes. Stir well to combine, season lightly again with salt and pepper, then cook slowly for a further half an hour, stirring from time to time, until the courgettes are soft but not turning to mush. If you don't cook the vegetables for long enough at this stage, the soup will lack body and the vegetables will retain an unwanted crunch.

Squish the tomato with your hand into a rough pulp. Avoid the temptation to use a knife. The hand squishing breaks down the tomato more effectively. Add the squished tomato to the pan along with the green beans. Pour over just enough cold water to cover, then continue to cook the soup at a low simmer for a further 15 minutes, or until all the vegetables are soft. Add the cooked white beans, along with 1 tbsp or so of their cooking liquid, to the pan.

Depending on what pasta you have to hand, either smash into small pieces wrapped in a folded clean dish towel (penne), snap into 1-cm/½-inch lengths (spaghetti or vermicelli), or leave whole (small soup pasta such as ditalini or short macaroni). Add the pasta to the pan and cook at a simmer for around 10 minutes, stirring well to avoid the pasta sticking.

When the pasta is cooked, so is your soup. It should be quite thick, although there will be enough well-flavoured broth to make the dish feel soupy. And remember, you'll be stirring in some pistou. The vegetables should be very soft but still intact and there should be only a hint of tomato, which is used it here for acidity rather than colour and flavour. At this stage, add a good glug of olive oil to your soup if you think it could use it (it probably could).

Serve the soup hot, but not quite piping, ladled into serving bowls and encourage your guests to stir in the pistou at the table.

PÂTES AU PISTOU
(HANDMADE TROFIE WITH PESTO, GREEN BEANS & POTATO)

Serves for 4, plus a bit extra

For the trofie:

500g/1lb 2oz/4 cups fine Italian semolina for pasta, plus extra for dusting

275ml/9¼fl oz/1⅓ cups lukewarm water

For the pesto:

⅛ garlic clove, peeled

50g/1¾oz pine nuts, lightly toasted

1 bunch of basil (Italian if possible), leaves picked

30g/1oz Parmesan cheese, grated

100ml/3½fl oz/½ cup olive oil

Sea salt

To serve:

1 medium red-skinned potato, peeled, cut into small cubes of less than 1cm/½ inch

200g/7oz fine green beans, topped

Pâtes au pistou, or pasta with pesto, is indisputably of Ligurian origin, but has been adopted by the Niçois, and indeed surely the British, as a quick, easy and tasty pasta dish. The Ligurians know best. They often eat their pesto with *trofie,* a short, thin, twisted shape made from just semolina flour and water, and always with some green beans and small pieces of potato thrown in the pot with the pasta. The Provençal *pistou* often contains no pine nuts, but here I do think that the Italians have it right. This is a proper Ligurian pesto rather than a *pistou.* I usually make pesto in a blender, but a pestle and mortar does the job nicely too: there are different schools of thought on this issue. *Trofie* are difficult to get right at first but, once you have the knack, they are simply time-consuming rather than tricky.

―――――――

To make the trofie, in a large mixing bowl, combine the semolina and warm water to form a dough. Knead the dough for a good 5–10 minutes until very smooth. Wrap the dough in clingfilm (plastic wrap) and allow to rest at room temperature for an hour.

Unwrap the dough. Keep it covered with a clean dish towel to stop the dough drying out while you work. Cut off a 1-cm/½-inch piece of dough and roll it into a long sausage of 1cm/½ inch diameter. Cut the sausage into individual pieces, like a small gnocchi, each 1cm x 1cm/½ inch x ½ inch.

Soak a clean dish cloth in cold water and keep it close by. Use the cloth to moisten your hands while you perform the next step; for some reason, it makes for nicer trofie. Wipe your hands with the damp cloth, then take one small 1-cm/½-inch piece of pasta. Place the pasta on the palm of one hand. Using the palm and fingers of your other hand, roll the pasta in a back and forth motion between your palms to make a 5-cm/2-inch long piece. A final roll with a 'flourish' with your hands as you release the pasta from the tips of your fingers onto the work surface helps to form a taper at each end. The pasta at this point should ideally be 5cm/2 inches long, 5mm/¼ inch thick, and tapered at each end.

Once all of your cut pieces of pasta have been turned into tapered trofie, it's time to twist the trofie around itself. This both looks nice and helps the pasta to catch the sauce. Take a tapered trofie and lay it at a 45-degree angle, either on the work surface or in your hand. Roll the end of a metal bench scraper or similar implement over the trofie, holding it at an elevation of 45 degrees. The trofie should half-twist around itself. When all the trofie are twisted, place on a tray lightly floured with semolina and set aside.

To make the pesto, crush the garlic with a pinch of salt until it is very smooth and pale in colour. Transfer to a blender with the pine nuts and blitz until smooth. Add the basil and blitz again. Add a small splash of water to help the basil to catch in the blender and to make a smoother sauce. Finally, add the Parmesan and olive oil, then blitz until all is smooth. Season with some salt.

To bring it all together, fill a large pot with water and bring to the boil. Season with salt, then add the cubes of potato. Cook for 5 minutes, then add the green beans. Continue boiling until both are cooked through – you don't want the beans to squeak or the potato to bite back.

Add the trofie to the pot. Cook to your preference (a nice al dente); if the trofie have just been made, rather than the day before, this will take only a couple of minutes. Drain the pasta, potato and beans, reserving the pasta cooking water.

In a large bowl, combine the pasta, potato, beans and pesto. Add a few splashes of the cooking water and stir together. The sauce should be loose enough to give a luxurious feel to the dish.

GRANDE BOUFFE

COUS-COUS

WITH GUILLAUME'S MUM

Cucumbers à la Crème

Baked Ricotta-stuffed Courgette Flowers

Broad Beans en Bedarcée

–

Le Cous-Cous: Lamb, Merguez, Chicken, Harissa Broth,

Turnips, Carrots, Chickpeas & Artichokes

–

Mistralou

–

Ganses, Strawberries, Ricotta & Honey

Guillaume, who sells us wine, happened to be visiting the restaurant for a tasting when I mentioned I was planning a special cous-cous dinner. He said his mum cooked the best cous-cous and that we should get her over to cook it with us, so we did. Chantal took the train to London from Paris.

Within ten minutes of her arrival at the restaurant she had happily donned an apron and taken charge. 'More spice! What have you been doing? Oh no, this won't do. Bon, Ecoutez! Does he speak French? Never mind. Your harissa tastes weird. I'll make that, put that down. This tastes quite nice, you know.'

Chantal filled our kitchen with a sweetness, warmth and generosity of spirit that has been hard to replicate.

Customers, initially baffled by the presence tableside of a mad mum waffling on in French, left rapturous. I am still asked by regular diners when she is coming back. Guillaume, for his part, shrugged and said 'It was just like at home.'

A 'cous-cous' is highly esteemed as a feast meal in France. Forget those sad pre-packed cous-cous salads that you buy at train stations, this is a dish for special occasions, and great for serving to a large group. My recipe serves four but everything can be easily multiplied for as many people as you need. The grain itself is rubbed painstakingly with butter and steamed gently over the stew: a revelation, and well worth the extra effort.

CHANTAL,

ECOUTEZ!

GUILLAUME'S MAMAN

Cucumbers à la Crème:
Serves 4

4 small cucumbers, ridged Lebanese or knobbly Italian ones, or 1 large cucumber
4 garlic cloves, unpeeled
1 tbsp red wine vinegar
1 tbsp olive oil
1 tbsp crème fraîche
1 tbsp mint leaves, chopped finely
Sea salt and freshly ground black pepper

Wash the cucumbers. Using a sharp vegetable peeler, cut the cucumbers into ribbons. Discard the mushy, seedy inner bits.

Roughly crush the garlic cloves, so they can express themselves in the marinade. Mix all the other ingredients together and season to taste.

Add the cucumbers to the marinade and leave to sit at room temperature for an hour or so. Before serving, remove the garlic and adjust the seasoning.

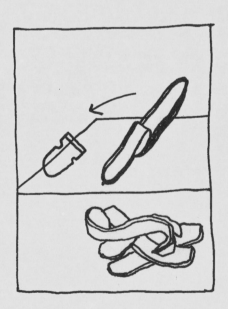

Baked Ricotta-stuffed Courgette Flowers

Serves 4

Baked courgette (zucchini) flowers stuffed with fresh cheese are much more delicate than their deep-fried counterparts, just take care not to overcook them.

4 fat courgette (zucchini) flowers (choose the bigger ones, without the courgette attached)
Olive oil
1 tsp honey, to serve

For the stuffing:
4 tbsp ricotta
20g/¾oz Parmesan cheese
2 tbsp chopped mixed herbs (parsley, chervil, mint)
Zest and 1 tsp juice of 1 unwaxed orange
Zest and 1 tsp juice of 1 unwaxed lemon
Salt and freshly ground black pepper

Preheat the oven to 180°C fan/200°C/400°F/gas mark 6.

Mix together all the ingredients for the stuffing. Fill the courgette flowers with the stuffing mixture.

Select an appropriate size roasting dish for the courgette flowers: it needs to be a snug fit. Drizzle the roasting dish with olive oil, place in the courgette flowers, then drizzle again with more olive oil. Season lightly with salt, and bake the stuffed courgette flowers in the oven for 10–12 minutes, or until warmed through and beginning to colour.

Before serving, drizzle the stuffed courgette flowers lightly with honey.

Broad Beans en Bedarcée

Serves 4

After much inquiry and research, I still have no idea what *en bedarcée* actually means. To us now, it means just-cooked broad beans tossed in a delicious cumin-spiced oil.

200g/7oz podded broad (fava) beans, outer skin removed if necessary
2 tbsp olive oil
2 garlic cloves, peeled and finely sliced lengthways
2 tsp cumin seeds, ground
2 tsp sweet paprika
1 tsp red wine vinegar
Salt and freshly ground black pepper

Boil the broad beans in lightly salted water for 1 minute, or until only just cooked. Drain the beans and leave to cool to room temperature.

Heat the oil in a pan and fry the garlic over a low heat until starting to turn golden brown and stick together. Reduce the heat to the lowest possible, then add the ground cumin and paprika. Cook, stirring, over a very low heat for a minute or two, taking care not to let the spices burn.

Remove the pan from the heat, add the broad beans and toss thoroughly in the spiced oil. Sprinkle in the vinegar and season to taste.

Serve the beans at room temperature.

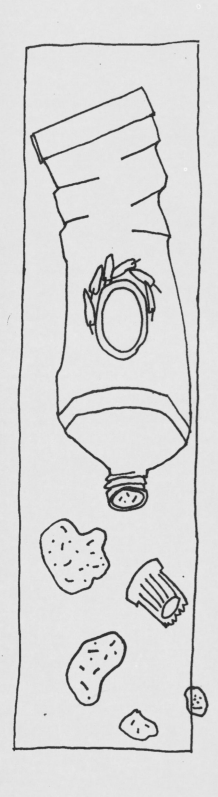

Le Cous-Cous
Serves 4

Rubbing the grains of cous-cous with butter and steaming them over the stew really does produce magical results. Before Chantal taught me this method I had always just poured over some boiling water and covered it for a couple of minutes. This does work in a pinch, and you'll still have something to soak up the stew, but the extra effort produces a cous-cous that is light, fluffy, buttery and gorgeous. A blob of fiery harissa is essential.

<u>For the stew</u>
4 pieces of lamb neck, 2.5cm/1 inch thick
4 pieces of lamb breast on the rib (1 rib per person)
4 chicken thighs
Olive oil
2 large onions, diced
6 garlic cloves, peeled and finely sliced lengthways
1 bunch of coriander (cilantro), leaves picked and left whole, stalks reserved and finely chopped
2 turnips, peeled
2 carrots, peeled
2 small courgettes (zucchini)
2 artichokes, stripped, peeled and choke removed
2 tbsp ground ras-el-hanout
1 x 250-g/9-oz can chickpeas (garbanzo beans), drained
½ x 250-g/9-oz can peeled plum tomatoes
4 Merguez sausages
Sea salt

Season the lamb and chicken well, then brown the meats in olive oil over a medium heat in a large pan. Remove the meat from the pan and set aside, then add the onions to the same pan with a pinch of salt. Fry the onions slowly for around 20 minutes, or until soft. Add the garlic and chopped coriander stalks. Continue to cook, stirring, over a low heat for a few minutes more.

Chop the other vegetables into bite-size chunks and add to the pan. It's important to make sure the vegetables are well coated in the fats from the meats, as this will give them flavour. Return the browned meats to the pan, add the ras-el-hanout and stir well.

Cook the stew over a low heat, stirring, for a few minutes, or until the spices have started to cook out and release their fragrance. Add the chickpeas, stir to mingle, then add the tomatoes. Cover with water, bring to the boil, then reduce to a simmer and cook for an hour and a half, or until the lamb is falling off the bone. Remove the chicken thighs before the end of the cooking time, if you think they're starting to go stringy.

After around 1 hour, start steaming the cous-cous over the stew following the instructions below.

When ready to serve, fry the Merguez sausages in a pan for approximately 5 minutes until cooked, but don't add them to the stew. Chantal says it 'washes off' their flavour.

Place the stew and Merguez sausages on a huge serving platter or bowl in the middle of the table. Sprinkle with coriander leaves. Serve with the cous-cous and some harissa (see page 15) that has been let down with a little of the stew broth.

For the cous-cous:
300g/10½oz cous-cous
200g/7oz butter/⅔ cup, softened
Sea salt

Place the cous-cous in a bowl, sprinkle with salt and cover with cold water. Leave for 10 minutes or so for the grains to fluff up, then drain.

Using your hands, rub the cous-cous with a third of the butter. The ultimate aim is to coat each individual grain in butter.

Arrange the cous-cous over the stew so that it will steam as the stew cooks. A purpose-made couscousière is ideal, obviously. We didn't have one at the restaurant. Some kind of drum sieve (strainer) or other shallow sieve is a good substitute, lined with clean dish towels or clingfilm (plastic wrap) and topped with a tight-fitting lid to keep the steam in. Whatever contraption you conjure up, it is key that no steam escapes.

After 20 minutes of steaming, take the cous-cous off the pan. Rub the half-cooked grains with the second third of the butter. Return to the pan and steam again for a further 15 minutes or until the grain is cooked through. Remove from the heat, rub the grains again with the remaining butter. Serve with the stew and sausages.

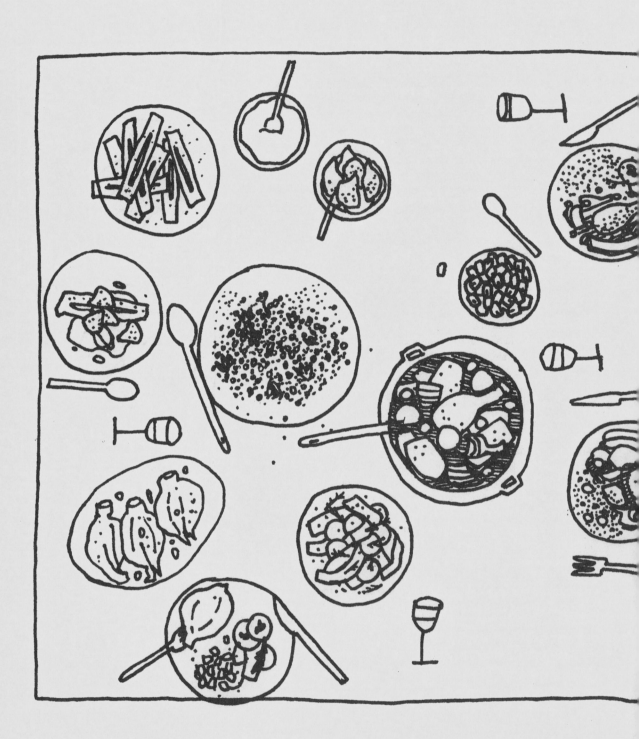

Ganses, Strawberries, Ricotta & Honey
Serves 4

A *ganse* is a flat, funny-shaped, sort-of beignet – or doughnut – from Nice. It's similar, I suppose, to the bugnes of Lyon. It's a crispy, sweetened, yeasted dough rolled out into thin strips and deep fried before being dusted with icing (confectioners') sugar. Ganses are made by the bucketload for the Niçois Carnival. Anyway, they are delicious, especially when eaten with some ripe or roasted fruit, fresh cheese and a drizzle of honey. This recipe makes a little too many – around 12 – but I imagine that having one too many little sugary doughnuts is a good problem to have. Besides, they are excellent with a morning coffee…

For the ganses:
125g/4½oz/1 cup plain (all-purpose) flour, plus extra for dusting
½ tsp dried yeast
1½ tbsp caster (superfine) sugar
A pinch of salt
1 egg
60g/2oz/½ stick very soft butter
½ tsp grated unwaxed lemon zest
½ tsp orange blossom water
Approximately 1 tbsp whole milk
Sunflower oil, for frying

To serve:
1 tbsp icing (confectioners') sugar
12 ripe strawberries
50g/1¾oz fresh ricotta
2 tsp honey

Sift the flour into a bowl. Make a well in the middle of the flour and mix in all the other ingredients except for the milk. When combined, add just enough milk to make a smooth, light dough. Cover the bowl and leave to prove for 1 hour at room temperature.

While the ganses dough is proving, cut the strawberries in half and macerate them in the icing sugar for about 20 minutes.

Dust a work surface lightly with flour and roll out the dough to a thickness of 2mm/¹⁄₁₆ inch. Using a ridged pasta cutter, cut the dough into rough rectangles about the size of a mobile phone. Using the same cutter, cut a single line down the middle of the rectangle from top to bottom, but leave a border of 2cm/¾ inch at both top and bottom edges. Repeat until all the dough is used up.

Deep or shallow fry the ganses in batches in hot sunflower oil, heated to 170°C/340°F, until a deep golden-brown colour. Remove the ganses from the oil with a slotted spoon and drain on paper towels.

Before serving, dust the ganses with icing sugar. Serve with the strawberries, a blob of ricotta, the juices from the strawberries and a drizzle of honey.

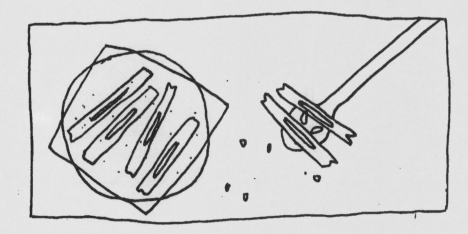

SALADE NIÇOISE

Serves 4

½ garlic clove, peeled, for rubbing

2 small artichokes, outer leaves removed, dark green bits peeled, choke removed

1 small, firm cucumber, or ½ a big watery one

12 nice radishes

1 white or red salad onion, as mild and sweet as possible

250g/9oz ripe tomatoes (the most delicious you can find, I like to use bull's heart)

2 tbsp olive oil

1 tbsp red wine vinegar

150g/5¼oz good-quality tuna in olive oil (such as Ortiz) or 8 salted anchovy fillets

A small handful of black olives (dark black Provençal for preference), pitted

½ bunch of basil, leaves picked

2 eggs, hard-boiled for 7 minutes and shelled

Salt and freshly ground black pepper

There is as much debate over the correct way to make a *salade Niçoise* as there is over how much water and ice to put in your pastis. These discussions have never troubled the Niçois: despite our efforts to ruin the reputation of this great dish, they have happily continued making this salad the way it should be. Jacques Médecin, former mayor of Nice and author of an authoritative cookbook on *la cuisine Niçoise*, was in part moved to write the book by his experience of the untraditional and frankly insulting: 'Over the world,' he declares in the introduction, 'I have had the unpleasant experience of being served up leftovers masquerading as *salade Niçoise*.' M. Médecin implores us: 'Whatever you do, if you want to be a worthy exponent of Niçoise cookery, never, never, I beg you, include boiled potato or any other boiled vegetable.'

I, for one, agree with Jacques. A *salade Niçoise* should be an expression of the southern French summer – crunchy, vibrant, strident and fresh. Squeaky green beans shouldn't get a look in here, let alone the humble spud. And please, avoid raw peppers. Feel free to improvise (a little). Tomatoes and cucumber are indispensable, and I love the crunch of sliced radishes. Artichokes, raw of course, add a delicate luxury, while raw broad beans are delicious when small and sweet. Courgette (zucchini) flowers wouldn't seem out of place. I love this salad served with just salted anchovies, but I do think that a little good-quality confit tuna is delicious too. Please shell out for some of the proper Spanish stuff in olive oil. Jacques says never to use both, but I'm sure he won't find out if you do.

———

Rub the inside of a serving bowl with the cut garlic. Prepare the artichokes and slice them thinly lengthways. Cut the cucumber and radishes into slices, but not too thin this time. Peel and slice the onion as thinly as possible. Cut the tomatoes into chunks, wedges or quarters depending on their size. Do not to slice them too thinly or the salad may become wet as the juices seep out.

Combine the vegetables in the serving bowl. Add the olive oil and red wine vinegar, then season with salt and pepper. Taste and adjust the seasoning.Mix in the tuna or anchovies, olives and basil. Taste again. Cut the hard-boiled eggs into halves or quarters, season lightly with salt and pepper, then arrange on top of the salad. Finish with an extra drizzle of olive oil, if you feel the salad needs it.

VEAL & PORK STUFFED TOMATOES

Serves 4

For the stuffing:

50g/1¾oz pancetta or unsmoked
    bacon, minced

100g/3½oz veal mince (rose veal
    if available)

100g/3½oz pork mince

30g/1oz chicken livers

20g/¾oz fresh breadcrumbs,
    soaked in milk

30g/1oz ricotta

20g/¾oz Parmesan cheese, grated

½ bunch of basil, chopped

½ bunch of fennel herb or chervil,
    chopped

2 thyme sprigs, leaves picked and
    chopped

½ tsp flaky sea salt

¼ tsp ground black pepper

¼ tsp fennel seeds, crushed

For the tomatoes:

8 or 12 vine (not plum) tomatoes,
    depending on the size

1 garlic clove, peeled, green
    sprout removed and finely sliced
    lengthways

8 or 12 whole basil leaves

A splash of olive oil

50ml/1⅔fl oz/2¾ tbsp dry white wine

40g/1½oz/2½ tbsp butter

6 tarragon sprigs

50ml/1⅔fl oz/2¾ tbsp double
    (heavy) cream

Salt and freshly ground black pepper

Apparently stuffed vegetables have a bad rep. Perhaps that's due to their use as a vessel for tired leftovers, or as an insipid and uninspired vegetarian option. Or perhaps they've simply been done to death – a seventies dinner party cliché, if I've ever heard of one. Well, phooey. No one told the cooks of the Mediterranean. They've been stuffing their vegetables for millennia to great effect: with fistfuls of fresh herbs, ample seasoning and a great deal of care. Aubergines (eggplant), peppers and marrow in particular are fantastic when stuffed with cracked wheat, fried onions, spices and herbs, then roasted slowly in the oven. I've had a lot of success with artichokes or courgette (zucchini) flowers stuffed with a punchy salt cod brandade and deep fried until crisp. But the real winners, I think, are tomatoes stuffed with meat and baked with tarragon and cream.

The veal adds a lightness to this dish that is lovely. If you can't get your hands on any, it's still great when made with beef and pork, or just pork. The chicken livers add a subtle depth of flavour but aren't completely essential. As obvious as it sounds, the key to this dish is getting your hands on some really great tomatoes. A tomato slightly smaller than the size of a tennis ball is ideal. The rest is pretty easy. Don't be deterred by the long list of ingredients. These are best made in summer, when the tomatoes are ripe and you can eat them in the sunshine, with a green salad, garlic-rubbed toast and plenty of chilled wine.

Feel free to use this mixture to stuff any number of vegetables: halved aubergines, courgettes, marrow, artichokes, little peppers, vine leaves (to be poached in tomato sauce and stock) and so on. All require some careful pre-cooking before adding the stuffing. These little meat-stuffed vegetables are known in Provence as *petits farcis*.

CONTINUED >

Preheat the oven to 200°C fan/220°C/425°F/gas mark 7.

If you have a friendly butcher, ask him to mince the pancetta or bacon as well as the veal and pork. This will save you much tedious chopping later.

Trim the chicken livers of any sinew and chop them as finely as possible. If it hasn't already been minced, finely chop the pancetta too. Soak the breadcrumbs in a little milk until soft. This *panade* will help to keep the stuffing smooth and soft. Discard any excess milk after the bread has softened.

Place all the stuffing ingredients together in a large bowl and mix well. Make a small patty of the stuffing mixture and fry it in oil to check for seasoning. If it needs more salt, add some, then check again until you are happy.

Cut the tops off the tomatoes but don't throw them away. Scoop out the seeds and pulp into a small sieve (strainer) suspended over a bowl. Season with a little salt, stir briefly and let the juices from the tomato seeds and pulp drop into the bowl while you finish stuffing the tomatoes.

Season the hollowed-out tomatoes well with salt. In the bottom of each tomato, place a fine slice of garlic and one basil leaf. Next, stuff the tomatoes with the veal and pork mixture. Replace the tomato hat, season again with salt and pepper, and drizzle lightly with olive oil.

Place the tomatoes in a roasting tray so they fit snugly. Choose your roasting tray carefully; there's nothing worse than the sauce evaporating away in too large a pan and catching on the bottom. Add the white wine and some of the tomato juices to the tray – roughly half wine to half tomato juices. There should be at least 1-cm/½-inch depth of liquid in the bottom of the tray so that there will be lots of cooking liquid left after the tomatoes have been roasted.

Dot the tomatoes generously with butter and then roast for around 20 minutes. After this time the tomatoes should be almost soft and the sauce will have reduced a little. Add to the tray a few sprigs of tarragon and the double cream. Swirl to mix the cream into the sauce and return the tray to the oven.

Reduce the heat of the oven to 160°C fan/180°C/350°F/gas mark 4 and let the sauce bubble away gently for another 10 minutes, or until the stuffing is cooked through, the tomatoes are soft but not collapsing, and the cream sauce has slightly thickened.

Serve the tomatoes either hot or still warm.

ROAST QUAIL, WARM OLIVE & ANCHOVY SAUCE

Serves 4

4 oven-ready quails

Olive oil

Bread and salad leaves, to serve

For the sauce:

2 tbsp olive oil

1 fat or 2 lean garlic cloves, peeled and sliced (not too thinly this time)

30g/1oz black olives, pitted

1 small thyme sprig

2 salted anchovy fillets

25g/1oz crème fraiche (regular, rather than reduced-fat)

Sea salt and freshly ground black pepper

This is a wonderful sauce, which is much more subtle than it might sound. It goes with all the usual stuff that olives and anchovies go with – in other words, almost everything.

———————

Preheat the oven to 220°C fan/240°C/475°F/gas mark 9.

Rub the quails generously all over with olive oil and season with salt and black pepper. Roast in the hot oven for 10–15 minutes, or until the quails are cooked through with only the slightest hint of pink on the breast and the legs are starting to pull away from the body. Quail is a forgiving bird; should you overcook it slightly, the meat will more often than not still be delicious. Remove from the oven and rest for 5 minutes in a warm place.

While the quails are roasting, make the sauce. Heat the olive oil in a small pan over a low heat. Add the sliced garlic and deep fry very slowly so that the garlic doesn't take on too much colour before it softens and tastes sweet. This should take about 5 minutes. Too high a heat will inevitably result in burnt garlic and a ruined sauce.

When the garlic is soft and sweet, add the olives. Continue to fry the olive with the garlic for a few more minutes, then add the sprig of thyme and the anchovies. Immediately remove the pan from the heat. The thyme will splutter and pop in protest, but the anchovies will yield and start to melt into the oil. When the sauce has cooled slightly and the anchovies have almost melted, stir in the crème fraîche. The aim here is not to produce an emulsified sauce – instead you are aiming for the sauce to split – so don't stir too much. Pour any resting juices from the quails into the sauce.

Spoon the sauce over the roasted quails. Mop up with good bread and soft, sweet salad leaves. Lamb's lettuce or oak leaf would do nicely.

RABBIT RICHARD OLNEY

Serves 4

4 rabbit legs or 1 whole rabbit, jointed

Olive oil

1 medium sweet white onion, halved and finely sliced into half moons

1 head garlic, cloves separated but not peeled

4 bay leaves

A small pinch of saffron

½ bottle (375ml/13fl oz) dry rosé

2 small cucumbers (Lebanese if possible)

4 juicy tomatoes

1 bunch of basil, leaves picked

Sea salt and freshly ground black pepper

This wonderful recipe is a Richard Olney classic: rabbit slow-cooked in rosé, saffron, cucumbers, tomatoes and basil. Cooked cucumber is somewhat unconventional, but delicious. Breaking down far enough to avoid being watery, the texture is a bit like a soft-braised courgette (zucchini), which would make a nice substitution if cooked cucumber feels like a step too far. Remember that in this case a little saffron goes a long way; the other flavours are delicate and too much spice might overpower. This is a light, summery braise, full of the flavours of Provence. A leafy salad, nothing with too much crunch, and some bread will be enough, as well as enough additional rosé to keep the whole table happy.

Preheat the oven to 160°C fan/180°C/350°F/gas mark 4.

Season the rabbit well with salt and pepper. Place a wide heavy-based ceramic pan, something with a tight-fitting lid, over a medium heat and add 1 tbsp olive oil. Brown the rabbit pieces until a light golden brown all over.

Add the sliced onions, garlic cloves, bay leaves and saffron, followed by the rosé. The rosé should cover the rabbit pieces; if not, top up with water to barely cover the meat. Cover the pan with the lid and bring to the boil. Just as the liquid in the pan has started to boil, place the pan in the hot oven for around 1 hour 30 minutes, or until the meat is soft and starting to fall off the bone. After an hour of the cooking time, check whether there is enough juice left in the pan. If too much has evaporated, add a splash of water.

Top, tail and peel the cucumbers, then slice them in half. Scoop out most of the watery seeds, then slice on a slight angle into 1.5-cm/½-inch thick pieces. Cut the tomatoes into small, angular bite-size pieces. Season both the cucumbers and tomatoes with salt and, once the rabbit is soft, add them to the stew. Drizzle the whole thing lightly with olive oil. Return the pan to the oven, this time uncovered, for a further 20 minutes, or until the rabbit has caught a little more colour and the vegetables have softened.

Remove the pan from the oven and assess the stew: it should not be too watery, but there must be enough strongly flavoured juices to mop up with bread and salad. If the stew seems a touch thin, cook it for a few more minutes, uncovered, over a low heat. If it seems a bit thick, add a glug more water. Taste the juices, as well as a small piece of rabbit, for seasoning, and if you think it needs it, add salt, a small knob of cold butter or an additional glug of extra virgin olive oil. Roughly tear the basil leaves into the stew, and it's ready.

RATATOUILLE

Serves 4

5 tbsp olive oil

1 medium white onion (as sweet as you can buy), halved and sliced thinly into half moons

2 proper Italian red peppers or, failing that, those twisted long red ones

2 aubergines (eggplants), cut into 3-cm/1¼-inch chunks

4 small, snappy courgettes (zucchini), none of that watery stuff, cut into 2.5-cm/1-inch pieces

4 garlic cloves, peeled, halved, green sprout removed and sliced thinly lengthways

A small bunch of thyme, tied with string

4 ripe medium vine tomatoes, skinned and cut into eighths

1 bunch of basil

Sea salt and freshly ground black pepper

For the record, the dish that the cartoon rat makes in the film is technically a tian of vegetables, and more specifically Michel Guerard's *confit byaldi*. As nice as it looks, a ratatouille it is not. Ratatouille is a stew of summer vegetables, the term coming from the old French and Occitan meaning 'to stir up'… although this can be misleading. A ratatouille must be delicately and carefully cooked in order to avoid that brown, watery mulch, which has been passed off as the real thing far too often. Don't be tricked by the received wisdom into thinking that you simply place all of the vegetables in a big pan together with some oil and salt, pop on a lid, then leave it to cook for 3 hours. This will result in a harmonious-tasting mush that will have inevitably caught on the base of the pan; the bitter brown then stirred violently back into the dish with a wooden spoon. The proper method demands much more attention, but as you will discover, the results are worth it.

Here's the thing, the cooking of the vegetables for a ratatouille should be done separately, or at least started apart, so that each piece of vegetable remains whole, but has started to mingle coyly with its friends in the pot. Start with some onion, cooked as slowly as possible, so that it ends up sweet and soft to the point of collapse. The tomatoes, which are added last, will break down into sauce easily, which is most welcome. The aubergines will ideally be rich with olive oil, soft but not broken. The courgettes will have frayed edges but hold the very slightest of bites. The slices of pepper will be juicy but intact. Right at the end, throw in a bunch of ripped basil, and perhaps add another glug of olive oil. You'll be rewarded with a stew that is light, vibrant, distinct and exciting to eat.

Add 1 tbsp of the olive oil to a heavy-based pan. Place over a low heat and add the sliced onion along with a small pinch of salt and a bundle of thyme. Cover with a lid and cook slowly for as long as it takes for the onion to go very soft and sweet: this will be at least 30 minutes, maybe 40 or more. Remove from the heat and set aside.

Meanwhile, grill the peppers. Heat an overhead grill (broiler), light a barbecue or simply turn on a gas hob flame. Rub the peppers lightly with olive oil and grill them until their skins are completely black and the flesh underneath is soft.

Put the blackened, softened peppers in a bowl and cover with clingfilm (plastic wrap). This will make it easier to remove the skins later.

In a separate wide pan or frying pan (skillet), add 2 tbsp of the olive oil and place over a medium heat. Season the aubergines with salt and fry until golden brown – add more oil if the aubergines soak it all up. Don't be afraid of using too much olive oil here; remember, you're making ratatouille. When golden brown and soft almost all the way through, add the aubergines to the pan with the onions.

Wipe out the pan used to cook the aubergines and repeat the process with the courgettes. Fry the courgettes in 1 tbsp of the olive oil until golden brown and soft, seasoning them with salt. This will be a slow process, as the courgettes catch and blacken easily. When the courgettes are soft but still have a slight bite, add them to the pan with the onions and aubergines.

Uncover the peppers and peel off the blackened skins and throw them away. Underneath the skin, the cooked flesh should be deeply smoky and sweet. Do not be tempted to wash the peppers to remove the blackened skin; it's much better to leave on a bit of smoky charred skin than to wash away the flavour. If there's any delicious pepper juice left in the bowl, don't throw that away either. Tear or cut the peppers into strips. I like the peppers to be outnumbered by the aubergines and courgettes, but that's just a personal preference. Add the strips of pepper and any juice to the pan with the other vegetables.

Wipe out the pan once more. In another 1 tbsp of the olive oil, fry the sliced garlic gently until it starts to stick together. Add the wedges of tomato and cook over a low heat until their edges start to fray and soften – you don't want the tomatoes to make a sauce in the pan, but you do want them to begin to break down and take on a hint of the garlic and oil flavour. Season with salt and pepper. Now, add the tomatoes to the assembly in the pan.

Return the pan to a low heat, half-cover with a lid and stew the vegetables together slowly for around 30 minutes, or until the tomatoes have broken down a little further but have not turned totally to sauce. Stir gently and infrequently to avoid making a mush of things. All the vegetables should be soft but not too mushy, all will be warm and gently steamy, and the juice that blips to the surface should give an ambrosial taste of the sunshine and a healthy amount (loads) of olive oil. (The cooking times above are rough guides, of course: depending on a number of factors, including, most importantly, how you like your ratatouille to be, you might want to keep cooking it for as long as an hour. Use your instincts.)

Roughly tear the basil and stir it through the vegetables. Add more salt and pepper if you think the ratatouille needs it, with a glug more olive oil if you dare.

You probably don't need me to tell you how to enjoy ratatouille, but here are some suggestions: with grilled, spatchcocked chicken; with roast quails wrapped in thin slices of cured ham; with grilled legs of lamb with olives and herbes de Provence; with cold slices of roast pork tossed with lettuces and anchovy sauce, et cetera, et cetera. Really a ratatouille could take pride of place on a summer table, either as part of a spread, next to a platter of grilled sausages. Or for a *vraie ratatouille en salade*, serve it on its own, at room temperature, with a few salad leaves and a vinegar-spiked reduction of its own cooking juices.

GRILLED CALVES' LIVER, BORLOTTI BEANS, CHOPPED ROCKET & PROSCIUTTO

Serves 2

2 slices of calves' liver, ideally around 1cm/½ inch thick, each weighing 150–200g/5¼–7oz

Olive oil

2 slices of prosciutto

Sea salt and freshly ground black pepper

For the beans:

500g/1lb 2oz fresh borlotti beans, podded

1 bay leaf

1 thyme sprig

1 tbsp white wine

2 tbsp olive oil, plus an extra glug or two

1 medium ripe tomato

1 tbsp good-quality red wine vinegar

1 bunch of domestic rocket (arugula), washed and roughly chopped

Juice of ½ lemon

Sea salt and freshly ground black pepper

Calves' liver is delicious. I like, if I can, to grill it over charcoal to add a bit of smoke to its meaty, mineral flavour. If you're not firing up the barbecue, this will be every bit as good seared quickly in a pan. It cooks in a matter of seconds, and there you have your rather elegant supper. Fresh borlotti beans mean that you are deep into summer. As Italian as the name we use is, these beans are very common in the South of France, grown locally and just as good as their Italian counterparts. Treat these beans delicately: simmer them slowly in water with white wine, herbs, tomato and olive oil and you'll be rewarded with a bean that holds it shape but turns perfectly tender. Here, remember that the sauce for the liver, and what holds the dish, is the oily juice from the beans, so cook them with care and season with attention.

———————

To cook the beans, put them in a pan with the herbs, white wine, 2 tbsp olive oil and enough water to cover the beans by 2cm/¾ inch. Do not add salt at this stage as sometimes it can mean that the skins stay a little tough: it's best to season at the end of the cooking time. Squish and tear the tomato into rough pieces with your hands and add them to the beans. Using your hands to do this is important as the skin and flesh will break down more easily and imbue the beans with a needed bit of acidity.

Bring to the boil, skim the surface of the water if necessary, then turn down the heat to a gentle simmer, cover with a lid, and cook the beans for around 45 minutes. Top up the water if the level threatens to go below the beans. Depending on the size and age of your beans, the cooking time might be slightly shorter or longer – taste the beans regularly until you are happy that they are completely soft but show no signs of falling apart.

Drain away some of the cooking liquid – keep the beans just covered, but not by too much, as the water will be seasoned as well as the beans. Season with salt, then add the red wine vinegar and a glug more olive oil. Taste the beans carefully: they should be full, rounded and have a pleasing balance of salt to vinegar. Remember that the beans are an accompaniment to the calves' liver, which is highly seasoned and will be topped with a slice of ham or two, so keep the seasoning solid but not strident. Keep the beans warm while you cook the liver.

Build a wood or charcoal fire under a grill. Make sure the bars of the grill are very clean and lightly oiled or the liver is likely to stick. Light the fire, then wait until the flames have died down but the embers are still white hot. Rub the slices of liver lightly with olive oil, then season with salt and pepper. Lay the liver over the hottest part of the grill and cook for 1 minute only on each side. If you're cooking the liver on the hob, place a non-stick frying pan (skillet) over a high heat until it's smoking hot. Add 1 tbsp of olive oil, wait until it too starts to smoke, then it's in with the liver. Cook the liver over a high heat for 1 minute only on each side. Try not to move the liver around too much in the pan, then it should form a nice crust.

When cooked properly, the liver will have a soft, bouncing resistance, a bit like a steak cooked to medium. I absolutely believe that calves' liver should be served an even pink, but other opinions differ. I have been severely challenged in the past by liver served very rare, but when cooked through it can be dry. Find a happy medium somewhere in between. Cook your liver to a shade of pink that suits you, then remove the pan from the heat and leave the liver to rest for a few minutes in a warm place.

Reheat the beans, if necessary. Reduce the amount of cooking liquid so that the juices are a loose saucy – but not soupy – consistency. Fold the roughly chopped rocket through the warm beans, then season with lemon juice and olive oil. A handful of herbs – tarragon, parsley – is welcome at this point, but not strictly necessary.

Pile the beans onto a serving plate. Lay the calves' liver on the beans, then drape over the slices of prosciutto.

SALMON BAKED IN FIG LEAVES WITH SAUCE VERTE

Serves 4

4 salmon fillets or sea trout (preferably wild, if you can find it), each weighing approximately 150g/5¼oz

Olive oil

4 or 8 fig leaves, depending on size

8 basil leaves or a sprig of oregano, thyme or marjoram

Sea salt

For the sauce verte:

50g/1¾oz spinach

50g/1¾oz watercress

50g/1¾oz flat leaf parsley, leaves picked

1 bunch of tarragon, leaves picked

1 bunch of chervil, leaves picked

2 egg yolks

100ml/3½fl oz/½ cup olive oil

100ml/3½fl oz/½ cup sunflower or groundnut oil

Juice of 1 lemon

Sea salt

Baking fish in fig leaves fulfils two purposes: it keeps the fish moist and it imparts a unique nutty, fruity flavour. However, the fig leaves must be fresh. Because of that, I don't make this dish often – after all, I don't even have a balcony at home, let alone a fig tree. If you have a friendly neighbour with a fig tree, ask them for some leaves. During the summer we order fig leaves through the vegetable supplier to the restaurant, and then we go a bit mad: we wrap monkfish and quails for grilling; we infuse custard to make a ice cream; or we turn the leaves into syrups for cocktails. Fanny's Fig Leaf Daiquiri was last summer's big hit. *Sauce verte* is a classic: a pale green mayonnaise flavoured with spinach and herbs. Served with baked salmon, the green-on-pink colour palette is a wonderful sight.

─────────────

Preheat the oven to 200°C fan/220°C/425°F/gas mark 7.

To make the sauce verte, bring a pan of salted water to the boil. Fill a bowl with iced water and place it next to the hob. Blanch the spinach, watercress and parsley in the boiling water for 10 seconds, then transfer to the iced water. When thoroughly chilled, remove the leaves from the water and squeeze well.

Place the leaves in a blender with the tarragon and chervil. Blitz until smooth, then set aside. Make a mayonnaise (see page 62) using half olive oil to half sunflower or groundnut oil. Too much olive oil in the mayonnaise can overwhelm the herbs. Instead of adding water, stir in the puréed herbs when the mayonnaise needs thinning. Season with salt and lemon juice.

Season the salmon fillets with salt and drizzle lightly with olive oil. Place each fillet on top of a fig leaf, or two leaves overlapping if they are small. Place two basil leaves on top of each piece of fish, then wrap the fig leaf around the salmon fillets to make a parcel. You can tie the parcel with string if you like, but I usually just place the side where the fig leaves overlap on the underneath.

Fit the fish parcels snugly into a roasting dish and place in the preheated oven. Roast for 10 minutes, or until the fig leaves have blistered and taken on some colour and the fish inside is just cooked. Ideally, for salmon, the fish will be warm but barely cooked in the centre.

Serve the salmon warm, still wrapped in the fig leaves, with the Sauce Verte on the side and maybe some buttery sautéed girolles mixed with boiled, dressed spinach leaves. Unwrap the parcels on the plate and eat the fish inside.

RED MULLET & MUSSELS EN PAPILLOTTE

Serves 4

2 medium–large red mullet, filleted (each fillet weighing approximately 100g/3½oz)

2 small or 1 large courgette (zucchini), peeled with a vegetable peeler into long thin ribbons

1 tbsp olive oil

20 mussels, cleaned

8 small plum or cherry tomatoes, halved or quartered depending on size

8 basil leaves

½ glass white wine

1 tbsp pastis

1 tbsp unsalted butter

Sea salt and freshly ground black pepper

Mullet and mussels are both particularly aromatic and marry well with white wine and a splash of pastis. A little cream inside is not a bad idea: feel free to improvise on the theme. These parcels are quick, easy, colourful and delicious.

———————

Preheat the oven to 200°C fan/220°C/425°F/gas mark 7. Place a heavy roasting tray in the oven to heat up.

Prepare the papillottes from parchment paper following the method given on page 23. Season the red mullet with salt and pepper. Season the ribbons of courgettes with a little olive oil and salt.

Drizzle the prepared parchment papillottes lightly with olive oil, then lay over the mullet fillets, courgette ribbons and mussels. Scatter over the plum tomatoes and the basil leaves. Drizzle over the wine and pastis, then more olive oil. Dot with the butter.

Seal the papillottes as described on page 23. Lay the parcels flat on the hot roasting tray leaving plenty of room between them. Place in the preheated oven and bake for 10 minutes, or until the papillotes puff up. The mullet should be cooked through and the mussels open.

Serve the sealed papillotes for your guests to open at the table, then dig in.

All this dish needs is maybe some good crusty bread to soak up the juices, but this would be lovely with a pilaf of nubbly Camargue red rice.

ROAST HAKE,
SAMPHIRE & TOMATO SALAD

Serves 4

A fat piece of hake or any other flaky white fish, on the bone, weighing approximately 1kg/2lb 4oz, scaled

2 tbsp olive oil

Branches of rosemary, thyme, bay and tarragon, all on the stalk, for a bed of herbs

1 unwaxed lemon, ½ sliced into rounds, plus ½ for juicing

1 large glass dry white wine (200ml/ 7fl oz)

1 tbsp butter

4 juicy large tomatoes (Amalfi Italian for preference)

100g/3½oz samphire, washed (this absolutely must be English or French as the imported Israeli stuff is bitter, stringy and horrible)

Olive oil

1 tbsp each roughly chopped parsley and tarragon leaves

Sea salt and freshly ground black pepper

Samphire and tomatoes are, I suppose, where the British summer meets its Mediterranean counterpart. These two ingredients combine really nicely, especially when dressed with plenty of herbs, lemon juice and olive oil. Both have a pleasing juicy, succulence going on. Samphire and tomatoes pair well with any fish. Grilled oily sardines or mackerel would be great, but here I've chosen a pristine piece of firm hake, which flakes nicely into the salad. The fish is roasted on the bone over a bed of herbs with a little wine. Cooking it this way ensures the moist flesh can be eased off the bone. This is especially delicious with a generous blob of homemade mayonnaise or aïoli served alongside. Some boiled and dressed lentils would also be a welcome addition to this dish, if used sparingly.

———————————

Preheat the oven to 180°C fan/200°C/400°F/gas mark 6.

Select an appropriate size roasting dish for the fish: it needs to be a snug fit. Drizzle the dish with olive oil and build a bed of herbs. Season the hake with salt and pepper both inside and out. Nestle the fish in the herbs, slide a few slices of lemon inside the fish with some tarragon stalks too. Pour over the wine, drizzle liberally with olive oil, then dot the fish with butter.

Roast the hake in the oven for 20 minutes, or until the flesh offers very little resistance when pierced to the bone with a skewer. If you can, it's best to remove the fish from the oven when it is almost cooked as it will continue to steam and cook on the bone while you assemble the rest of the dish. If the wine threatens to boil away during cooking, add a splash of water. Ideally there will be some buttery, winey juices left in the bottom of the dish.

To bring it all together, cut the tomatoes into fat chunks, then season with salt and pepper. Fill a large pan with water and bring to the boil. Cook the samphire in the boiling water for only a minute or two, or until soft and succulent. (Do not add salt.) Drain and set aside. Combine the tomatoes with the samphire, while it's still warm, and dress them with olive oil, lemon juice and chopped herbs.

Arrange the still-warm tomato and samphire salad on a serving platter. Flake the hake flesh off the bone in big pieces and lay them just to the side of the salad. Drizzle any buttery, winey juices from the roasting dish over the fish.

A crusty baguette would do a first-class job of mopping up the juices here, making an impromptu open sandwich of warm, buttery fish and juicy tomatoes.

PANNA COTTA & CHERRIES POACHED IN PASTIS

Makes 4 (generous) portions

For the panna cotta:

600ml/1 pint/2 cups double (heavy) cream

1 vanilla pod or 1 tsp vanilla extract, preferably one with little black seeds in it

Rind of ½ unwaxed lemon, peeled with a vegetable peeler

1½ leaves of gelatine

75ml/2½fl oz/3 tbsp whole milk

75g/2½oz/⅓ cup icing (confectioners') sugar

For the poached cherries:

100ml/3½fl oz/½ cup pastis

100ml/3½fl oz/½ cup water

50g/1¾oz/¼ cup caster (superfine) sugar

1 thyme sprig

400g/14oz finest French dark red cherries, stalk removed and pitted

Poaching cherries in pastis results in a deep, dark crimson liquid. Sweet, sour and with a heady aniseed hit, it's something syrupy, exotic and vivid to pour around your white vanilla-speckled set cream. Any leftover cherry liquor is a treat when mixed with some Crémant (or Champagne, darling) for a sort of southern Kir Royale.

Pour 450ml/15¼fl oz/1¾ cups of the cream into a pan. Add the vanilla and lemon rind, then bring to the boil. Turn the heat down and simmer until the cream has reduced by one-third. Remove the cooked lemon rind. If using real vanilla, remove the vanilla pod, split it lengthways and scrape the seeds back into the cream.

Soak the gelatine in the cold milk for about 15 minutes or until soft. Remove the gelatine, bring the milk to a boil, then return the gelatine to the milk and stir until dissolved.

Pour the milk and gelatine mixture through a sieve (strainer) into the hot cream, stir, then allow to cool. Lightly whip the remaining cream with the icing sugar and fold into the cooled cooked cream.

Pour the panna cotta mixture into your preferred moulds. I like to use individual dariole moulds that are wider than they are tall, as it makes for a prettier plate when turned out, but you can use anything you have to hand. They should be approximately 150ml/5fl oz capacity, but make do with what you have. Leave the panna cotta in the refrigerator to set for at least 2 hours.

To poach the cherries, bring the pastis, water and sugar to a boil with the sprig of thyme. Add the cherries. Cook at a low simmer for about 10–15 minutes, until the cherries have softened slightly and the poaching liquor has turned a deep red. Remove from the heat and allow the cherries to cool in the liquid. Refrigerate until cool.

To turn out the panna cotta, dip the moulds into a pot of boiling water for just a second or two. This will melt the very outside of the panna cotta and allow it to slip easily from the mould. Turn out each panna cotta into a shallow bowl, then spoon over the cherries and some of the crimson liquor.

RUM BABA &
ROAST REINE CLAUDE PLUMS

Makes approximately 8 little babas

For the babas:

80ml/2¾fl oz/⅓ cup milk

1½ tsp dried yeast

2 tsp sugar

A small pinch of salt

3 eggs, beaten

300g/10½oz/2 cups plain
   (all-purpose) flour

125g/4½oz/1 stick unsalted butter,
   cubed and softened

50g/1¾oz currants soaked in rum

For the rum syrup:

200ml/7fl oz/1 cup dark rum

400g/14oz/2 cups caster (superfine)
   sugar

4 star anise

4 cinnamon sticks

8 cloves

For the plums:

8 Reine Claude plums (greengages),
   halved and stoned

1 tsp icing (confectioners') sugar

2 tbsp unsalted butter

A few thyme sprigs

To serve:

Whipped cream sweetened with sugar

A splash of dark rum

I absolutely love rum baba: a spongey vehicle for indecent amounts of rum and whipped cream, with jammy roast plums providing some much-needed acidity. These babas are smaller and less spongey than many, especially the Neapolitan equivalent, which are huge, light, syrupy balloons. There's nothing wrong with that, but I prefer this version. My recipe, I am told, is extremely contentious, possibly due to the addition of currants.

———————

Gently warm the milk to blood temperature. Dissolve the yeast in the milk, then stir in the sugar and salt. Leave in a warm place for 10 minutes to activate. Crack the eggs into a large bowl and add the activated yeast mixture. Add half of the flour and mix through to make a wet batter. (I use an electric stand mixer fitted with a dough hook.) Cover the bowl with a dish towel or clingfilm (plastic wrap), and leave in a warm place for 1 hour to prove. After the first prove, add the remaining flour and knead for a few minutes to make a dough. Dot the softened butter over the top in little knobs, cover, and prove for a further hour.

After the second prove, mix the softened butter into the dough and add the rum-soaked currants. Grease some small dariole moulds generously with butter. Use moulds that are taller than they are wide – approximately 65mm x 60mm/2½ inches x 2¼ inches. Transfer the dough into the moulds, filling each one no more than two-thirds full. Cover with a cloth and leave the filled moulds to prove for around 30 minutes, or until the dough has risen and is approaching the rim of the mould.

Preheat the oven to 170°C fan/190°C/375°F/gas mark 5. Place the plums in an ovenproof dish, sprinkle over the sugar and leave to macerate for 15 minutes. Dot the plums with the butter and top with a sprig or two of thyme. Place the babas on a tray, leaving ample space between each mould. Place the babas and plums in the oven and bake for 20 minutes, or until the babas are golden and a 'mushroom' has risen over the top of each mould and the plums are jammy.

Meanwhile, make the rum syrup. Place the rum, sugar and the spices in a pan, then pour in 800ml/27fl oz/3½ cups cold water and bring to the boil. Boil together for about 10 minutes until syrupy, then keep warm.

Remove the babas from the oven. Allow them to cool slightly before removing from their moulds. Slide a knife around each mould to ensure the babas have not stuck. Pour the syrup into a small pot. One by one, submerge the babas in the syrup until all the babas are sodden. Serve them while still warm alongside the roast plums and a dollop of lightly whipped, sweetened cream with a little extra rum splashed on top.

NOUGAT ICE CREAM WITH SALTED HONEY & FENNEL BISCUITS

Serves 8 or more

For the ice cream:

60g/2oz shelled pistachios

60g/2oz skinned blanched almonds

500ml/18fl oz/2 cups double (heavy) cream

500ml/18fl oz/2 cups whole milk

10 egg yolks

120g/4⅓oz honey

30g/1oz sugar

35g/1¼oz glucose or invert sugar syrup

Grated zest of ¼ orange

½ tsp orange blossom water

75g/2½oz soft nougat, chopped or crumbled into 1-cm/½-inch pieces

For the biscuits (makes about 16 biscuits; the dough can be frozen):

180g/6⅓oz/1½ cups plain (all-purpose) flour, sieved

1 tsp baking powder

½ tsp fennel seeds

100g/3½oz/7 tbsp unsalted butter, diced and softened

95g/3⅓oz caster (superfine) sugar

50g/1¾oz honey

Flaky sea salt

This recipe for nougat ice cream was influenced by an idea in *The Alice B. Toklas Cookbook* and has been on the menu at Sardine since the restaurant opened. I love the nougat found in the South of France that has whole toasted fennel seeds running through it. Instead of putting fennel seeds through the ice cream – which I'm sure would be delicious – we make a salted honey and fennel biscuit to serve alongside. The biscuits are very easy, baked from frozen, and go with everything. The glucose or invert sugar syrup helps to make the ice cream softer, but is not strictly necessary. You can always replace it with the same quantity of honey instead.

───────────

To make the biscuits, place the flour, baking powder and fennel seeds in the bowl of an electric stand mixer. Add the butter, sugar and honey, then mix with paddle attachment until the dough comes together.

Tip out the dough onto a clean work surface and bring it together by hand until you have a smooth, firm dough. Divide the dough in half and roll into two logs, each approximately 5cm/2 inches thick. Wrap the logs of dough in parchment paper. If baking the same day, place in the refrigerator until thoroughly chilled. Otherwise, place in the freezer until need and bake from frozen.

To bake the biscuits, preheat the oven to 160°C fan/180°C/350°F/gas mark 4. Unwrap the logs of dough and place them on baking trays, at least 10cm/4 inches apart. Bake them for 20 minutes (or 15 minutes if refrigerated), pressing from time to time with the base of a heavy pan to flatten the biscuits out. Eventually the biscuits should be fully flattened: the ideal thickness for the biscuits is 5mm/¼ inch. After about 20 minutes the biscuits should be an even, deep golden brown.

Remove the biscuits from the oven and allow to cool slightly. While still warm and soft, cut each biscuit into fingers, ideally 10cm/4 inches long and 2cm/¾ inch wide, but really any shape will do. Sprinkle the biscuits liberally with flaky sea salt and allow to cool completely before serving.

To make the ice cream, preheat the oven to 170°C fan/190°C/375°F/gas mark 5.

On separate roasting trays, roast the pistachios and almonds in the preheated oven for 8 minutes, or until aromatic and just taking on a tiny bit of colour. Keep the roasted pistachios whole, but chop the roasted almonds into chunks – the size is up to you. Put the chopped almonds in a spaghetti basket or wide-meshed sieve (strainer), then shake to remove any fine dust. This might seem a bit of a faff but it's worth it as any almond dust will give the ice cream an unpleasant grainy texture.

Meanwhile, bring the cream and milk slowly to the boil in a pan. Turn off the heat before it boils over. While you wait for the milk and cream to boil, whisk the egg yolks in a large bowl with the honey, sugar and glucose or invert sugar syrup (if using). The mixture should be as smooth as possible, but not aerated.

Pour the hot milk and cream slowly and gradually into the egg and honey mixture, whisking continually as you pour. Do not add too much hot liquid to the eggs in one go as they may scramble.

Once all the hot milk and cream has been added to the eggs, transfer the mixture back to the pan. Cook very slowly over a low heat, stirring all the while with a rubber spatula or a wooden spoon, until the custard reaches 82°C/180°F, or thickens to the point when it coats the back of a wooden spoon and a line drawn with your finger over the spoon remains unbroken. Pour the cooked custard through a fine sieve into a deep tray, that will fit in your refrigerator. At this point, add the roasted nuts to the custard.

Leave the tray of custard to cool to room temperature, stirring occasionally to avoid it forming a skin, then refrigerate until thoroughly chilled.

Once chilled, stir in the orange zest, orange blossom water and the nougat pieces. Next, churn in an ice-cream maker according to the manufacturer's instructions. Alternatively, place the tray in the freezer, stirring the mixture every 30 minutes until the mixture is evenly frozen.

I like to serve a couple of scoops of ice cream per person with a biscuit nestled in the bowl alongside.

GRILLED PEACHES & NOUGAT PARFAIT

Serves 4

For the peaches:

4 peaches

1 tbsp olive oil

1 tbsp crème de cassis or other fruit liqueur

1 rosemary sprig, for brushing the peaches

For the nougat parfait:

3 egg whites

70g/2½oz/⅓ cups sugar

190ml/6½fl oz/¾ cup double (heavy) cream

70g/2½oz nougat, crumbled into small chunks

When grilling peaches over charcoal, it doesn't take long for the soft fruit to turn sticky and aromatic. A little olive oil brushed over the cut side of the peaches prevents them from sticking to the grill: use a sprig of rosemary to brush the peaches for bonus points. A little crème de cassis thrown into the mix gives them an extra fruity dimension. This nougat parfait is an easy, no-churn alternative to ice cream. The nougat we use is a soft Spanish turrón that freezes into chewy chunks. If you can't find this type of nougat then you can substitute the same quantity of ground hazelnut praline.

To make the nougat parfait, whisk the egg whites to soft peaks in a bowl using an electric mixer. With the motor still running, slowly trickle in the sugar. In a separate bowl, lightly whip the cream until it sits in soft folds. Fold the softly whipped cream into the beaten egg whites, then gently stir through the nougat. Transfer the parfait mixture to a plastic container with a lid and freeze for around 3 hours, or until set.

Halve the peaches and remove their stones. Mix together the olive oil and crème de cassis. Using the rosemary sprig, brush the peaches with this oily concoction. Place the peaches cut-side down over a charcoal fire or alternatively place the peaches cut-side up under an overhead grill (broiler). Grill the peaches, turning them once and basting them occasionally with the olive oil and cassis mixture. The peaches should be marked black by the hot bars of the grill, and softened but not falling apart.

Serve the peaches while still hot with a scoop of frozen parfait on top, so the parfait and nougat melt into the warm fruit.

CHOCOLATE MOUSSE, HAZELNUT BISCUITS & CHANTILLY

Serves 6

For the chocolate mousse:

170g/6oz good dark (70%) chocolate

170g/6oz cold butter, cubed

A couple of pinches of salt

1 shot of espresso, or 25ml/2 tbsp strong coffee, allowed to cool

170g/6oz caster (superfine) sugar, plus 2 tsp for the egg whites

4 eggs, separated

30ml/2 tbsp rum or brandy

1 tbsp water

For the biscuits (makes about 15):

60g/2oz hazelnuts

100g/½ cup caster (superfine) sugar

25g/1oz plain (all-purpose) flour, sifted

2 medium egg whites

½ tsp vanilla extract, paste or (if you can afford it) the seeds from ½ vanilla pod

For the Chantilly cream:

250ml/9fl oz/1 cup double (heavy) cream

2–3 tbsp icing (confectioners') sugar

A splash of brandy, cognac or Armagnac

Chocolate mousse is up there with my most hated desserts, or at least it was until I discovered this recipe, which is based on Julia Child's version. This mousse is less airy fairy than others, with a good sticky texture to it. These hazelnut biscuits are extremely crunchy. Ensure there is a lot of brandy in your Chantilly cream in order to cut through all the richness.

————————

Melt the chocolate, butter and pinch of salt together over a bain-marie of simmering water. Take care to ensure that the bowl does not touch the water below. Try not to over-stir while melting as this can cause the mixture to split. When melted and mixed, add the cooled coffee slowly to avoid splitting.

Meanwhile, in another bowl over a bain-marie, beat the egg yolks, sugar, rum and water together with a whisk, until the mixture has thickened slightly (like runny mayonnaise). Cool the thickened egg yolks over ice, stirring the mixture as it cools. Chill over the ice until cold and thick. Fold the chocolate/butter mixture into the egg yolks.

Meanwhile, beat the egg whites with a small pinch of salt. When the egg whites begin to froth and just take shape, drizzle in the 2 tsp of sugar. Continue to beat until the egg whites hold their shape in soft peaks. Fold a third of the egg whites into the chocolate, then repeat until all is incorporated. Pour gently into a container and chill for 3–4 hours until set.

To make the hazelnut biscuits, preheat the oven to 180°C fan/200°C/400°F/gas 6. Roast the hazelnuts for about 10 minutes, until a golden brown all the way through. Remove from the oven and allow to cool until you can handle them. Meanwhile, mix the flour, sugar, egg whites and vanilla together until well incorporated. Roughly chop the hazelnuts and add them to the mixture. Line a tray with parchment paper and spoon out the biscuits, about a tablespoon of the mixture for each one, leaving as much space as possible in between each one, as they spread out an awful lot. Bake in the preheated oven for 10-12 minutes, until golden brown and crisp. Allow to cool completely, then peel the biscuits off the parchment. These keep for a week in a sealed container.

To make the Chantilly cream, whip some double cream with some icing (confectioners') sugar and a splash of brandy, cognac or Armagnac. How much sugar and booze I will leave up to you (I like it very boozy).

Heat a spoon in some simmering water, then scoop out your chocolate mousse onto plates. Serve with the hazelnut biscuits and the Chantilly cream.

AUTUMN

Autumn, I think, is my favourite season. I've never been particularly happy in the heat, and I quite like the smell of wet leaves – time for a walk in the woods. For the past couple of years, I've been trying to work out what cooking Provençal actually means when the nights start to draw in and there's a chill in the air. For all that summer represents the best known of the repertoire, autumn is an opportunity to cook as the southern French do when the tourists go home.

An English autumn is the season of wild mushrooms, quince, apples, plums and wild berries, fresh nuts, furred game, of Keats's 'mists and mellow fruitfulness'. In Provence, apart from the grape harvest, they celebrate mushrooms, sweet chestnuts and autumn squashes, and generally enjoy having their province back from the barbarian hordes.

It's one of the best times of year for produce: there's a point where the summer stuff overlaps with that of autumn – the last of the ripe tomatoes are, for a brief time, together with the first of the red bitter leaves, and the first pumpkins arrive just as the last courgettes (zucchini) leave. The new season's squashes seem to come just in time, as if they knew that the weather has started to turn, and we're tentatively thinking again about starches instead of salads.

The coming of colder nights inevitably means that we need a bit of comforting. The food becomes somehow a bit less vibrant and a bit more mellow, a bit less zingy and a bit more rounded. There's still room for some big flavours, but at this time of year it's not so much about acidity, colour and contrast, but a harmony, cosiness and reassuring depth.

BLACK FIG & TOMATO SALAD

Serves 4

8 Provençal black figs, in a perfect
   state of ripeness, of course

4 delicious tomatoes – bull's heart
   for preference, but anything
   spectacular will do

1 tbsp red wine vinegar or Champagne
   vinegar (highest quality)

2 tbsp olive oil

12 basil leaves

Sea salt and freshly ground black
   pepper

This recipe is one to be made as summer gives way to autumn, and only when both figs and tomatoes are spectacularly good. Provençal black figs are to be sought out, as they are rightly famous for their perfumed scent and sweet, delicate flavour. Choose a tomato that is coloured a dark red from growing in a whole summer's sun. The rest is pretty easy – a few leaves of basil, some good vinegar and the best olive oil you can get.

Good, fresh cheese is an obvious accompaniment to tomatoes and figs. Mozzarella, obviously, and good buffalo or sheeps' milk ricotta, but also young goats' milk cheese, something with a light and moussey texture, shaved with a knife over the salad. I wouldn't say no to a piece of toast either, rubbed lightly with garlic and drenched in good olive oil.

Tear the figs in half with your hands. Cut the tomatoes into wedges around the same size as half a fig. In a bowl, season the tomatoes well with salt and black pepper. Drizzle over the vinegar and the olive oil, and toss to combine. Add the figs and basil leaves to the tomatoes and toss again, ever so briefly. Arrange the salad on a plate and then eat it.

RAW CEP & FRESH COBNUT SALAD

Serves 4

A few small, firm ceps (weighing
    around 150g/5¼oz in total), cleaned

50g/1¾oz Parmesan cheese shavings

1 tbsp chopped parsley

Juice of ½ lemon

2 tbsp olive oil (use your best stuff)

A big handful of fresh cobnuts
    (around 15–20 nuts), shelled

Sea salt and freshly ground black
    pepper

Raw ceps have an intriguing flavour. This salad is another 'must' during the short cep season, and should be made only with the finest, tautest specimens. Use small, firm ceps as, apart from anything else, you risk finding a maggot wriggling around in your salad. Cobnuts are a type of cultivated hazelnut, and are in season fresh at the same time as the mushrooms. Prise away the shell and you are left with a soft, milky white nut to eat. If you cannot find cobnuts, use fresh hazelnuts instead.

―――――――

Slice the ceps as thinly as you can with a sharp knife or a mandoline and place in a mixing bowl. Add the Parmesan shavings, chopped parsley, lemon juice and half the olive oil. Season with salt and pepper. Toss gently to dress the salad. Taste carefully to check the balance of lemon juice and salt, then adjust as necessary. Arrange the salad on a big plate and drizzle over the rest of the olive oil. Using a Microplane fine grater, grate the fresh cobnuts over the salad, covering the sliced ceps with a fine snow of fresh nuts.

PANISSE & POSSIBILITIES

Makes enough for 4 as a snack

100g/3½oz/¾ cups Italian chickpea
flour (farina di ceci)
1 tbsp olive oil
1 lemon
Parmesan cheese
Sea salt and freshly ground black
pepper

Panisse is perhaps the most famous fried chickpea (garbanzo bean) snack. Panisse originated, predictably, in Liguria, and was brought many moons ago to Nice and down the coast to Marseille. In both big cities it's a smash hit: deep fried in batches, sold on the street and scarfed down by the dozen. Panisse is for some an acquired taste. But bear with me! Imagine, if you will, a vat of polenta made out of fine-milled chickpea flour, cooked down to a thick paste, set into a block, cut into a variety of different shapes, and fried in oil until crispy outside and wobbly within, like weird chips. In Marseille they shape panisse into logs before slicing into rounds. Home cooks, cooking smaller batches, often set dollops of thick batter onto oiled saucers or shallow plates overnight before turning them out and slicing. The final shape matters not too much, but the thicker the slice, the more wobble will be left inside – it's up to the individual cook to decide on the ratio of soft to crispy they would like.

Panisse are pleasingly versatile. By all means serve them like they do in Nice: as thick-cut, gastropub-style chips, stacked like Jenga, with a rich daube of beef. They are fantastic shallow fried in olive oil with a scattering of rosemary, a wedge of lemon, a bit too much salt and eaten slightly too hot. An ideal snack for the cook who prefers to drink cold beer.

On that note, panisse are an inspired addition to any *petite friture* (see page 26) of little fish and shellfish, of salted anchovies sandwiched between sage leaves, or of various fried variety meats, wild mushrooms and so on. In Sicily, where they are known as panelle, they are stuffed into a soft bun to make a southern Italian chip butty. I'm sure they don't put any salt and vinegar in it down there, but I might venture a little smear of anchoïade (see page 20) would do the trick quite nicely.

CONTINUED >

Sieve the chickpea flour into a large pan and then slowly whisk in 400ml/ 14fl oz/1¾ cups cold water. Add a pinch of salt and then whisk in the olive oil.

Slowly bring the mixture to the boil (or more accurately, a 'gloop'). Lower the heat and continue to cook slowly, stirring frequently, for around 25 minutes or until the mixture is very thick. There will be lumps, but do not fret. Transfer the mixture to a blender and whizz until smooth or, if you have one, use a stick blender to blitz your panisse batter into submission. Return the batter to the pan and cook for a further 5 minutes.

Lightly oil one or more receptacles for the panisse: a shallow tray, perhaps, or a sundry collection of plates and saucers. A word of warning: if you neglect to oil the receptacle thoroughly, your panisse will stick to it and infuriate you. I speak from experience.

Pour the batter into the prepared tray or plates, keeping the panisse to a depth of no more than 1cm/½ inch, or 5mm/¼ inch if you like them a little more crisp. Smooth the top of the batter as best you can with a spatula. Cover the surface of the panisse with parchment paper to avoid a skin forming. Place the panisse in the refrigerator and leave to set for a few hours, or preferably overnight.

When your guests have arrived and the cold beers have been opened, it's time to fry. Remove the chilled panisse batter from the refrigerator and cut into your preferred shape: anything from long, thin, irregular strips to regimented, rectangular chips. Pour olive oil into a large, shallow pan to a depth of 2cm/¾ inch and place over a medium–high heat. Carefully slide the panisse pieces into the hot oil and fry until golden and crisp on all sides. At this stage, I like to add some sage leaves or rosemary sprigs to the oil so that they too can crisp up, before removing the whole assembly to drain on paper towels.

Sprinkle the panisse readily with salt. Serve with a squeeze of lemon juice, some grated Parmesan and lots of freshly ground black pepper.

CRISPY PIG'S EARS & APPLE AÏOLI

Makes enough for a small party

2 pig's ears

A few thyme sprigs

Rock salt

1kg/2lb 4oz duck fat, or enough to
    cover the pig's ears

Sunflower oil, for deep frying

For the apple aïoli:

2 apples

1 garlic clove, peeled and green
    sprout removed

2 egg yolks

200ml/7fl oz/1 cup extra virgin olive
    oil

Juice of ½ lemon

Salt

A delicious crispy snack. Making these pig's ears requires a bit of slow cooking in duck fat and so it's worth pairing up the cooking with another confit recipe, such as duck legs or rillettes, to save both on time and precious fat. Note also that you will need to salt the pig's ears overnight. The sauce hails from the Basque country, I believe, and is a happy union of apple sauce and garlic mayonnaise. What's not to like? This apple aïoli is equally good with grilled game birds, including quail and pigeon.

Heavily salt the pig's ears and thyme sprigs and leave overnight. In the morning, discard the thyme, rinse the ears well and pat them dry with paper towels.

Preheat the oven to 140°C fan/160°C/325°F/gas mark 3.

To prepare the pig's ears, melt the duck fat slowly in an ovenproof pan or casserole. When the fat is liquid, carefully lower in the pig's ears. Cover with foil and place in the hot oven and cook for 2 hours, or until the ears are soft. If you're preparing ahead, place the ears in a suitable container and pour over the liquid duck fat. Leave to cool and place in the refrigerator. If party time is soon, remove the pig's ears from the fat and place on a tray to cool. When cool enough to handle, slice the ears as thinly as you can with a large, sharp knife.

To make the apple aïoli, roast the apples in the hot oven with a little salt until they are very soft and have started to caramelise. Leave to cool. Once cool, mash the apples to a paste. In a pestle and mortar, crush the garlic to a fine white paste with a pinch of salt. Transfer the garlic paste to a small mixing bowl and add the egg yolks and apples, then smash everything together. Using a hand whisk, slowly add the olive oil drop by drop, making sure that the oil is fully incorporated before adding more. Continue adding the oil in a slow, steady stream, whisking it in until a mayonnaise starts to form. Add a little lemon juice and, if the aïoli looks too thick, a splash of water. Season the aïoli to taste with salt and more lemon juice. Set aside in the refrigerator until needed.

While being deep fried, pig's ears tend to explode so it's advisable to use a deep pan with a snug-fitting lid that you can deploy as a shield. Fill the pan with sunflower oil and heat to 180°C/350°F. Carefully lower the pig's ear slices into the hot oil and cook briefly. Once the explosions have died down, the pig's ears will be crispy and delicious. Remove the slices from the oil and drain on paper towels. Season liberally with salt and serve with the apple aïoli.

DEEP-FRIED PRAWNS & ROUILLE

Serves 4

Milk, for dunking

Semolina flour, for dusting

A mound of prawns commensurate with appetites (best for this are small, whole, shell-on prawns)

Sunflower oil, for deep frying

Salt

For the rouille:

1 fat or 2 small garlic cloves, peeled, green sprout removed

A pinch of salt

1 tbsp fresh bread, crust removed

2 salted anchovy fillets

A small pinch of saffron

1 egg yolk

½ tsp cayenne pepper

100ml/3½fl oz/½ cup olive oil

1 tbsp good red wine vinegar

1 tsp lemon juice

Rouille is a rust-coloured, saffron-and-cayenne-spiked mayonnaise. It does a fine job livening up a bowl of bouillabaisse, but it would be a shame if that were the only time rouille made an appearance on the dining table. It's a great accompaniment to anything deep fried. By this I mostly mean chips, obviously, but rouille is equally great with seafood. When we made this dish at the restaurant, we used Cardigan Bay prawns that came in still alive and kicking. I regret to say that we threw the prawns straight into the deep-fryer still jumping – a swift and noble death. Live or not, this is delicious made with fresh, small, shell-on prawns, which I like to eat whole, head and all. Tiny brown shrimp are just as nice cooked this way, but may need a light batter to bind them together. Barbecued prawns are equally delicious with rouille, and remind me of holidays in France like nothing else. Rouille should be thick, deep, strong, mysterious and pretty bloody spicy.

To make the rouille, in a pestle and mortar, crush the garlic to a fine white paste with a pinch of salt. Transfer the garlic paste to a food processor, add the bread, anchovy fillets and saffron threads, then blitz to a thick but smooth paste. Add the egg yolk and cayenne pepper and blitz again. Start to add the olive oil very slowly, drop by drop at first, making sure that the oil is fully incorporated before adding more. Continue adding the oil in a slow, steady stream. As the emulsion starts to thicken, add a few drops of vinegar and lemon juice along with a splash of water, then continue adding more oil. It's important to add the vinegar, lemon juice and water gradually so that the rouille is less likely to split. As it is stabilised by the bread and anchovies, a rouille is harder to split than an aïoli, but I have managed it. When all the oil has been incorporated, taste the rouille for salt and acidity and adjust as necessary to find a nice balance.

Pour the milk into a shallow bowl and place the semolina flour in another. Dunk the prawns first in milk and then roll them in flour. If you prefer an extra crunchy coating, repeat this process.

Heat the oil in a deep pan to 180°C/350°F. To check the temperature, drop a small cube of bread into the hot oil. If it floats immediately in a mass of bubbles, the oil is hot enough. Deep-fry the prawns for one minute, until crispy. Remove form the oil, drain on paper towels and sprinkle with salt. Serve with the rouille.

SARDINES STUFFED WITH SWISS CHARD & PINE NUTS

Serves 4 as a starter

12 whole sardines, scaled and gutted (ask your fishmonger to do this for you)

Olive oil, for drizzling

Salt and freshly ground black pepper

For the stuffing:

1 bunch Swiss chard

Olive oil, for frying

2 garlic cloves, peeled, halved, green sprout removed, sliced finely lengthways

1 tsp fennel seeds

1 tbsp pine nuts

1 tsp chopped dried red chilli (those big red Spanish ones are good, if you can get them)

1 tbsp chopped mixed herbs (parsley, tarragon, chervil and fennel are all great, but whatever soft herbs you have to hand will do nicely)

A pinch each of grated unwaxed orange zest and lemon zest

1 tbsp fresh breadcrumbs

1 tsp freshly grated Parmesan cheese (controversial, say the Italians, with fish, but what do they know?)

Salt and freshly ground black pepper

This is an incredibly simple way to prepare sardines, and it is really much less fiddly than one might imagine. Swiss chard is a hugely popular vegetable in Nice. It figures in much of Niçois cooking, not least in the *tourte aux blettes*, an exceedingly eccentric sweet chard, pine nut and raisin tart. Much less controversial is this versatile savoury stuffing, which is surely Moorish in origin. Optional extras in the stuffing include saffron, raisins and anything else North African, such as chopped salted lemon, coriander seeds, or go the whole hog and make a *chermoula* instead. This is also excellent inside a chicken or quail.

———

To make the stuffing, wash the Swiss chard well, then separate the leaves from the stalks. Trim any discoloured or black bits from the stalks and chop them finely. Add the stalks to a pan of well salted boiling water, then add the leaves too and boil until soft. Drain and cool, then squeeze both the stalks and leaves to remove any excess water. Chop the leaves finely, combine with the stalks and set aside.

Heat 2 tbsp of olive oil in a pan and fry the garlic, fennel seeds and pine nuts slowly until all are golden brown. Introduce the chopped Swiss chard to the pan and cook gently in the oil for 5 minutes, stirring frequently. Add the dried chilli, mixed herbs, orange and lemon zests and the breadcrumbs. Stir to combine, then take the pan off the heat and allow everything to cool. Add the grated Parmesan and check the seasoning. If you've cooked the greens gently, the mixture should both look and taste vibrant, rather than sludgy and brown. If you think the stuffing mixture looks dry, add a little more olive oil.

Preheat the oven to 180°C fan/200°C/400°F/gas 6.

Once the stuffing mixture is cold, place as much as possible inside the cavities of the sardines. Place the fish in a roasting tray, season with salt and pepper and drizzle with olive oil. Roast the sardines in the hot oven for 5 minutes or until cooked through. Alternatively, barbecue the sardines over a hot charcoal grill. This method creates a very delicious dish, but unless you faff around securing the fish with wooden toothpicks, some of the stuffing will fall out and incinerate on the hot coals. I can't say I bother with the wooden sticks bit!

Whichever way you choose to cook your fish, eat the sardines hot and with a good squeeze of lemon juice.

FRIED CEPS & PERSILLADE

Serves 2

2 nice fat ceps (weighing around
   100g/3½oz each), cleaned

1 tbsp olive oil

2 tbsp unsalted butter

Salt and freshly ground black pepper

Slices of hot buttered toast, to serve

For the persillade:

1 garlic clove, peeled, halved and
   green sprout removed

2 tbsp picked parsley leaves

Fresh ceps, porcini or penny buns are – no matter what you call them – highly sought after in France. It's much easier to buy this mushroom over there, because the French know how fine the eating is. In Britain we seem yet to grasp the concept quite properly. I can't say that growing up we ever had fresh ceps on the family dining table, despite the fact that they grow all over our island. When there are no ceps to be found in the woods, whole villages in rural France are known to be thrown into depression: a sorry state of affairs, indeed.

Nowadays I am most likely to go out and forage for my own ceps: my wife is Polish and thus an expert in wild mushrooms. Otherwise, when in season, fresh ceps are available from select greengrocers; Borough Market in south east London is always a good bet. Ceps are expensive produce to buy, but they are worth every penny, of course.

There are many good ways to cook ceps. This is one of the simplest.

———————

First, make the persillade. Finely chop the garlic and then the parsley. Combine them both and then very finely chop them together. Set aside.

Cut the ceps into 5-mm/¼-inch thick slices.

Heat the olive oil in a wide, heavy-bottomed pan. When the oil is hot, add the ceps and cook over a medium–high heat for a minute or two on each side, or until the ceps have taken on a nice bit of colour. Add the butter to the pan. Season the ceps with salt and pepper and cook them in the butter for another couple of minutes. Toss the persillade into the pan with the ceps and the foaming butter.

To serve, slide the ceps out of the pan onto waiting slices of hot buttered toast.

An optional extra would be either a slice of prosciutto or some good cooked ham. Fried ceps also make an ideal garnish for ham, egg and chips. Just saying.

SQUASH & MUSSEL SOUP

Serves 4

3 tbsp olive oil

1kg/2lb 4oz mussels, cleaned

1 glass dry white wine

2 medium white onions, finely diced

½ head celery, finely diced

4 garlic cloves, peeled, halved, green sprout removed and finely sliced lengthways

1 tbsp fennel seeds

1 dried Spanish chilli, chopped

2 bay leaves

1kg/2lb 4oz tasty winter squash or pumpkin ('Delica' or 'Violino' for preference, ideally not butternut squash)

1 ripe tomato or 1 peeled plum tomato from a jar

1 tbsp double (heavy) cream

1 tbsp parsley, finely chopped

Sea salt and freshly ground black pepper

This might seem an unlikely pairing but the combined flavours here are delicious. The fennel seeds in the soup's base bridge the gap to tie the two principal ingredients together, a hint of chilli adds a lovely warmth and a swirl of cream completes the picture: there's something at once exotic and deeply comforting about this soup. This is one of those rare occasions when I am persuaded that a soup should be puréed until smooth.

———————

Heat 1 tbsp of the olive oil in a decent-sized pan with a lid and throw in the mussels, followed by the white wine. Cover with a tight-fitting lid and cook quickly for a few minutes until the mussels have opened. Take care not to overcook the mussels – as soon as they open, they are ready. Discard any mussels that refuse to open.

Strain the mussels, keeping the winey broth. Leave the mussels and the broth to cool while you make the soup base. Heat the remaining 2 tbsp of olive oil in a heavy pan. To make a soffrito, add the onion, celery, garlic, fennel seeds, chilli, bay leaves and a pinch of salt. Sweat the whole lot together slowly for at least half an hour, or until the mixture is completely soft and tastes rounded and sweet.

Peel the squash or pumpkin, remove any seeds, and cut into 2-cm/¾-inch chunks. Add the squash to the soffrito and stir to combine. Squish the tomato with your hands into small pieces and throw that in too. Cook over a low heat for a few minutes to start the cooking process, then add the mussel cooking liquor and top up with water. Bring to the boil, then cook the soup over a medium heat for around 40 minutes, or until the squash has softened and tastes great.

While the soup is cooking, shell the mussels and set aside: I think it's best to refrigerate the cooked shellfish to be on the safe side. Transfer the soup, in batches if necessary, to a blender and purée until very smooth. You can, if you like, pass the soup through a sieve (strainer) for a smoother result, but honestly, life is too short. Taste the soup for seasoning. It's almost finished. It should taste full, rounded, and with a touch of acidity from the wine and tomato.

Put the soup back into the pan and reheat. Add the cooked mussels along with any juices that have leached out into the container. Simmer slowly for a few minutes to reheat, then pour into bowls. Drizzle over a swirl of double cream, scatter over the parsley, and add a grind or two of black pepper.

BRAISED OCTOPUS,
SWEET POTATO & AÏOLI

Serves 6, depending on the size of your octopus

6 small sweet potatoes (or 3 whoppers)

Aïoli (see page 173)

Fennel fronds or parsley

For the octopus:

1 octopus (double sucker for preference, frozen, defrosted and soaked for a few hours in a couple of changes of water)

2 tbsp olive oil

2 bay leaves

1 tsp fennel seeds

1 dried (Spanish) red chilli or 1 fresh mild red chilli

1 glass dry white wine

2 tbsp sweet wine from Languedoc (Rivesaultes, Muscat, Banyuls)

2 tbsp brandy, Cognac or Armagnac

For the tomato sauce:

2 tbsp olive oil

1 medium white onion, finely diced

2 garlic cloves, peeled and sliced lengthways

1kg/2lb 4oz fresh tomatoes, skinned (score the skin, immerse briefly in boiling water, refresh in iced water and then peeled) and halved

Freshly ground black pepper

I always used to boil octopus. Nothing wrong with that, at all. If I'm making a salad with potatoes and herbs, or planning to grill a tentacle or two over a hot fire, then I still do. When I am not boiling octopus, the rest of the time I'm drawn again and again to this irresistible recipe.

I suppose some might call it a *daube de poulpe* – an octopus stew – but this method is simpler than the name makes it sound. It's really just a way of cooking an octopus in its own juices, which results in a pot full of something reduced, rich and powerful. Tomatoes add another dimension of flavour and a wonderful colour, and I take great pleasure in pouring in various boozes and seeing where the stew ends up: sometimes just dry white wine, other times rosé, always a glug of brandy, very occasionally some pastis towards the end, and on special occasions a good glug of sweet wine, although not all of these at once, you understand.

Sweet potato and aïoli are unlikely sounding companions to this dish, but this combination of rich seafood, punchy garlic and sweet, smoky starch is one that must, must be tried. This is another recipe from Lulu Peyraud that has become a favourite of ours to cook at the restaurant.

Wrap the sweet potatoes well in foil and place them directly on the hot coals or embers of a barbecue. Cook the potato parcels for a good hour, turning them once or twice, until the potatoes are soft all the way through. The skin will blacken, but this is a good thing. Besides, the skin can be peeled off where too far gone, leaving a delicious smoky flavour to the flesh. Alternatively, roast the foil-wrapped sweet potatoes in a hot oven at 220°C fan/240°C/475°F/gas mark 9 until a similar result is achieved.

Next, grapple with your octopus. It should have previously been frozen in order to tenderise the flesh, then defrosted thoroughly ready for you to prepare it. Wash the octopus well. Cut the tentacles into 2-cm/¾-inch pieces. Open the head out flat and cut into 2-cm/¾-inch squares. Put the octopus pieces in a large colander to allow some of the water to run off.

Meanwhile, make a tomato sauce. Heat the olive oil in a pan, add the diced onion and garlic and fry over a low heat for 20–30 minutes or so until soft. Add the halved, skinned tomatoes and cook them with the onions and garlic until they break down and begin to look like a tomato sauce. Season with black pepper but do not add any salt at all.

Heat the other 2 tbsp of olive oil in a large, heavy pot. Keep the octopus nearby, ready to put in the pot. The idea is to sizzle the aromatics quickly in the hot oil, but not to burn them, so don't throw them in and then spend a minute searching for the octopus! When the oil is hot but not quite smoking, throw in the bay leaves, fennel seeds and chilli, followed almost immediately by the octopus.

Now comes my favourite bit. As soon as the octopus is added to the hot oil, it will fry for a few seconds before relenting and releasing its juices. The contents the pot will swell pleasingly, and the octopus will suddenly be cooking in its own copious broth.

Add the tomato sauce to the pot, followed by the wines and the brandy, return to the boil and then turn down the heat to a low simmer. Cook slowly, stirring occasionally, for around an hour, or until the octopus is soft but holds a slight bite under the tooth and the gravy around it has reduced to a rich, oily, thickened sauce. I prefer to leave the consistency of the sauce to your personal preference: Lulu reduces hers to the point where the sauce coats the pieces of octopus, but I like to leave a little more liquid in mine as I find it can become both overly intense and riotously salty.

Note that I have added no salt to this recipe thus far: an octopus when cooked this way can sometimes be very salty in itself and so no extra is needed. Add a pinch of salt only if you think it needs it.

Serve a spoonful of the octopus stew with pieces of steaming sweet potato and large blobs of aïoli. Scatter liberally with herbs: fennel fronds and parsley both work well.

SALT-BAKED GUINEA FOWL

Serves 2–4, depending on the size of
the bird

1 guinea fowl (approximate weight
1.5kg/3lb 5oz)

Thyme sprigs

6 garlic cloves, unpeeled

½ unwaxed lemon

Around 2kg/4lb 8oz rock salt

500g/1lb 2oz fine salt

Black pepper

For the gravy:

The giblets and the wing tips of
the bird

Chicken stock, if you have any to hand

1 shallot, cut in half

Tarragon sprigs

Parsley stalks

Black peppercorns

A glug of brandy, Armagnac or
Calvados

1 tbsp cold butter, cut into cubes

Sea salt

I've always struggled with guinea fowl. It tends towards the dry, while that promised hint of gaminess never seems to materialise. Remembering an incredible lamb shoulder baked in sea salt at 'that posh restaurant in Paris' – pink and juicy, yet soft and falling off the bone – it struck me that guinea fowl was a prime candidate for the same treatment. Success! The fowl emerged from its salty cocoon moist and delicious: simultaneously steamed and roasted, fully seasoned, but not overly so. It turns out this recipe is very easy – the only potential pitfall is spilling salt all over your kitchen floor. You'll need a lot of salt, so buy a big bag of it. This method also works very well with chicken.

––––––

Preheat the oven to 220°C fan/240°C/475°F/gas mark 9.

Take the guinea fowl and place the thyme, garlic, and the lemon inside it. Put a small circle of foil over the opening to stop the salt crust getting inside. Season with black pepper only (no salt!) and set aside.

Put the salt into a big bowl. Add just enough water to dampen it and make it workable – think wet sand. In a deep oven dish, spread the salt in a layer around 1cm/½ inch thick. Put the guinea fowl on top. Bury the bird in the salt, making sure that it is completely encased by a covering of around 1cm/½ inch thickness.

Bake in the hot oven for 40 minutes.

Meanwhile, make a gravy. Roast the wing tips and giblets in the hot oven until a deep golden brown. Deglaze the tray or pan with the chicken stock or water, add the other ingredients and then simmer for about half an hour, or until the bird is done. Strain the gravy into a small pan and simmer quickly until reduced by half. Add a little salt to taste, but don't go overboard with the seasoning at this stage as you'll be adding some savoury resting juices later on.

Check that the bird is cooked by inserting a skewer through the salt crust into the flesh – try to aim for the thickest part of the thigh, nearest the bone. If the skewer is hot to the touch, then it's ready. If the skewer is only warm, give the bird a further 5 or 10 minutes in the oven. This stage of the cooking is the trickiest – it's hard to check if the bird is cooked through the salt crust as you can't be completely sure which bit you are probing. The good news is that it's hard to dry out the bird as all the moisture is kept inside the crust. A digital temperature probe helps (it should read 70°C/160°F).

When you are confident that the guinea fowl is cooked, remove it from the oven and let it rest inside the salt crust for around 10 minutes. This is a good opportunity to leave it on prominent display to show how clever you are.

When you are ready to serve, crack the salt crust with a pestle, a rock hammer, a baseball bat or similar to remove any hard pieces of salt, then brush away any loose grains like an archaeologist. Set aside while you finish the gravy.

Bring the gravy to a gentle simmer, add any juices that have gathered in the resting bird and whisk in a few small cubes of cold butter. Check the gravy for seasoning – it shouldn't be too salty – and keep warm.

Joint and carve the guinea fowl, then pour the sauce over the top.

This needs nothing more complicated to accompany it than some plain boiled spinach, dressed with a little olive oil and lemon juice. But it would be equally delicious with a handful of sautéed buttery girolles and a light cream sauce (make a very light roux, add chicken stock, some cream, and simmer). Other possible routes include a mayonnaise mixed with a few chopped fines herbes and a touch of mustard, boiled new potatoes, buttered runner beans, a green sauce with anchovies and capers, a tarragon-soaked bread and boiled egg sauce, a small pile of raw choucroute and so on.

GROUSE, GRAPES & RED WINE

For 1 person (multiply as is fit)

1 grouse, drawn, claws removed

1 tbsp olive oil

½ slice of sourdough, a piece the right size to sit your grouse on top

200g/7oz (red) Muscat grapes

1 large glass red wine – the posher the better, obviously

1 tbsp cold, cubed butter

Salt and freshly ground black pepper

An absolutely delicious way with grouse, this dish feels decidedly more exotic than the usual beige bread sauce that we Brits are so fond of. Bravo!, I say, to the Ancient Romans for bringing this kind of cooking to Gaul. While this is almost certainly not a traditional Provençal dish, I hope that you agree that it gets into the spirit of things quite nicely. Partridge, pigeon and quail can all be cooked in this way, but the intensely gamey flesh of the grouse marries well with the sweet sauce that results. A highly encouraged optional extra is piece of toast, fried until crisp in the fats rendered from the bird, to soak up the resting juices as the grouse sits on top. This will need a peppery green salad – watercress is traditional with game for a reason, and is an excellent choice here.

Preheat the oven to 220°C fan/240°C/475°F/gas mark 9. Rub the grouse lightly with oil, this will help the seasoning to stick. Season the grouse well with salt and a little black pepper.

Heat the olive oil in a deep-sided ovenproof pot. Brown the grouse slowly on all sides until a deep, golden brown all over. Remove the grouse and set aside while you fry your toast. There should be enough fats in the pan, but if it looks a little dry, add a bit more oil. Fry your slice of bread on a medium heat until it is golden brown. Remove the fried slice and replace with the grouse.

Add the grapes and the wine to the pan with an additional splash of water. Bring the wine to the boil, then put the pot into the hot oven. Roast the grouse for 10–15 minutes depending on the size of the bird (I find that 12 minutes usually works) or until the breast starts to rebound a little when squeezed. You want the meat to be an even pink all the way through. Remove the grouse from the pot and rest for at least 5 minutes in a warm place atop the piece of toast.

Meanwhile, carefully reduce the sauce a little. Squish the grapes to encourage them to release their juice. When the sauce tastes intense and delicious, whisk in the cubes of butter. Check the seasoning and add more salt, if necessary. The sauce should taste rounded, full, nicely sweet and lightly acidic from the wine, and there should hopefully be a lot of it. If you think the sauce has over-reduced, add a splash of water and taste again.

Put the piece of toast with its grouse topping onto a plate. Arrange the grapes around the bird and pour the sauce all over the grouse.

POACHED HALIBUT, SPINACH & SAFFRON BUTTER SAUCE

Serves 4

For the sauce:

100ml/3½fl oz/½ cup white wine

50ml/1⅔fl oz/2¾ tbsp white wine vinegar

½ shallot, sliced

4 black peppercorns

1 bay leaf

200g/7oz/⅔ cup butter, very cold, cut into small cubes

A pinch of saffron

Lemon juice (optional)

Salt

For the fish:

1 bay leaf

1 thyme sprig

1 tarragon sprig

Some parsley stalks

½ leek, or 1 shallot

1 celery stalk

1 tsp black peppercorns

t tsp salt

1 tsp white wine vinegar

4 wild halibut fillets (approximate weight 125g/4½oz each), or 4 pieces turbot or brill, cut into tranches on the bone (approximate weight 150g/5¼oz each)

For the spinach:

500g/1lb 2oz spinach, washed

Lemon juice

1 tbsp olive oil

Sea salt and freshly ground black pepper

On the rare occasions that we are able to source wild halibut, poaching it gently in a *court-bouillon* is a delicate way of cooking this fish, and one that highlights its quality. Poached fish cries out for some kind of fat, and this butter sauce certainly provides it. *Beurre blanc* with poached fish is an obvious classic. A pinch of saffron turns the sauce a brilliant orange hue, reminiscent of fish stews of the South of France. Of course, you can substitute any firm-fleshed white fish, such as turbot or brill on the bone.

――――――――

For the sauce, put the wine, vinegar, shallot, peppercorns and bay leaf in a pan, bring to the boil, then simmer until reduced to 2 tbsp. With this sauce, the idea is to evaporate almost all of the liquid and then to replace it with butter. Strain the liquid through a sieve (strainer), squeezing to extract all the liquid. Discard the solids, then add the saffron to the warm reduction. This reduction can be stored for later use.

Gently heat the reduction in a pan. Whisk in a couple of cubes of butter. When this has almost all disappeared, add the same amount again. Repeat until the butter is used up. Never boil or simmer the sauce as it may split.

Season the sauce with salt and possibly a squeeze of lemon juice, if it needs it. Pour the sauce into a bowl and let sit in a warm place while you cook the fish; you might need to stir the sauce from time to time. If the sauce should go cold, it can be very gently reheated while you whisk – just be careful not to split it!

Tie the vegetables, herbs and stalks tightly together with string. Put this bundle in a pan (one big enough to poach the fish in later) with the peppercorns and cold water. Bring to the boil, then reduce the heat and simmer for 10 minutes. Fish out and discard the herbs and peppercorns, now your court-bouillon is ready. Season the court-bouillon with 1 tbsp salt and 1 tsp white wine vinegar.

With the water barely at a simmer, gently lower in the halibut and poach for around 5 minutes, or until cooked through. Test the fish with a sharp skewer; there should be no resistance between the flakes. Carefully fish out the halibut. If the halibut has any skin still on, remove it now using a fork.

Cook the spinach for a few seconds in salted boiling water. Remove with a slotted spoon and squeeze out all the liquid. Dress the warm spinach with salt, pepper, lemon and olive oil. Keep warm. To assemble, pool some sauce on a plate and sit the poached fish in the middle. Serve the spinach alongside.

CASSOULET (AND A SLIGHTLY UNTRADITIONAL BRUNCH...)

Serves 4

1 medium white onion, diced

8 garlic cloves, peeled

2 tbsp duck or goose fat (optional, but in keeping with tradition, otherwise olive oil is also fine)

250g/9oz pork belly, skin on

2 bay leaves

A large thyme sprig

A couple of parsley stalks

250g/9oz white beans – fresh, unsoaked, Coco de Paimpol for preference when in season (dried and soaked Coco de Paimpol when not in season), or otherwise large dried cannellini beans, soaked overnight and drained

2 peeled plum tomatoes from a can

4 fat Toulouse sausages

2 confit duck legs, from a can or jar, or homemade for extra points

A handful of fresh breadcrumbs

1 tbsp chopped flat-leafed parsley (optional)

(For the brunch version: 4 slices black pudding and 4 eggs)

Sea salt and freshly ground black pepper

Much has been written about cassoulet. It's the sort of dish that has the paysans of Languedoc waving their arms around at that town down the road who make it in a slightly different way. The sanctity of the dish is taken so seriously that there is a brotherhood – the Grande Confrérie du Cassoulet – that defends the glory and quality of cassoulet in Castelnaudary, in part by conducting surprise taste tests of the cassoulets offered by local chefs. Absolutely fantastic. To the English, who have nothing approaching a real food culture, it's all rather hilarious. I hope that one day we will realise who had it right all along.

I'm sure the inhabitants of Carcassonne or Auch would spit indignantly into my pot of cassoulet, and well they might, for this version is a cross between the Toulousian and Castelnaudarian version of the dish: duck confit, of course, Toulouse sausages, natch, but pork belly instead of the more traditional shoulder, and no lamb. The breadcrumbs are apparently a Toulouse-only addition. Heretics. In the restaurant we make a version of this for brunch on the weekend, with all of the above, plus black pudding and eggs: cue vigorous arm waving.

The beans are an important part of this dish. You want a bean that is plump enough to absorb a lot of the fats, to go creamy without going mushy, and soft enough to help to form a delicious crust. A difficult brief! We have had great success with the white Coco de Paimpol, but more traditional, and harder to find, are Coco de Saissons or Tarbais beans, the latter of which come with an impressive price tag.

CONTINUED >

Fry the diced onion and the garlic slowly in the duck fat or olive oil until soft, seasoning well with salt. This will take at least 30 minutes. Season with black pepper. Meanwhile, take the skin off the pork belly in one piece. Roll the bay leaves, thyme sprigs and parsley stalks up in the skin and tie tightly in two places with string to make a sort of porky bouquet garni.

Put the onion mixture, beans and pork skin bundle into an ovenproof pot large enough to accommodate all the ingredients. Squish and tear the tomatoes with your hands into the pot. Add a big pinch of salt, enough to season the beans. Give everything a good stir to mix.

Preheat the oven to 160°C fan/180°C/360°F/gas 4.

Cut the pork belly into four pieces. Season with salt, and brown in a small amount of duck fat until a deep golden colour on all sides. Also brown the sausages and add, along with the confit duck legs, to the pot, pushing them down under the beans. Tip in half the fat from the pan – it would be a shame to waste it! Add enough water to cover the beans.

Briefly fry the breadcrumbs in the remaining fat until lightly coloured and reserve for later. Heat the assembly briefly on the stove top until it starts to bubble, then cook in the preheated oven with a lid on for two and a half hours. After an hour, remove the lid and sprinkle the breadcrumbs on top. Continue baking with the lid off so that the cassoulet forms a delicious crust. For an extra thick crust, you can stir the first layer of crusty breadcrumbs into the stew before adding another layer.

Remove from the oven, allow to cool, and then serve. Chopped parsley on top is optional and possibly heretical, but does add a welcome freshness.

For the breakfast version, follow the recipe as described above, but with a few small changes. Make the cassoulet the day before you plan to breakfast, but hold back the breadcrumbs. Cool the stew and refrigerate it overnight. In the morning, reheat the stew slowly and keep warm. Briefly fry the slices of black pudding before adding them to the pot with the other meats. Fry all the breadcrumbs until crispy and set aside while the cassoulet warms. When the cassoulet is hot, make a few divots around the bobbing meats and crack the eggs into the holes. Season the eggs lightly with salt. Top with the parsley and the fried breadcrumbs. Return the pan to the oven until the egg whites are set but the yolks are still soft.

A spritely green salad dressed with walnut oil and vinegar helps to cut through a bit of the fat. If you're having it for breakfast, a Bloody Mary pretty much does the same job. Besides, no one wants salad for breakfast.

RED PEPPERS COOKED IN RED WINE WITH BASIL & CRÈME FRAÎCHE

Serves 4

4 large Italian or French red peppers, deseeded

2 tbsp olive oil

6 garlic cloves, peeled and finely sliced

1 glass red wine (something fruity)

1 bunch of basil, leaves picked

1 tbsp crème fraîche

Sea salt and freshly ground black pepper

This is a fantastic side dish to have on the table on a summer's day, to be eaten warm with grilled meats and oily fish, or allowed to cool and scarfed with some fresh, young cheese and plenty of bread. The key is to stir fry the peppers over a high heat in plenty of olive oil before adding the wine – you want the peppers to take on a little colour. Do try to seek out proper peppers from southern Europe: something that has seen a bit of sun in its life.

———————————

Cut the peppers into rough strips or long chunks, about 7.5cm/3 inches wide. Heat the olive oil in a big pan and add the peppers. Stirring frequently, fry the peppers over a high heat for about 5 minutes, or until they start to soften and have taken on a little colour. Throw in the garlic, reduce the heat to medium, then stir the vegetables for a few minutes until you're satisfied that the garlic has lost its pungent raw flavour.

Season the peppers with salt and black pepper, then add the red wine. Reduce the heat to low and cook the peppers for a good 40 minutes, or until they are soft and beautifully sweet. Frequently check the liquid level in the pan: if it threatens to dry out and catch, add a little water. You don't want the peppers to be swimming in a soupy liquid, but a little of the acidic, oily juices is a good thing.

Throw the basil leaves in whole, then stir them into the hot peppers to wilt. Remove the pan from the heat and allow to cool slightly.

When ready to serve, blob the crème fraîche into the pan and half-stir it into the peppers. It's much better when the crème fraîche isn't completely amalgamated as the colours are more vivid and each bite of the peppers is slightly different.

This dish is good with so many things, but here's a short list: grilled pork chops; grilled lamb chops (with oregano instead of basil, maybe); steak; mackerel and particularly nice, this one, salmon or sea trout grilled until crispy outside and silken pink within.

GRANDE BOUFFE

AN AUTUMNAL GRAND AÏOLI

Gougères
Turnip Top Toasts
Lardo, Chestnuts & Honey
–
Le Grand Aïoli:
Salt Cod, Braised Octopus, Artichokes, Cauliflower, Pink Fir Potatoes, Carrots,
Purple Sprouting Broccoli, Boiled Eggs & Radishes
–
Apple & Walnut Cake

Now, aïoli is (arguably) garlic mayonnaise, but a *grand aïoli* is something much more spectacular. A riot of poached vegetables, aïoli, salt cod, snails and sometimes octopus, it's one of the most quintessentially Provençal feasts there is, and a splendid celebration of summer. The idea is that you take a piece of each thing and dip it in aïoli as you go – a smear of golden, garlicky sauce, slightly bitter from olive oil, is a perfect foil to the saline hit of the cod and the appealing blandness of the boiled vegetables.

While a *grand aïoli* pairs very well with a chilled rosé, the truth is that this meal is always somehow seems appropriate whatever the season. We cooked this meal in the autumn, on Hallowe'en I seem to remember. Safe to say, the vampires were warded off.

An autumnal *grand aïoli* presents certain opportunities, too. Wild mushrooms are always welcome, especially whole roasted ceps, or fat pieces of deep-fried hedgehog mushrooms. Roasted squash, pumpkin

or sweet potatoes add a lovely sweet, comforting note, and when cooked in embers, add a delicious bit of smoke that works very well with the sauce. Bobby beans, fried courgette (zucchini) flowers, langoustines, big juicy tomatoes, a little quick stew of squid cooked in rosé… all of these things and more work well, but think about balance where you can.

At the meal's centrepiece is of course the aïoli, so make it strong, balanced and delicious, and whatever you do don't run out of it. The accompaniments are up for debate, but vegetables are the most important. Use whatever is in season and tasting good. I love a bit of salt cod with mine, to offset the slightly bland vegetables, and either boiled snails or braised octopus to add a bit of extra wobble to the proceedings.

We baked the apple and walnut cake in an enormous tray and cut it into squares, but a regular cake tin is more sensible. Ours took so long to cook that it was still warm from the oven – an unintentional happy ending!

SQUEEZE

Gougères
Makes enough for a small party

Light, moreish little cheesey choux things. Buy some quality Comté or Swiss Gruyère for this.

Makes enough for a small party, and 'too many' gougères always seem to disappear as if by magic.

125ml/4fl oz/½ cup cold water
50g/1¾oz/¼ cup cold unsalted butter, cubed
1 tsp caster (superfine) sugar
A pinch of salt
70g/2½oz/½ cup plain (all-purpose) flour, sifted
3 whole eggs, or 2 if large
50g/1¾oz/¼ cup Comté or Gruyere, cut into small (5-mm/⅛-inch) cubes

First, make the pastry. Put the water, butter, sugar and salt in a pan and bring to the boil, whisking continually. Cook for a couple of minutes, whisking all the while, then add the flour all at once. Reduce the heat to low and stir with a wooden spoon until the dough comes together. Continue to stir and cook for around 5 minutes, until the pastry comes away from the sides of the pan and feels stiff enough to stand your spoon up in it.

Transfer, ideally, to a stand mixer and slowly beat in the eggs one by one. Continue to work until the pastry is almost at room temperature. Put into a bowl, cover and put in the refrigerator until cold. When cold, add the cheese, cut into small cubes.

Preheat the oven to 180°C fan/200°C/400°F/gas mark 6.

When ready to cook, pipe out your little gougère buns onto a baking tray lined with parchment. They should be a little smaller than the size of a golf ball. Put the tray in the oven and bake for around 35–40 minutes, or until a light golden brown, puffed and crisp. Don't open the oven door for the first half an hour of the cooking time. When done, the gougères should sound hollow when tapped on the bottom. Pierce each bun with a toothpick or similar so that any excess steam can escape – this will stop them becoming soggy. Allow to cool a bit, but warm gougères are obviously better.

Turnip Top Toasts
Serves 4

One of my favourite little toasts: braised greens are always fantastic on toasts as a little snack. Turnip tops are mildly bitter and make for a satisfying bite. A little fresh ricotta is a delicious optional extra.

1 handful turnip tops (cima di rape)
1 garlic clove, peeled, halved, sprout removed, and sliced lengthways
1 dried Italian chilli, or ½ fresh mild red chilli
A pinch of fennel seeds
Small sourdough loaf
2 tbsp olive oil

Wash the turnip tops and trim off any woody stalk. Boil in heavily salted water for a few minutes until soft. Drain, allow to cool, and squeeze well of water. Chop the turnip tops finely. Fry the garlic, chilli and fennel seeds slowly in half of the olive oil. When the garlic starts to stick together, add the turnip tops. Braise slowly for around 5 minutes, stirring from time to time. Turn off the heat and keep warm

Toast some thin sourdough bread until nice and crunchy. Top with the warm braised greens and drizzle with a little more oil.

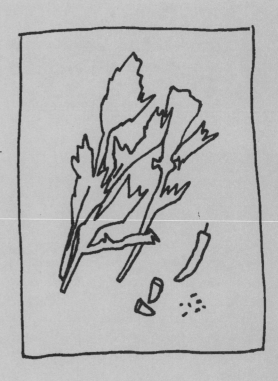

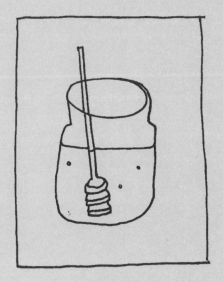

Lardo, Chestnuts & Honey
Serves 4

My friend Max's mum hails from Piedmont, and he introduced me to this excellent little taste of autumn: warm roasted chestnuts draped in melting lardo and drizzled with honey. The mealy, bland sweetness of the chestnuts needs something to lift it, and a slice of quality salted back fat does just this. Max strongly insists that the honey must be an excellent chestnut one. I put a bit of thyme on the chestnuts too, but I'm not sure if he'd approve.

2 or 3 roast chestnuts, per person
1 thin slice of Lardo di Colonnata, per person
1 sprig of thyme, picked
1 tbsp chestnut honey

Preheat the oven to 140°C fan/160°C/325°F/gas mark 3.

Warm the chestnuts in the oven. Put them on a serving plate and drape the slices of lardo over the top so all of the chestnuts are covered. Put a leaf or two of thyme on each chestnut. Drizzle the lot with the chestnut honey.

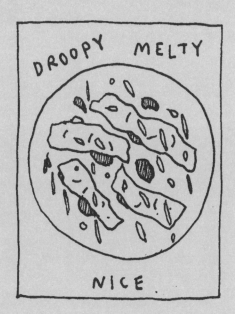

Le Grand Aïoli
Serves 4

The most important of sauces, aïoli is more strident than soothing and is best when one doesn't skimp on garlic. Originally, this would have been made with only garlic, salt and oil, resulting in a fiery, powerful and volatile paste. The addition of a little egg yolk is a good thing but I definitely think, and must insist, that the only oil involved must be extra virgin olive oil as you really want those bitter, peppery flavours to stand out. At the restaurant, we usually make big batches of aïoli and so do so in the food processor. If you are making a lot of it, then this is a good way to go, but smaller batches are best off made with a pestle and mortar. Aïoli, of course, goes with everything.

For the aioli:
1 fat or 2 small garlic cloves, peeled and green sprout removed
1tsp fine salt
2 egg yolks
200ml/7fl oz/1⅓ cup extra virgin olive oil
Juice of ½ lemon

To serve:
500g/1lb 2oz salt cod
½ quantity of Braised Octopus (see page 154)
4 artichokes, prepped for boiling
½ cauliflower, cut into large florets
12 Pink Fir potatoes, washed
4 carrots, peeled and halved lengthways
½ head purple sprouting broccoli, cut into large florets
4 eggs, hard-boiled and shelled
1 bunch radishes, washed
1 quantity of aïoli

To make the aïoli, crush the garlic with a good pinch of salt to a fine white paste in the mortar with the pestle. Add the egg yolks and emulsify as best you can. Add the olive oil very slowly, at first drop by drop, then in a slow stream. As the emulsion starts to thicken, add a few drops of lemon juice and a few of water, then continue with the oil. It's important to add the lemon juice and water gradually to avoid splitting the mixture. When all the oil is incorporated, taste the aïoli for salt and lemon juice to find a nice balance. You shouldn't be able to taste any raw egg. If you can, the aïoli needs more oil. If it looks a little too thick and 'rebounds' when you try to dip something into it, it needs another splash of water.

To serve alongside the aïoli, simmer the vegetables (except the radishes) separately in salted water until cooked. The artichokes need particularly careful and slow cooking. I might do them last to avoid discolouring the water. The vegetables should be soft, with no 'al dente' rubbish going on, but not mushy.

Poach the salt cod at a low simmer in unsalted water. Peel off the skin and separate into large chunks if not portioned already.

Reheat the vegetables by dunking briefly back into the pot of water. Drain well.

Arrange the salt cod, vegetables and eggs on a large platter – arrange by type, and try to find a nice contrast of colour across the platter – whites next to vivid colours, greens next to oranges, and so on. The rich, saucy braised octopus can happily sit in a little bowl of its own.

Place a huge bowl of aïoli in pride of place on the table and set about demolishing it.

Apple & Walnut Cake
Serves 8–10

100g/3½oz/½ cup dark muscovado sugar
100g/3½oz/½ cup light soft brown sugar
200g/7oz/⅔ cup unsalted butter, softened
3 eggs
½ tsp vanilla extract
100g/3½oz plain yogurt
125g/4½oz/1 cup rye flour
125g/4½oz/1 cup plain (all-purpose) flour
2 tsp baking powder
½ tsp fine salt
½ tsp ground cinnamon
A good grating of nutmeg
50g/1¾oz walnuts, crushed a bit
4 apples (weighing about 500g/1lb 2oz)
2 tbsp demerara sugar
Yogurt or crème fraîche, to serve

Preheat the oven to 180°C fan/200°C/400°F/gas mark 6. Grease a 24-cm/9-inch cake tin and line with parchment paper.

Using an electric mixer, cream together the sugars and butter until light and fluffy. Beat in the eggs, one at a time. Add the vanilla extract and yogurt and mix well.

In a separate bowl, whisk together the flours, baking powder, salt, cinnamon and nutmeg. Add to the butter mixture and beat just until incorporated.

Grate three of the (unpeeled) apples and fold into the cake mixture along with the walnuts.

Scrape the batter into your prepared cake tin and smooth the top. Peel and slice the remaining apple and arrange on top of the cake – the pattern doesn't matter too much, but overlapping concentric circles always looks nice. Sprinkle with demerara sugar and bake for about 45 minutes, or until a skewer inserted comes out clean. Serve with yogurt or crème fraîche.

PORK CHOP, ROAST PUMPKIN, TROMPETTES DE LA MORT & WALNUTS

Serves 4

4 pork chops

1 pumpkin or squash ('Delica' or 'Violino' varieties are particularly good, but please no butternut squash – depending on size, you may only need a half)

6 garlic cloves, unpeeled, crushed with the flat of a knife

1 tomato from a jar, ripped into small pieces

A few thyme sprigs

2 tbsp olive oil, plus extra for frying

50g/1¾oz walnuts

200g/7oz fresh trompettes de la mort mushrooms, washed in water, drained well and dried out

2 tbsp butter

2 tbsp roughly chopped parsley

Sea salt and freshly ground black pepper

This pumpkin, mushroom and walnut trio is a fantastic accompaniment to pork, amongst other things. Trompettes de la Mort are a favourite wild mushroom, with a striking black hue and a distinct flavour. It's only food, of course, but I do think these colours are autumn on a plate.

Perhaps you don't need instructions on how to cook a pork chop, but here's a recipe anyway. I aim for a chop weighing 300g/10½oz all in. Remove the rind but leave the fat on – trim it a little if it seems excessive, but as my Welsh grandma used to say, it's the best bit. Season well with salt and pepper. For best results, grill the chops over a wood and charcoal fire (although a heavy pan never fails), but avoid any flare-ups as the fat drips onto the coals. Balance the chop fat-side down for a time to render the fat edible. The best pork is always cooked pink. Rest the chop for 5 minutes after cooking. Drizzle with oil while the pork is resting and you'll have a ready-made sauce to pour over when it's time to eat.

———————————

Pre-heat the oven to 180°C fan/200°C/400°F/gas mark 6.

Remove the seeds from the pumpkin, then cut into 3-cm/1-inch thick wedges. Place the pumpkin wedges in a roasting dish along with the garlic, tomato and thyme. Drizzle with the olive oil, season with salt and black pepper, then toss to coat everything evenly. Rearrange the thyme sprigs so they sit underneath the pumpkin wedges (they are less likely to frazzle away to nothing). Add 3 tbsp water.

Cover the dish with foil and roast in the oven for 30–40 minutes, until the pumpkin is approaching soft. Remove the foil and continue to roast for a further 15–20 minutes, until the pumpkin has coloured and is soft all the way through. The garlic should be soft and sweet. Remove from the oven and keep warm.

On a separate small tray, roast the walnuts for 4–5 minutes until they have coloured slightly and their flavour has intensified. Remove from the oven and set aside. Meanwhile, over a medium heat, fry the mushrooms in the butter and a bit of olive oil. Season with salt and pepper, then stir in the chopped parsley.

To serve, arrange the warm pumpkin and any oily juices on a platter. Spoon over the warm, buttery mushrooms, and scatter with chopped roasted walnuts. Eat with the pork chop.

GIROLLES, GRILLED POLENTA, SPINACH & CRÈME FRAÎCHE

Serves 4

1 litre/1¾ pints/4¼ cups water

200g/7oz coarse polenta (not instant)

Olive oil

250g/9oz girolles, cleaned but not washed

1 tbsp butter

½ garlic clove, peeled and sliced finely lengthways

1 tsp picked thyme

1 tbsp chopped parsley

400g/14oz spinach

Juice of ½ lemon

4 tsp crème fraîche

Parmesan cheese, to serve (in a block, not grated)

Sea salt and freshly ground black pepper

I often cook far too much polenta – something happens to me in the whisking stage and I get overexcited – but when this happens, I use the excess to make set polenta. Once set, polenta can be sliced, rubbed with oil and grilled over hot coals: crispy and blackened on the outside, creamy and wobbly within. It's a fine foil for buttery wild mushrooms. A few shavings of Parmesan add a savoury spike, while a dollop of crème fraîche ties it all together.

First make the polenta. Bring the water to the boil in a pan and whisk in the polenta, adding it in a thin stream while you whisk. Reduce the heat to low and cook, stirring occasionally, for around 1 hour, until very thick. Season lightly with salt. Rub a deep-sided tray lightly with olive oil and pour in the polenta. Smooth the surface as best you can. Allow to cool then place in the refrigerator to set overnight. The next day, turn out the set polenta and cut into fingers: I aim for pieces that aren't too large – about 10cm/4 inches x 3cm/1 inch.

Light a barbecue or heat a cast-iron grill pan. Alternatively heat a top-down grill (broiler) in the oven. The heat, particularly if cooking over coals or wood, should be very hot or the polenta will stick. Rub the polenta lightly with olive oil and grill on both sides until crispy, golden brown and slightly blackened in places. Leave the polenta alone while it crisps up – if you attempt to move it too early, it will make an almighty mess. Set aside and keep warm.

Meanwhile, fry the girolles in 1 tbsp olive oil over a medium heat. When they have taken on some colour, turn down the heat, add the butter, garlic and thyme, and season with salt and pepper. Continue to cook for a few minutes until the girolles are cooked through and the garlic has fried gently and mellowed. Throw in the chopped parsley, stir, and keep warm.

Meanwhile, bring a pot of water to the boil. Season the water heavily with salt, and dunk the spinach in. Cook the spinach for no more than a few seconds before removing to a tray with a slotted spoon. Press the spinach to squeeze out the water – there will be a lot of it but you must be thorough. Drain off the water and drizzle the squeezed spinach with olive oil and the lemon juice.

Put the grilled polenta on plates. Arrange the dressed spinach next to it, and spoon the girolles and all their buttery juices over the top of and around the polenta. In the middle of this trio, dollop a teaspoon of crème fraîche. Grind over some black pepper, add shavings of Parmesan and drizzle with olive oil.

STEAK NIGHT

A few recommendations on choosing and grilling steaks… Firstly, buy your meat from a proper butcher. Meat has become far too cheap. It should be a rare and expensive treat. Pay full whack for the best you can afford, it'll be worth it. For those in London, I recommend H.G. Walter in Baron's Court, the Ginger Pig at various locations or The Butchery in Bermondsey; all of which sell terrific beef at terrifying prices.

As to what cut to choose, it's down to personal preference. We cook a lot of onglet in the restaurant, because it's more affordable and the flavour is outstanding. It should be grilled rare, as it can tend towards toughness if overcooked. It's not the most tender cut, but since when was that the point? If it's a special occasion I would go for sirloin – for ease we cook them off the bone – in thick-cut, half-kilo steaks. Oh, and there's a T-bone steak, of course. But then again, maybe a côte de boeuf.

Whatever you choose, take it out of the refrigerator a good hour before you're going to cook it, season it generously and grill it over hot wood and charcoal embers: wood for the flavour, charcoal for the extra heat. Rest it for about half as long as you've cooked it for. At this stage a drizzle of olive oil or a big knob of butter will go some way to creating delicious resting juices to be spooned back onto the steak later.

BRAISED TURNIPS, GIROLLES & HORSERADISH CRÈME FRAÎCHE

Serves 4, as a side for a big steak

Olive oil

200g/7oz girolles, cleaned

125g/4½oz/½ cup unsalted butter

400g/14oz little turnips, with their tops, whole if very small or halved if larger, peeled

A few thyme sprigs

2 garlic cloves, peeled and lightly crushed

250ml/8fl oz/1 cup chicken stock (or use vegetable stock or water)

Sea salt and freshly ground black pepper

For the horseradish crème fraîche:

¼ fresh horseradish root, peeled

2 tbsp crème fraîche

Juice of ½ a lemon

Salt

This was on the menu at Chez Panisse during the week that I worked there. Little turnips with their tops, braised in butter and a little chicken stock, make a wonderful side for a steak, particularly when a few girolles are thrown into the mix.

———————

For the horseradish crème fraîche, finely grate the horseradish into the crème fraîche. Season to taste with lemon juice and salt.

Heat 1 tbsp olive oil in a wide, deep pan and sauté the girolles until they are nicely coloured, soft, but not completely cooked. Season with salt and pepper. Pour out of the pan and set aside for later.

Melt the butter in the pot and add a glug of olive oil to stop the butter from colouring too much. Put in the peeled turnips. Stir the turnips around in the butter so that they take a little colour on all sides. Add the thyme and the garlic. Cook for a few minutes, stirring, until the turnips are an attractive golden brown. Add half the chicken stock and cover the pot with a lid. Reduce the heat to very low and cook for around 15 minutes.

After 15 minutes, check to see if the stock has evaporated – the turnips should have absorbed most of it. Wash the turnip tops well, chop them finely, and add to the pot with the turnips. Next, add the other half of the stock and re-cover. Cook for a further 10 minutes, or until the turnips are soft and golden and there is a small amount of liquid remaining.

Introduce the cooked girolles to the turnips and stir everything happily around.

Serve with steak and the horseradish crème fraîche.

SWISS CHARD & ANCHOVY GRATIN

Serves 4

1 big bunch Swiss chard

125g/4½oz/½ cup unsalted butter

4 fat garlic cloves, peeled and finely
   chopped

2 tbsp plain (all-purpose) flour

250ml/8fl oz/1 cup whole milk

A grating of nutmeg

8 salted anchovy fillets

2 tbsp fresh breadcrumbs

1 tbsp olive oil

This is one of my favourite dishes from one of my favourite cookbooks, Richard Olney's *Lulu's Provençal Table*. For me, it represents the very best of Provençal grand-mère cooking. It's an absolutely wonderful thing: very simple to make, with bags of rustic charm and an awful lot of garlic. Extremely good with steak, especially when you don't stint on the anchovies, but equally good with grilled or roast lamb, pork or chicken.

———————

Preheat the oven to 180°C fan/200°C/400°F/gas mark 6.

First, prepare the Swiss chard: wash it well and separate the leaves from the stalks. Trim the stalks of any black or grey bits and chop into small pieces. Bring a large pot of salted water to the boil. Boil the stalks for a few minutes until soft but not mushy. Add the leaves and cook for a further minute. Drain the chard and squeeze it very well to remove the water.

In a nice big pot or deep-sided pan, melt the butter. When frothing, add the chopped garlic. Cook on a very low heat for a minute or two, until an overwhelming scent of garlic fills the room. Add the squeezed out Swiss chard and stir everything around. Cook for a further minute or two, then sprinkle over the flour. Stir the flour around in the butter for a minute to cook it out slightly, then add the milk bit by bit, stirring all the while: this in effect is a rather rustic method of making a béchamel. When all the milk has been added, you should have a wet, smooth Swiss chard béchamel. Cook the Swiss chard for 10 minutes on a low heat. Add a little more milk if the mixture looks too dry – bear in mind we will be gratinating this in the oven so it will dry out a little more. Season with salt, pepper and grated nutmeg, leaving a little leg room on the salt as the gratin will be topped with salty anchovies.

Pour the gratin into a baking dish. Criss-cross with the salted anchovy fillets, sprinkle with the breadcrumbs and drizzle with the olive oil. Bake the gratin in the hot oven for around 30 minutes, or until the breadcrumbs are golden brown and crispy and the gratin is bubbling hot underneath. Allow to cool a little before serving.

POTATO & LOVAGE BEIGNET

Serves 4

1 tbsp plain (all-purpose) flour

1 egg

1 tbsp sparkling water

1 tbsp double (heavy) cream

1 tsp fine salt

1 tsp sugar

1 spring onion (scallion), shredded

1 tbsp chopped picked lovage or
tarragon

400g/14oz floury potatoes, peeled

Sunflower oil, for frying

Flaky sea salt

This fried, grated potato cake has a rich, fluffy centre and frazzled edges – like an enriched tempura batter. Lovage is a herb with a strong celery taste that stands up well to frying, but tarragon is delicious here too.

Put the flour in one half of a mixing bowl. In the other half, place the egg, water and cream. Beat the egg and liquids together, then incorporate them slowly into the flour to make a smooth batter. Add the salt, sugar, spring onion and lovage or tarragon.

Using a box grater or a grating attachment, grate the potatoes on the thickest side of the grater. Add the potatoes to the batter. Move them around with your hands to coat. You can let them sit for a while in the batter.

Heat the oil in a pan. When the oil reaches 180°C/350°F, form the potatoes into rough patties and carefully slide them into the pan. Fry for a few minutes on both sides until golden brown and crisp. Drain on paper towels, sprinkle with flaky sea salt, and serve.

CEP, BREAD & BONE MARROW SAUCE

Serves 4

1 piece bone marrow, soaked for a few
hours in cold water

1 tbsp dried ceps, soaked in hot water,
drained and chopped

1 tbsp black pepper, ground

4 tbsp fresh breadcrumbs (no crusts
allowed)

200ml/7fl oz/1 cup beef, veal or
chicken stock or, even better, the
broth from a Pot-au-Feu

50g/1¾oz/¼ cup unsalted butter

50g/1¾oz Parmesan cheese, grated

Salt

The ceps, stock and bone marrow make for a pretty meaty sauce, mellowed by breadcrumbs, Parmesan and a touch of butter.

Pop the soaked marrow out of the bone. Break the marrow into pieces and melt in a pan. Add the soaked, chopped ceps to the hot marrow fat in the pan. Fry for a minute or two over a low heat until the ceps start to smell. Add the black pepper and fry for 30 seconds to release the oils in the spice.

Add the breadcrumbs and stock. Whisk the sauce as it cooks, breaking the breadcrumbs into smaller pieces. Cook for 5 minutes over a low heat, whisking from time to time, until you are left with a thick, smooth(ish) sauce. Add water if it looks too thick. Whisk in the butter and Parmesan. Season to taste.

BLACK TRUFFLE BUTTER

Makes 4 discs of butter, enough for a meal for 4

50g/1¾oz/¼ cup good unsalted butter

10g/⅓oz of summer black truffle or 5g/¼oz of Périgord black truffle

½ tsp lemon juice

1 tsp Cognac, Armagnac or brandy

Flaky sea salt and freshly ground black pepper

Should you get your hands on some fresh black truffle, well done you. I'm sure you don't need suggestions on what to do with it, but this recipe comes in well handy if for some reason you have too much (!) and are worried that it might go off, or if you have a few scraps lying around to use up. Grating truffles into butter preserves them nicely, and can be kept in the freezer for a rainy day when you might need cheering up.

Butter fats are a good friend to truffles in general, and serve to enhance and enrich their flavour: a willing vehicle. Summer truffles are much more affordable than the winter Périgord ones, but often need help. This method squeezes a lot of flavour out of them. A glug of fine brandy adds an interesting backnote, and a little squeeze of lemon provides some lift.

Truffle butter is a luxurious thing to put on your steak while it rests, but obviously has myriad other uses: tossed through pasta, melted into scrambled eggs, stirred into a hot pea soup, spread onto hot toast, to be eaten with steak tartare or raw veal, melted onto grilled, spatchcocked quails… I could go on for hours here.

Soften the butter, either by leaving out at room temperature or by whizzing in the blender until smooth. Finely grate the truffle into the butter and add the other ingredients. Mix together well and taste for salt – remember that this butter will be used to top a salty delicious steak, so it won't need fully seasoning. The butter should be very smooth with no lumps of cold butter – whizz or beat it well.

Transfer the butter onto a piece of parchment paper, spreading the butter out into a rough line. Roll the butter up into a cylinder, and twist the ends of the parchment to seal. Fold over the ends of the twists and wrap the whole thing in clingfilm (plastic wrap). Store in the refrigerator for a week or two (until the shelf life of the butter), or freeze.

When your steak (côte de boeuf, please) comes off the grill and is still piping hot, plop a few discs of the butter on top. The truffle butter will mingle with the resting juices. You will need some fluffy, crisp chips to smush into the juices, but I trust you have this angle covered.

DOMINO POTATOES

Serves 4

1.25kg/2lb 12oz red potatoes (such as
   Desiree), peeled
200g/7oz/²⁄₃ cup unsalted butter
4 bay leaves
Salt

These are potatoes stacked like dominoes and baked in clarified butter with bay leaves and sea salt. The closest relation to this in the traditional repertoire is *pommes Anna*. These potatoes are ever so slightly less faff than all that. Delicious with a steak, obviously, but since these are potatoes cooked in butter they are delicious with anything. You'll need a mandolin, or failing that, a sharp knife and a lot of patience.

———

Preheat the oven to 180°C fan/200°C/400°F/gas mark 6.

Slice the potatoes an even 1mm/¹⁄₃₂ inch thick. It works better when the potatoes are sliced shorter rather than longer – across the width rather than along the length, if that makes sense, as they are easier to stack.

Once the potatoes are sliced, stack them loosely in your hands, then lay them in a roasting dish, stacked like dominoes on top of one another. Spread them in lines across the tray. Try not to stack them either too flat (they will crisp up too much) or too tightly (they will steam and not crisp properly).

Meanwhile, clarify the butter: melt the butter in a pot and bring to a simmer. Cook very gently for a minute or two, then skim off the milk solids from the butter and discard. It doesn't matter if you don't get them all.

Pour the butter all over the stacked potatoes, season with salt, and tuck the bay leaves in amongst the potatoes. Cover the dish with foil and bake in the oven for 45 minutes.

Remove the foil and check to see whether the potatoes are soft. If not, re-foil and return to the oven. Baste the potatoes with the butter, and return, uncovered, to the oven. Bake for a further 15 minutes, or until the potatoes are golden brown and crisp.

Remove from the oven, pour off some of the excess butter (keep for another batch of potatoes), and allow to cool slightly before serving.

ROAST BONE MARROW, SNAILS & PERSILLADE

Serves 4

4 'trugs' of bone marrow (10-cm/
4-inch lengths of marrow, split
lengthways like a little boat)

1 small can of French pre-cooked
snails (about 16 snails in all),
drained of any liquor

1 fat garlic clove, peeled, halved and
green sprout removed

1 tbsp picked parsley

1 tbsp fresh breadcrumbs

1 tsp grated Parmesan cheese

Sea salt and freshly ground black
pepper

We were introduced to this over-the-top little side dish by the chef Henry Harris when he came to cook at the restaurant. Henry is a master of the classic but moreover of the desirable – things that you really want to eat. We grilled some côte de boeufs and rested them in butter while the little bone marrow boats roasted in the oven, manned by a crew of happy snails fizzing with garlic, parsley and breadcrumbs. Hello, sailor.

––––––––––

Preheat the oven to 200°C fan/220°C/450°F/gas mark 7.

Soak the trugs of bone marrow in cold water for a few hours to remove the blood and soften the marrow. Remove the marrow from the bones and break into 2-cm/¾-inch chunks. Return the marrow to the bones and dot with snails. Season with flaky sea salt and ground black pepper.

Chop the garlic and parsley finely together to make a persillade. Mix with the breadcrumbs and Parmesan. Sprinkle the persillade over the marrow and snails.

Roast the bone marrow boats in the hot oven for 15–20 minutes, or until the marrow is hot and fudgey, the snails roasted in the marrow fat and the persillade starting to crisp nicely.

Serve with the steaks, some kind of potatoes and a nice watercress salad.

CLAFOUTIS

Serves 4–6

3 tbsp cold unsalted butter

70g/2½oz/½ cup plain (all-purpose) flour, sifted

100g/3½oz/½ cup caster (superfine) sugar, plus 2 tbsp extra for sprinkling

A pinch of salt

3 medium eggs

280ml/9½fl oz/1 cup plus 2 tbsp whole milk

400g/14oz fruit (plums or apricots should be stoned, but cherries and prunes can be left with their pits inside – just warn your guests!)

Icing (confectioners') sugar, to taste

1 tbsp kirsch (if using cherries) or brandy (for any other stone fruit) (optional)

Cooking in a restaurant is frustrating sometimes in that some dishes are unachievable – a dessert like a clafoutis, one of the simplest, most comforting desserts in the home cook's repertoire, needs a good 40 minutes at least to bake. In a restaurant this means either a too-long wait or inevitable wastage, so I only get to cook this when we are serving a set menu. Clafoutis is a baked eggy batter into which can be suspended many different fruits, from cherries (unpitted of course), to apricots, plums and brandy-soaked prunes.

———————————

Melt 1 tbsp of the butter and set aside to cool. Whisk together the sifted flour, caster sugar, salt, eggs, melted butter and milk to make a smooth batter. Set aside while you prepare the fruit.

Stone the fruit, if necessary. If you feel the fruit is too acidic, macerate in icing sugar to taste for 15 minutes. At this point you can add a splash of kirsch or brandy, if you feel so inclined.

Preheat the oven to 180°C fan/200°C/400°F/gas mark 6.

Grease a ceramic baking dish with butter. Add the fruit to the dish, then pour over the batter. Top the batter with fine slivers of cold butter, and sprinkle with the extra caster sugar.

Bake in the oven for around 35–40 minutes, or until the clafoutis has risen, the fruit has gone jammy and the top is an attractive golden brown.

Remove from the oven, allow to cool slightly and serve warm.

FIG LEAF ICE CREAM & ROAST FIGS

Serves 8

For the ice cream:

10 small or 4 large fresh fig leaves

500ml/18fl oz/2 cups whole milk

500ml/18fl oz/2 cups double (heavy) cream

6 egg yolks

175g/6oz/¾ cup caster (superfine) sugar

For the roast figs:

8 ripe black figs

1 tbsp caster (superfine) sugar

1 tbsp eau de vie or grappa

Fig trees grow all over Britain but rarely bear fruit, so you'll have to buy the figs themselves, but a spot of urban foraging means that you'll have a few green fig leaves to use to infuse the cream. Fresh fig leaves impart an intriguing taste, fruity, nutty and reminiscent of coconut, that makes for a delicious milky ice cream, particularly when served with the jammy, sweet roast fruit.

First, make the ice cream. Preheat an overhead grill (broiler). Lay the fig leaves on a baking tray and grill for 2 minutes or until the fig leaves have started to take on a little colour and smell wonderfully nutty. Allow to cool, then shred the fig leaves with a knife.

In a heavy-based pan, slowly warm the milk and cream to scalding point. Meanwhile, beat the egg yolks with the sugar. Whisk a little of the hot milk and cream into the egg mixture. Continue adding the hot milk and cream, a little at a time, until the egg yolks have been tempered. Combine all together, whisking fast, so that the eggs don't scramble.

Cook the custard until it thickens slightly and coats the back of a spoon and you can draw a line with your finger through it and have it hold. Alternatively, use a thermometer and cook to 82°C/180°F.

Pour the custard through a sieve (strainer) into a tray and allow to cool, then refrigerate. Churn the ice cream in an ice-cream maker and freeze.

When ready to cook the figs, preheat the oven to 180°C fan/200°C/400°F/ gas mark 6.

Halve the figs and toss with the sugar and eau de vie or grappa. Arrange on a baking tray and roast in the oven for 15–20 minutes or until soft and jammy.

Serve the warm roast figs and any leftover juices in the tray with the fig leaf ice cream.

SWEET ORANGE BLOSSOM FOUGASSE WITH CHERRIES & WHIPPED CREAM

Makes 1 tray of brioche, enough for 8 people

2 tsp fresh yeast (or 1 tsp dried)

150ml/5fl oz/²⁄₃ cup warm water

500g/1lb 2oz strong white bread flour, plus extra for dusting

2 tsp fine salt

50g/1¾oz/¼ cup caster (superfine) sugar, plus extra for sprinkling

2 medium eggs

1 tbsp crème fraîche

70g/2¹⁄₂₀z/¼ cup unsalted butter, cubed and softened, plus 100g/3½oz/½ cup butter, cubed, for later

Zest of ½ unwaxed lemon and ½ unwaxed orange, grated

1 tsp orange blossom water, plus extra for brushing

20 cherries, pitted

To serve:

100ml/3½fl oz/½ cup double (heavy) cream, whipped

1 tbsp icing (confectioners') sugar

1 tbsp grappa or eau de vie

Fougasse d'Aigues Mortes hails from a town in the Camargue, and is a sweet fougasse that has much in common with a brioche. Flavoured heavily with orange blossom water, it's delicious on its own, particularly for breakfast, but I thought it might be nice with cherries pushed into it before it bakes: buttery, floral and with jammy fruit running through it. A little sweetened whipped cream, particularly with a touch of added booze, is a nice addition.

———

Activate the yeast by stirring together with a splash of lukewarm water. Allow to activate for 5 minutes in a warm spot.

Mix together the flour, salt, sugar and the activated yeast. Make a well and add the eggs and crème fraîche, followed by the rest of the water, bit by bit, and knead until you have a smooth, light, puffed and aerated dough. Put the softened butter in the mixing bowl and mix until smooth again.

Cover with clingfilm (plastic wrap) and let the dough rise in a warm spot for 3–4 hours. Alternatively, leave the dough to prove overnight in the refrigerator.

When ready to bake, preheat the oven to 180°C fan/200°C/400°F/gas mark 6. Line a baking tray with parchment paper.

On a lightly floured surface, roll out the dough into a rectangular shape: do not work it too much. Put the rectangle of dough on the prepared baking tray.

Using your finger or the handle of a wooden spoon, make holes in the dough just as you would for focaccia, but deeper. Make the holes in lines so that it looks neat. Sprinkle a few drops of orange blossom water into each hole. Insert a cherry into each hole too, followed by a cube of pre-cut butter. Brush all over with extra orange blossom water.

Bake in the preheated oven for 10 minutes. Then remove the tray from the oven, sprinkle the brioche heavily with caster sugar and return to the oven for a further 5 minutes.

Remove from the oven and allow to cool slightly before tucking in. Serve with the whipped cream, to which you have added icing sugar and a good glug of grappa or a fruity eau de vie.

WINTER

By winter, long gone are the summery salad days of ripe tomatoes, plump figs, goats' milk and honey. 'À la Provençale', the culinary term used across France, no longer seems to apply for all of the essential ingredients – aubergines (eggplant), peppers, tomatoes, courgettes (zucchini), olive oil and sunshine – are no more. For the keen cook, however, the winter season offers a wealth of opportunities that the average tourist will never see. The year does not stop as summer fades, and so one makes do with what one has at hand.

Thrillingly, for this cook at least, the en-vogue ingredients during the Provençal winter are similar to what we have here in Britain, and there is no more worrying that the tomatoes might not quite be as good as those at the market in Aix, or that the aubergines we buy from the supermarket on the high street are inferior to what the handsome, moustachioed farmer has on his table at the local market. We're not cooking ratatouille any more: we've moved on to potatoes, carrots, cabbage and turnips, and I'd challenge any southern French farmer to beat us at our own game. What ingredients we don't grow ourselves can be easily sourced, albeit at a cost, and a piece of beef from a good British butcher will, I'm happy to report, usually be much better than one can find in France; our horseradish just as fiery, the red wine for the stew no less powerful for being imported: we're on an even footing.

Provençal winter cooking is about anchovies and olives, salted for winter; grassy new season's olive oil, pounded into a rousing aïoli; squeaky fresh Florence fennel, braised until soft and sweet; rich, mealy chestnuts cooked slowly into a soup; the solemn, staid, but wholly delicious ritual of the Christmas Eve Gros Souper (and its thirteen desserts); black truffles on everything, bien sûr. Provence holds most of its azure colour throughout the season, but while we might well suffer under more severe skies, much of the cooking is available to us, and very much at hand.

RAW CHOPPED SEA BASS, OYSTERS, RAZOR CLAMS & CUCUMBER

Makes 8 shells, enough for 4 people as a starter

8 live rock oysters in the shell

6 live razor clams

150g/5¼oz wild sea bass fillet, skinned and pin-boned

½ small cucumber, peeled and cut into 5-mm/¼-inch dice

½ tsp parsley, finely chopped

½ tsp chives, finely chopped

1 tbsp olive oil

2 tsp lemon juice

½ tsp crème fraîche

1 tsp freshly grated horseradish

Sea salt and freshly ground black pepper

Coarse rock salt, to serve

I first encountered a mixed seafood and oyster tartare at the age of twenty-one, while living in Paris. After saving for months, I went for a blowout meal at Café Constant on Rue St. Dominique including a delicious mélange of raw salmon, seabass, oysters, ginger and caviar, served in the shell. I urge you to buy a piece of wild sea bass from a fishmonger for this dish, as the farmed and frozen supermarket equivalent is nowhere near nice enough to be eaten raw. Razor clams are delicious raw, providing you aren't squeamish about the cut pieces wriggling about on your chopping board.

———————

Shuck the oysters, leaving them on the half-shell. To do this, holding the oyster with its flat side facing upwards, insert an oyster knife into the pointed hinge. Wiggle the knife to and fro, slowly pushing it in, and when you have some purchase, twist the knife until you hear a 'pop'. Continue twisting your knife back and forth, and slide the knife into the oyster along the top of the shell. Take care not to puncture the oyster itself. Cut through the small muscle on the inside of the top shell, then open the oyster. Brush off any stray pieces of shell, reserving any juices that leech out. Strain the juices through a sieve (strainer) to remove any grit. Chill the oysters in the refrigerator. Wash the rounded bottoms of the shells, dry and set aside to use later for serving.

Using a small, sharp knife, run the blade inside the shell down the side of the live razor clam. Peel back one half of the shell and remove; be careful as razor clam shells are very brittle and liable to shatter. Use the knife to cut the razor clam away from the shell as you pull it out. Cut away the digestive sac and any other dodgy-looking, gritty black bits. Wash the clams well in cold water.

Using a very sharp knife, chop the sea bass and oysters into 5-mm/¼-inch or 1-cm/½-inch dice. When cutting raw fish into tartare, cut thin strips first, arrange the strips in a line and then cut through them horizontally to make cubes. Don't set about hacking the fish up willy-nilly as your knife won't cut cleanly without mushing the fish. Cut the razor clams into thin (2-mm/¹⁄₁₆-inch) slices. Combine the raw fish in a bowl. Add the cucumber and the herbs. You might not need it all; it's better to have more fish than cucumber in the mixture. Season with salt and a little black pepper, then dress with the olive oil, lemon juice and crème fraîche. Add a little of the reserved oyster juices to add a briney depth to the mixture, but not so much that it is watery. Taste carefully for seasoning and adjust with more salt and lemon juice, if necessary.

Spoon the tartare into the reserved oyster shells. Grate a little fresh horseradish over the top. Plate the filled oyster shells atop small piles of rock salt to serve.

BAKED OYSTERS WITH PASTIS, TARRAGON & BREADCRUMBS

Serves 4, as a starter

½ fennel bulb, with fronds

50g/1¾oz/¼ cup unsalted butter, softened

¼ garlic clove, peeled and sliced thinly lengthways

A pinch of grated unwaxed orange zest

A tarragon sprig, leaves picked

A splash of pastis

50g/1¾oz/⅔ cup fine fresh breadcrumbs

12 oysters

Sea salt and freshly ground black pepper

To serve (optional):

Fennel

Rocket (arugula)

Watercress

Baked oysters suffer from a slightly cheesy, Americanised reputation. Not so these buttery, crispy, pastis-spiked baked oysters, which have an immediate, simple appeal. Note, please, the lack of cheese here. The flavours are more stripped back. I first ate something similar to this, using absinthe in the place of pastis, at the amazing restaurant Camino in Oakland, California (sadly now closed), where the oysters were baked in a wood fire over masses of wild fennel. They emerge still sizzling, the fennel frazzled and smelling of wood smoke, with the breadcrumbs crisp, and the absinthe butter pooling into the upturned half-shell, mingling with the oyster juices.

─────────────

Preheat the oven to 220°C fan/240°C/475°F/gas mark 9.

Discard the tougher outer leaves of the fennel. Reserve the fennel fronds or herb and set aside, then finely dice the rest. Heat a small knob of the butter (about 1 tbsp) in a pan, then add the fennel, garlic and orange zest. Cook for a minute, then add a splash or two of water and continue cooking until the fennel is soft. Transfer to a bowl and leave to cool.

Finely chop the tarragon and fennel fronds or herb. Combine the butter, cooked fennel mixture, chopped herbs, pastis and breadcrumbs, and season with salt and pepper. Everything should be well incorporated, with no big bits of unblended butter. The mixture should taste herby, slightly sweet from the fennel, with a good hit of aniseed from the pastis and just a hint of orange zest.

Shuck the oysters, leaving them on the half-shell. Hold the oyster with its flat side facing upwards and insert an oyster knife into the pointed hinge. Wiggle the knife to and fro, slowly pushing it in, and when you have some purchase, twist the knife until you hear a 'pop'. Continue twisting your knife back and forth, and slide the knife into the oyster along the top of the shell. Take care not to puncture the oyster itself. Cut through the small muscle on the inside of the top shell, then open the oyster. Brush off any stray pieces of shell.

Top the oyster with a tablespoon or so of the pastis butter. Lay the oysters in a roasting dish, making sure they fit snugly. Use any leftover fennel fronds or tarragon stalks, piles of rock salt or fresh seaweed to balance the oyster shells so they don't fall over and spill their cargo. Bake the oysters in the hot oven for about 5–6 minutes, or until the topping has simultaneously melted and turned crispy. Eat immediately. Serve with a small salad, if you fancy, of raw shaved fennel, rocket and roughly chopped watercress.

SALSIFY & SAUCISSON EN PAPILLOTTE

Serves 4, as a starter

4 thin or 2 fat sticks of salsify

50ml/1⅔fl oz/2¾ tbsp white wine

1 thyme sprig

1 bay leaf

2 garlic cloves

A pinch of whole coriander seeds

A good glug of olive oil

40g/1½oz good saucisson, peeled and finely julienned into 2-cm/¾-inch lengths

50g/1¾ oz baby spinach

50g/1¾ oz/¼ cup unsalted butter

4 small thyme sprigs

1 tbsp finely chopped mixed parsley and chervil

To serve:

Fried breadcrumbs

Grated Parmesan cheese (optional)

Salsify is the loveliest of root vegetables, with a rather elegant artichoke-like flavour. As such I tend to treat it as if it were an artichoke: peeling, cutting into lengths and keeping in lemony water, before simmering slowly in water, wine, olive oil and herbs. Sometimes I like to fold pre-cooked salsify into a piece of parchment paper, where it will steam nicely with some white wine and plenty of butter. A small amount of julienned saucisson imparts a lot of flavour, and plenty of fresh herbs provide a lift. This parcel would be equally delicious with mussels and a little finely chopped bacon.

Prepare some lemony water for the salsify to stop it from going brown. Peel the salsify one by one, wash well, cut into 8-cm/3-inch lengths and drop into the lemony water while you prepare the rest. Put half of the white wine, the thyme, bay, garlic and coriander seeds into a pot with the prepared salsify and top up with water. Add some salt to taste. Bring the salsify to the boil, then immediately turn down to a slow simmer. Cover the salsify with a cartouche of parchment paper to keep it under the water. Cook for around 10 minutes or until the salsify is just soft.

Preheat the oven to 200°C fan/220°C/425°F/gas mark 7.

Remove the salsify from the water and allow to cool. While the salsify is cooking, prepare the papillottes: cut four 40-cm/15-inch pieces of parchment paper. Fold the pieces in half to double the thickness. Drizzle the top half of the papillotte with olive oil, then lay over the cooked salsify in neat rows. Leave enough room to both fold the parcel over and crimp it well on all sides. Scatter over the saucisson, spinach and herbs, and dot with the thyme and the butter. Sprinkle with the remaining white wine, then fold over the parcel and seal it well on all sides by folding it over two or three times – start with the bottom of the fold, then do the outsides, then finally the open part of the parcel.

Double check they are properly sealed, and put the papillottes onto a flat tray and into the oven. Bake for 8 minutes, or until the parcels are puffed up and full of steam. Put the papillottes onto plates and encourage your guests to rip into their bags at the table. Some crispy breadcrumbs fried in olive oil and some grated Parmesan are good things to have ready at the table.

ARTICHOKE & BONE MARROW GRATIN

Serves 4

1 piece of bone marrow, soaked in cold water for an hour or two

1 tbsp unsalted butter

1 tbsp plain (all-purpose) flour

250ml/8fl oz/1 cup homemade light chicken stock

2 tbsp double (heavy) cream

8 stem artichokes, tough leaves snapped off, topped, choke removed, green tough stem peeled, cut into 5-mm/¼-inch slices, and kept in lemony water until ready to use

1 tsp picked thyme leaves

2 tbsp grated Gruyère cheese

2 tbsp fresh breadcrumbs

Nutmeg, to taste

Sea salt and freshly ground black pepper

Cardoon and bone marrow gratin is a classic dish from the French Alps. I've never seen a cardoon in Britain, so the artichoke – a member of the same family – is a good substitute. This is rich, rib-sticking, wintery stuff, delicious just with a salad or served alongside roast or grilled meats. The consistency of the sauce, which is like a béchamel but made with light chicken stock and cream instead of milk, is key – too thick and the gratin will be too heavy, but too light and the contents will float away, adrift in a sea of sauce. Adjust the consistency as you see fit, either by cooking the sauce further or by adding an extra splash of cream to thin it.

Preheat the oven to 180°C fan/200°C/400°F/gas mark 6

Place the bone marrow in a roasting tray and roast in the hot oven for only a few minutes until it starts to change colour. Remove from the oven and slide the marrow out of the bone. Set aside to cool. When completely cool, slice into 5-mm/¼-inch slices.

Make a roux by melting the butter in a pan over a low heat and then whisking in the flour. Cook for a few minutes over a low heat, then whisk in the chicken stock little by little. When all of the stock has been incorporated you should have a thickened but not gloopy sauce. Add the cream and cook for 5 minutes over a low heat. Season lightly with salt, pepper and nutmeg.

Lightly butter a small gratin dish and layer the sliced artichokes, bone marrow and thyme. Season as you go with salt and plenty of pepper. Add half of the grated Gruyère as a layer halfway up the gratin dish. Cover with the sauce, then the breadcrumbs and the rest of the grated Gruyère.

Bake in the hot oven for 30–40 minutes, or until the artichokes are soft, the cheese melted and the top browned and bubbling.

FENNEL & RADICCHIO GRATIN

Serves 4

3 bulbs of Florence fennel

2 garlic cloves, peeled and finely sliced

1 head of radicchio

4 tbsp double (heavy) cream

4 tbsp fine fresh breadcrumbs

1 tbsp olive oil

Parmesan cheese

Sea salt and freshly ground black pepper

A delicious wintery gratin that is simplicity itself. Boiling fennel might seem intuitively wrong but a quick dip into simmering water will soften and mellow the bulb into something plump enough to soak up the creamy juices. This gratin is best eaten alongside a fat pork chop.

Preheat the oven to 180°C fan/200°C/400°F/gas mark 6.

Cut the tops off the fennel bulbs. If there are any, pick the fennel herbs off the tops. (If there are none, where are you buying your fennel?!) Split the fennel bulbs in half, remove the outer layers, setting them aside for making soup or stock. Cut the fennel bulbs into sixths or eighths depending on the size of the bulb. Make sure you cut through the root so that each piece holds together.

Bring some water to the boil with a good pinch of salt in a pan and cook the fennel over a low heat at a simmer for a few minutes until the root piece of each segment yields when pierced with a skewer. Remove the fennel and drain well.

Grease a gratin dish with butter and place the fennel and sliced garlic into the dish.

Remove the outer leaves of the radicchio, cut it in half, then slice through the root into similar (although thinner) segments than the fennel, of about 1-cm/½-inch thickness. Mingle the radicchio in the gratin dish with the fennel. At this stage add the chopped fennel herb, if you have it. Pour over the cream and mix. Season with sea salt and black pepper. Scatter over the breadcrumbs, drizzle with olive oil and grate over some Parmesan.

Bake in the oven for 30 minutes, or until the gratin is bubbling and the breadcrumbs and Parmesan form a crisp golden brown crust on top.

RED WINE BAGNA CÀUDA

Serves 4

200ml/7fl oz/1 cup red wine

2 fat or 4 small garlic cloves, peeled, halved and green sprout removed

10 salted anchovy fillets

150g/5¼oz/⅔ cup very cold unsalted butter, cut into small cubes

2 tbsp olive oil, plus extra for drizzling

Freshly ground black pepper

2 nice carrots, peeled and halved lengthways

4 celery stalks, peeled if stringy, any leaves reserved

2 artichokes, prepared and halved (keep in lemony water until ready cook)

A handful of sprout tops

Bagna càuda is another Piedmontese recipe that has been assimilated into the Provençal repertoire. A 'warm bath' of anchovies, olive oil, butter and garlic, into which can be dipped, fondue-style, raw or cooked vegetables: cardoons, artichokes, carrots, celery, potatoes, radishes, bell peppers and so on. This recipe is unconventional in that it contains a reduction of red wine, which turns the sauce a wonderful purple colour and adds a some wintery heft, and also that the sauce is served drizzled over the vegetables rather than on the side. I tend to go heavier on the butter than the olive oil, both because I enjoy the smooth comfort of a sauce rich with butter fat, but also because when too much oil is added the sauce tends to split. I prefer serving cooked vegetables with this dip, which makes it feel more like a starter than a snack. Sprout tops may not be usual, but they are cheap, delicious and – when upturned – hold the sauce like little boats.

Bring the wine and the garlic to the boil in a pan over high heat. Turn the heat down to a simmer and cook until the garlic is completely soft and the red wine has reduced to around 2 tbsp. At this stage, remove from the heat and mash the garlic with a fork into the wine as finely as possible – the smoother the better. Reduce the wine and garlic mixture further to 1 tbsp of thickened liquid, then add the anchovies. Cook slowly over a very low heat until the anchovies melt into the liquid.

Whisk the mixture together until as smooth as possible. There should be only a little thick reduction left in the pan. Over a very, very low heat or a bain marie, whisk in the cold butter one cube at a time. Don't be tempted to add too much butter at once or the sauce might split. If you feel the mixture is too thick, let it down with a splash of water. Continue incorporating the butter until it has all been used up. Slowly whisk in the olive oil, adding it in a thin stream. Check the sauce for seasoning: it should be salty enough from the anchovies. Grind in some black pepper and keep the sauce warm over a pan or bowl of hot water.

Cook the vegetables in a pan of well-salted, simmering water until soft but not mushy and certainly not falling apart. Be sure not to overcook the sprout tops in particular. Drain the vegetables, arrange either on a large serving dish or individual plates, then pour over the sauce. Drizzle with extra olive oil. Chop the celery leaves and sprinkle over the top. Finish with a generous grind of pepper.

CHICKPEA & SAUSAGE SOUP WITH AÏOLI

Serves 4

250g/8¾oz dried chickpeas (garbanzo beans), soaked overnight in plenty of cold water with 2 tsp bicarbonate of soda

1 bay leaf

1 thyme sprig

1 peeled tomato from a can, ripped up into pieces

2 tbsp olive oil

2 medium white onions, finely diced

½ head of celery, finely diced

2 garlic cloves, peeled

1 tsp fennel seeds, lightly crushed

For the meatballs:

100g/3½oz pork mince

25g/1oz pancetta, minced

1 tbsp fresh breadcrumbs, soaked in milk until soft and then squeezed

2 tsp grated Parmesan cheese

1 tsp crushed fennel seeds

1 thyme sprig, picked and chopped finely

1 tbsp finely chopped parsley

A pinch of salt and freshly ground black pepper

Aïoli, to serve (see page 173)

This idea came about from reading Leslie Forbes' delightfully illustrated *A Table in Provence*. Traditionally, I think, this is a big old boiled stew of chickpeas with whole sausages, to be eaten in two parts: first the broth, then the meat and chickpeas (garbanzo beans) with a splodge of aïoli. I think I might have read the recipe wrongly, and I ended up with a brothy chickpea soup in which I poached some little meatballs of sausage meat. If you've ever eaten at Moro in Clerkenwell, London, where they do a cracking butifarra with white beans and alioli, you'll know that the best bit is when the garlic sauce seeps into and enriches the already sticky, porky broth. There's much of the same here.

Drain the chickpeas and put them in a large pan with some cold water, the bay leaf, thyme and tomato. Don't add salt at this stage. Boil the chickpeas for an hour or two until very soft, topping up the water if necessary. When the chickpeas are cooked you want a nice amount of broth leftover. Season the chickpeas and their broth with salt.

Meanwhile, start the soffrito. Heat the olive oil in a pan big enough to fit the finished soup. Add the onion, celery and garlic and fry slowly for about 30 minutes, until very soft and sweet. Add the crushed fennel seeds and cook for a further 5 minutes.

Add the cooked chickpeas and their broth to the cooked soffrito. Bring to the boil and cook at a simmer for 30 minutes while you prepare the meatballs.

To make the meatballs, combine all the ingredients in a bowl. Form into small meatballs around the size of a hazelnut. Poach the meatballs gently in the soup until cooked through. Throw in the chopped parsley and taste for seasoning. Pour the soup into bowls and top with a spoon of aïoli.

CHICKEN LIVER & CEP PARFAIT

Serves 4

250g/9oz chicken livers

200g/7oz/⅔ cup butter

3 eggs

2 dried ceps, soaked in 4 tbsp hot
water (reserving the soaking water)

2 tbsp brandy

2 tbsp Madeira wine or port

1 bay leaf

1 thyme sprig

1 scant tsp fine salt (curing salt makes
the parfait keep longer but can be
hard to get)

Pinch of quatre-épices (optional)

To serve:

Slices of thin toast

Cornichons

A parfait is the smoothest of preparations, an impossibly rich, silky concoction of eggs, butter and chicken liver. Ours has a reduction of brandy and Madeira, given an extra earthy note with some dried ceps.

———————

Firstly, take the liver, butter and eggs out of the refrigerator. Bring them to as near to room temperature as possible before you make the parfait, otherwise you will struggle to achieve a smooth texture.

Meanwhile, pass the cep soaking water through a sieve (strainer) to remove any grit and put into a pan along with the ceps, brandy, Madeira, bay and thyme. Reduce this liquid by two-thirds, then allow to cool to room temperature. Strain again and discard the mushrooms and herbs.

Preheat the oven to 140°C fan/160°C/325°F/gas mark 3.

Trim the chicken livers of any sinew. Blitz the chicken livers with the butter and eggs in a blender (a smoothie maker-type of blender gets the mixture smoother). Slowly add the boozy reduction and emulsify with the chicken liver. Pass the resultant mixture through a sieve using a bench scraper or similar. Season the mix with the salt and a pinch of quatre-épices if you like it. At this stage, taste the mixture for salt and add more if you think it needs it.

Pour the parfait into a small terrine or stainless steel container. Cover tightly with foil. Put the terrine into a deep-sided roasting tray. Pour in boiling water until the water comes over halfway up the side of the terrine. Carefully transfer the bain-marie to the oven without sloshing boiling water all over your arms. Bake for 50 minutes. Lift up the foil to check the parfait: it should have a slight wobble to it. If it looks a little loose, return to the oven and check every 5 minutes until you are confident.

Remove the terrine from the oven and the bain-marie. Allow to cool to room temperature, then cover with clingfilm (plastic wrap) and chill in the refrigerator. When the parfait is cool, create a seal by pouring clarified butter over the top and the chilling. This parfait is best set overnight in the refrigerator.

When ready to serve, remove the clarified butter from the parfait. Heat a spoon in boiling water and scrupulously scrape off the greyed outer layer. Either spoon out rochers of parfait onto individual plates or, if your terrine is attractive enough, plonk it on the table and let guests help themselves. Serve with hot, crisp slices of thin toast and some good-quality cornichons.

BACON, CHESTNUT, ROSEMARY & POTATO SOUP

Serves 4

2 tbsp olive oil

60g/2oz smoked French bacon or pancetta, cut into large lardons

2 medium white onions, finely diced

½ head celery, finely diced

1 carrot, peeled and finely diced

2 fat garlic cloves, peeled, green sprout removed and finely sliced lengthways

1 tsp fennel seeds

½ tsp picked rosemary leaves (no more, don't overdo it)

A few dried ceps, soaked in boiling water and roughly chopped (soaking water reserved)

100g/3½oz cooked (vacuum-packed) chestnuts, broken in half

500g/1lb 2oz red potatoes, such as Roseval or Desiree, peeled and cut into 1.5-cm/½-inch chunks

1 litre/1¾ pints/4 cups light homemade chicken stock, or just water

Sea salt and freshly ground black pepper

To serve:

Olive oil

Grated Parmesan cheese

Bacon, chestnuts, rosemary and potatoes are all the best of friends. Together this foursome creates a thick, warming soup that should be left chunky, unblitzed and *bien rustique*. If you have some to hand, a handful of dried ceps adds a musky depth of flavour. A slick of grassy, buttery, slightly bitter olive oil helps everything to meld together nicely. Grated Parmesan is optional, but very much encouraged.

———————————

Heat the olive oil in a large heavy-based pan. Slowly fry the bacon lardons over a low heat until golden brown but not too crispy. Add the onion, celery, carrots, garlic and fennel seeds. Add a good pinch of salt. Slowly fry this soffrito in the oil for at least 30 minutes, stirring from time to time, until sweet and very soft.

Chop the rosemary finely, add to the pan and stir. Cook over a low heat for a couple of minutes, then add the ceps. Cook for a further few minutes, then add the chestnuts and potatoes. Add the stock or water plus the soaking water from the dried ceps. Don't drown the soup in liquid. Initially, add just enough liquid to cover the vegetables by an inch or so and then top up the liquid as it reduces; it's far better to add liquid in this way rather than have a soup that is far too liquid from the start.

Bring the soup to the boil over a high heat, then reduce to a simmer. Cook the soup for about 30 minutes, until the potatoes are soft and everything tastes full, sweet and generally great. The chestnuts will have broken up a bit during the cooking, but if you feel that too many of them remain in big pieces, mash them against the side of the pan a bit with a wooden spoon. The soup should be quite thick, but not so thick that it's just vegetables in a bowl. Season again with salt and black pepper to taste. Drizzle with your best olive oil and grate over the Parmesan before serving.

1ST ANNUAL BLACK TRUFFLE DINNER

Raw Veal Toast, Ossau Iraty, Baby Spinach

–

Cauliflowers Cooked in Butter

–

Poularde en Demi Deuil, Morel Cream Sauce

–

Brie de Meaux à la Truffe

Truffles are not an ingredient that most people eat every day, but I can stretch to at least once a year: if you can get your hands on some good truffles, then it makes sense to make an event of them. Black truffles found in Provence are much esteemed as some of the best in the world. The season runs from November to March, and restaurants throughout the region offer up set menus featuring truffle in every course.

Black truffles differ from white truffles: they are more earthy, mushroomy, perhaps less perfumed or heady, but just as infectious. Italian white truffle menus are an exercise in restraint. Care is taken not to overwhelm the taste of the white truffle with a buttery vehicle for the prized tuber: egg pasta with Parmesan, white risotto, wet polenta. The nice thing about the black truffle is that, more so than the white truffle, it stands up well to cooking. Plus the black truffle's cheaper price tag means you can chuck a (little) more of it about, add it to sauces, whip it in butters and shave extra on top.

We started with a hand-chopped veal tartare, seasoned with lemon juice, olive oil, pepper and salt, with some shaved sheeps' milk cheese, Ossau Iraty, spread on a piece of thin toast with a grated truffle and Cognac butter. Cauliflowers, cooked whole in butter and scented with bay, white wine and nutmeg, collapsed into florets when prodded with a fork, ready to be dusted with Parmesan and grated truffle.

The main course is a Lyonnais classic, *Poularde en demi deuil* (chicken in half-mourning), a reference to the veil-like appearance of the black truffle slices stuffed under the skin. A fine French black-leg chicken is stuffed carefully with thick slices of truffle soaked in Madeira, then poached gently in stock.
A piece of poached chicken is napped with an indecent morel cream sauce, and you're away. For dessert, instead of inventing some truffley concoction, we cut a whole Brie de Meaux in half and stuffed it with truffled mascarpone cream. Much better.

2 GRAMS

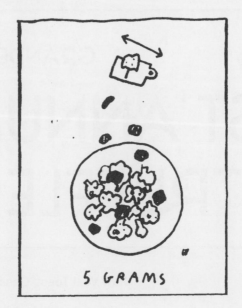

5 GRAMS

Raw Veal Toast, Ossau Iraty, Baby Spinach
Serves 4

200g/7oz veal topside or fillet
Lemon juice
Olive oil
50g/1¾oz Ossau Iraty (or Manchego or Pecorino)
4 thin slices of toast, or more if you fancy
1 tbsp truffle butter (see page 185)
A small handful of baby spinach
Sea salt and freshly ground black pepper
Black truffle, to serve

Remove any fat and sinew from the veal. Chop it into small dice using a very sharp knife – the best way is to cut thin strips off the piece and then dice them. Season the veal with salt (be generous or it will be tasteless), pepper, lemon juice and olive oil.

While the toast is still hot, spread the slices with the truffle butter.

Dress the spinach with a little oil, salt and lemon juice.

Put the diced veal onto the buttered toast. Shave over some Ossau Iraty with a knife, set the spinach next to it and grate (not shave) over some black truffle.

Cauliflowers Cooked in Butter
Serves 4

1 cauliflower
150g/5¼oz/⅔ cup butter
½ glass white wine
2 garlic cloves, unpeeled
2 bay leaves
A grating of Parmesan cheese
Sea salt and freshly ground black pepper
Black truffle, to serve

Cut the cauliflower in half. Discard the very bottom woody part, keeping the leaves and inner stem. Season with salt. Heat the butter in a pan large enough to fit both cauliflower halves. When it starts to bubble, add the cauliflower, cut-sides down. Fry over a medium–low heat for a few minutes, until the cauliflower takes on some colour. Turn the cauliflower over so the rest of it takes up some butter and colours a bit too. Turn it cut-side again, then add the white wine, garlic cloves and bay leaves. Cover with a lid, reduce the heat to low and cook, covered, for 1 hour. Lift the lid from time to time to take a peek. The stem should be soft when poked with a skewer, the butter should smell nutty, and the wine reduced to a scant buttery sauce. If it's looking a little dry before the cauliflower is cooked, add a splash of water. Check the seasoning for salt, then lift the cauliflower straight onto waiting plates. Pour over what sauce there is, grind over a little black pepper, grate over a small amount of Parmesan, then shave over the black truffle.

COOK REAL SLOW.

Poularde en Demi Deuil, Morel Cream Sauce
Serves 4

For the chicken:
8 thick-ish slices of black truffle (2-mm/¹⁄₁₆-inch thick)
2 tsp Madeira wine
1 chicken (approximate weight 1.5–2kg/3lb 5oz–
4lb 8oz)
1 medium onion
1 celery stalk
1 carrot
1 bay leaf
1 thyme sprig
A pinch of whole black peppercorns
Black truffle, to serve

For the sauce:
500ml/18fl oz/2 cups chicken stock (reserved from
the poaching pan)
3 tbsp cold unsalted butter, cubed
1 tsp plain (all-purpose) flour
50g/1¾oz fresh morels (or a small handful of dried
morels soaked in hot water)
A good splash of Cognac
2 tbsp double (heavy) cream
Sea salt and freshly ground black pepper

Soak the slices of truffle in the Madeira wine for
10 minutes. Prepare the chicken for poaching. Slide the
soaked truffle slices carefully under the skin of the breast
of the chicken, at regular intervals. Put the chicken into

a large pan with all the other ingredients and top up with
cold water. Bring the chicken to the boil from cold, skim
well, reduce to a simmer for 5 minutes, then turn off the
heat and cover with a tight-fitting lid. Let the chicken sit in
the hot water for at least an hour, until the liquid has cooled
– this will cook the chicken slowly and keep it succulent.

Next, prepare the sauce. Reduce the chicken stock by half.
In another pan, melt 1 tbsp of the butter and add the flour.
Whisk together to make a light roux, then slowly whisk in
the reduced chicken stock bit by bit, whisking all the while
to keep the sauce smooth. When all the stock has been
incorporated, cook at a slow simmer for about 15 minutes.

Meanwhile, fry the morels in 1 tbsp of the butter and
season with salt and pepper. Add the Cognac, bubble
briefly, then tip the lot into the simmering sauce. Add the
double cream and continue to simmer slowly for
5–10 minutes. Check the seasoning and adjust the salt to
taste. The sauce should not be so thick as to be cloying,
but it should coat the back of a spoon nicely. Whisk in the
remaining 1 tbsp cold cubed butter just before serving.

Carve the chicken into pieces on the bone. Serve with
the hot morel cream sauce and some plain boiled spinach
dressed with lemon juice. Shave loads of truffle on top.

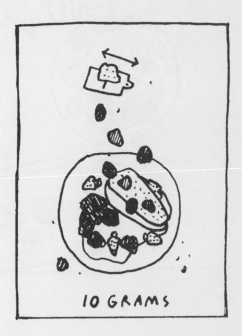

10 GRAMS

CHEESE NOT CAKE!

Brie de Meaux à la Truffe
Serves 4

You could just grate some truffle onto some cheese, and
I certainly wouldn't complain, but if you have time then this
is a nice way to impart truffle into your cheese. Also great
with Brillat Savarin, Camembert, Coulommiers or anything
else soft, creamy and sweet.

1 x 350-g/12-oz piece of Brie de Meaux
1 tbsp mascarpone cheese
1 tsp double (heavy) cream
1 tsp finely grated black truffle
A small pinch of quatres-épices, or failing that just some
black pepper and nutmeg
Fine salt, to taste
Thin slices of toast, crackers, biscuits or bread, to serve

The day before, cut the cheese in half laterally. Mix
together all the other ingredients and stuff the cheese
with the mixture. Put the other half of the cheese back
on top, wrap it back up and let it mature overnight in
the refrigerator.

Take the cheese out of the refrigerator at least an hour
before serving – you want this one to be soft and just
starting to run. If you're using Brillat Savarin it's nice with
honey. Serve with thin toast, crackers, biscuits or bread.

POT-AU-FEU

Broth with Bone Marrow Dumplings

–

Le Pot-au-Feu:

Beef Ribs, Chicken & Morteau Sausage

Potatoes, Cabbage & Carrots

Horseradish Cream, Auntie Mary's Pickled Red Cabbage, Cornichons, Mustard, Green Sauce

–

Blood Orange Sorbet

Pot-au-feu is arguably one of France's national dishes, and I would argue that it's possibly the most quintessential home-cooked family favourite of the lot. *Pot-au-feu* means, literally, 'pot on the fire'. At its most simple, it's a plate of boiled beef and some vegetables, with a bit of the broth over the top. It comes from a time when the peasants would keep a pot over the fire and just kept the broth bubbling and simmering forever, and on a Sunday, if you could afford a chicken or a bit of beef, it would go in. In this way evolved a sort of master stock: in lean times filled with humble root vegetables, and others filled with various mixed meats, a French *bollito misto*.

The two dishes sit side by side, but there are a few differences: a pot-au-feu is usually a simpler affair, with fewer different meats and maybe just mustard as an accompaniment, but I like to include at least three in mine: heavy, fatty beef short ribs, a plump chicken and some smoked Morteau sausage from the Jura. A whole veal shin would be a wonderful addition:

I had originally planned to include it when we cooked this meal at the restaurant, but we couldn't get any, so there you go. Accompaniments can stretch to as many as you have to hand: good, smooth hot Dijon mustard, and a wholegrain too, fresh grated horseradish mixed into cream, an oily green sauce spiked with salty anchovies, capers and tarragon, and some pickles to cut through the richness. Cornichons are traditional in France of course, but my Auntie Mary, late of Llandewi, Powys, made a sharp red cabbage pickle which goes rather nicely here.

A traditional start to a *pot-au-feu* is a bowl of the broth, perhaps with a toast topped with boiled bone marrow. For this meal we made instead some juicy little bone marrow dumplings, an idea from my friend Eliot, to float on top. To finish, a sharp, sweet blood orange sorbet: in season in winter, and a much needed icy hit of citrus to blow through all the meat, fat and potato that precedes it.

For the Pot-au-Feu

Serves 8, depending on appetites

It makes a big difference if you can make the time to salt the short ribs and the chicken overnight before starting the stew in the morning – a depth of flavour to the meat that is hard to achieve otherwise. The stew will need to cook for a good 4–5 hours, so leave yourself plenty of time. You'll obviously need a nice big pot. The dumplings and accompanying sauces can be made while the pot-au-feu is simmering away.

2kg/4lb 8oz beef short ribs, on the bone, cut into lengths that will fit in your pot
1 chicken (approximate weight 2kg/4lb 8oz)
2 red onions, halved but not peeled
2 celery stalks
2 bay leaves
1 thyme sprig
A good pinch of whole black peppercorns
4 cloves
2 allspice berries
2 Morteau sausages
4 carrots
1 medium-sized, firm white cabbage
2kg/4lb 8oz potatoes (red, like Roseval or Desiree)

The day before you want to cook, salt the short ribs and the chicken with fine salt, the short ribs quite heavily. The next day, put the short ribs into (lightly salted) cold water and bring to the boil. It sounds silly but seasoning this cold water with a small amount of salt is important, as otherwise the beef can lose the salt that you have taken the care to put into it the day before. Discard the water and repeat the process with more cold, lightly salted water. This process will remove a lot of fat and impurities from the beef, along with any rancid fat flavours.

When the beef has been brought to the boil twice, start the stew: cover the beef with cold, unsalted water, and add the onion and celery. The onion and celery are for flavour, and will be overcooked by the time the meat is ready, and will be discarded at the end. If you have some muslin, make a little pouch with the herbs and spices, and pop this in too. If not, you'll have to carefully fish out the herbs and spices later.

Bring the water to the boil, then turn down to a slow simmer. Skim the surface of the Pot-au-Feu regularly, for a good few minutes at the start, then briefly at least every half an hour, especially just after you add the other meats. Cook the short rib for 3 hours at a gentle simmer, until it is starting to soften and is (use your best judgement), three-quarters cooked. Slip in the chicken and poach gently alongside the short ribs – skim well after you have added it – for just over an hour. Scoop out some of the broth and boil the Morteau sausages separately in this for about 45 minutes. The Morteau sausages make the broth fiercely smokey and so it is best to keep separate, so that the smokiness can be controlled as you add some of their broth back in.

When the short ribs are starting to fall off the bone, but before they disintegrate into a sinewy mess (about 4 hours simmering should usually do the trick), take them out of the broth. Remove also the chicken, which should be cooked after about an hour and a quarter or an hour and a half in the broth, and portion into eight pieces on the bone. The Morteau sausage should be cooked after 45 minutes of fast simmering. Cut the sausage into 3-cm/1¼-inch thick slices. Set the meats aside.

Strain the pot-au-feu broth and mix in some of the broth that the Morteau sausages were cooking in, until you think the amount of smoke you can taste is about right. If you think it needs it, season the broth carefully with salt. Peel the carrots and cut in half. Cut the cabbage in half, then

into 3-cm/1¼-inch wedges along the root so that the cut piece will stay intact after cooking. Peel the potatoes and cut into big pieces. Simmer all of these vegetables in the broth, taking care not to overcook them. They should be soft but, please, not mushy. Set aside.

Check again the seasoning of the broth, as you are about to serve it. Simmer a few of the dumplings in the broth for a few minutes, then pour into bowls and eat.

After the broth has been eaten, put the meats and vegetables to reheat with some more of the broth. Serve everything very hot, the meats on a platter together with the vegetables, and the piquant sauces on the side. Moisten with the broth and sprinkle with coarse salt, if necessary.

For the dumplings:
40g/1½oz/⅓ cup self-raising (self-rising) flour
40g/1½oz fresh fine breadcrumbs
30g/1oz melted bone marrow
1 tbsp butter, melted
1 large or 2 small eggs
1 tbsp finely chopped parsley
1 thyme sprig, picked and finely chopped
Sea salt and freshly ground black pepper

Mix the flour and breadcrumbs together in a bowl. In a separate bowl, mix the melted bone marrow, melted butter and eggs. Whisk in the flour and breadcrumbs, followed by the herbs and the salt and pepper. Roll the mixture into small balls, according to personal taste, but ideally no bigger than a 10 pence piece. Keep in the refrigerator until ready to use.

For the accompaniments:

Horseradish cream: Finely grate some fresh horseradish and mix it into some double (heavy) cream, some salt and some red wine vinegar. Don't overmix or the sauce will thicken too much. It should be pretty fiery.

Green sauce: Chop some parsley, tarragon, chervil, salted anchovies, capers and a scrap of peeled garlic all very finely together. Mix in some Dijon mustard, a squeeze of lemon juice and lots of olive oil.

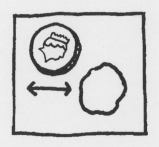

Auntie Mary's pickled red cabbage: Shred a red cabbage as finely as you can. Weigh the cabbage and then weigh out 2 percent of this weight in fine salt. Mix and rub the fine salt well with the cabbage. Bring a pan to the boil with half vinegar, half cold water. Auntie Mary used to use malt vinegar, I think, I used white wine vinegar – both are nice. Add enough sugar to make it a little bit sweet as well as sour. Cool the pickling liquor to room temperature then pour over the cabbage in a sealable jar. Keep for at least a few days before using, but then it keeps for months. Thanks, Mary.

Blood Orange Sorbet
Serves 8

I have never followed an exact recipe for blood orange sorbet as it all depends on how sweet the oranges are. The basic method is to juice some blood oranges and then mix that juice with some sugar syrup.

Make a strong sugar syrup by boiling caster (superfine) sugar with a little cold water. Cool to room temperature, then whisk little by little into the blood orange juice. When the juice tastes slightly sweeter than desired (when frozen the mixture will taste less sweet), add in a glug of booze. Campari is traditional in Italy, but any kind of Amaro would be good after a meal like this, or if you wanted something French you could go for Suze, a Gentian aperitif with an aromatic, bitter taste. Don't add too much booze, however, as it will stop the sorbet from freezing altogether. I find that if you add just enough so you can taste it in the mixture, it works nicely, preventing the sorbet from freezing too hard as well. Some of the zest from the oranges adds a touch of bitter balance, and lemon juice helps to balance the acidity if you need some more.

If you have an ice-cream maker, cool the mixture before churning according to the instructions. If you don't, pour the mixture in a flat tray and place in your freezer. Stir the mixture every 30 minutes or so with a fork, until eventually you have a delicious frozen granita. The recipe below is a rough guide.

10 blood oranges, juiced
Zest of 2 unwaxed blood oranges, finely grated
150g/5¼oz/⅔ cup caster (superfine) sugar
Lemon juice, to taste
Booze, to taste (optional, see above)

Grate the zest of 2 of the blood oranges and then juice all 10 of them. Make a strong sugar syrup with the water and sugar. Mix the sugar syrup into the orange juice and zest. Cool, then freeze, then eat.

NEW SEASON'S OLIVE OIL DINNER

Toast, Salt, Oil

–

Chickpea, Black Cabbage & Bread Soup, Olive Oil

–

Daube de Bœuf, Potato Gnocchi & Olive Oil

–

Fresh Cheese, Herbs, Hazelnuts, Honey & Olive Oil

–

Olive Oil Cake, Poached Quince & Crème Fraîche

A menu to cook as autumn gives way to winter. The Provençal olive oil season comes later than most, and I've found it hard to get hold of, not to mention riotously expensive. We usually use Tuscan oil in the new season. New season's olive oil is bright, lime green; fresh, fruity and peppery, it deserves to be treated as a star ingredient in itself. The food to cook to celebrate the oil harvest should defer to the oil's pride of place: the dishes should be comforting, starchy and slightly muted – no huge flavours or eccentric combinations here, just a vehicle for a few good glugs of the green stuff.

First, a Tuscan tradition, bruschetta: the first thing eaten when the oil comes off the press is often a piece of toast, drizzled liberally, and I mean liberally, with oil and topped with a few flakes of good sea salt. The toast should be good sourdough with enough holes that the oil can run out of them and down your chin. *Ribollita*, the famous soup, is another Tuscan job, re-imagined slightly with soft chickpeas (garbanzo beans) instead, made pappy with stale bread, green with finely chopped cabbage, and lifted with a grating of cheese.

So far, so northern Italian, but now over the border to the *daube de bœuf*, a recipe we love to cook. This is rightly a Provençal classic: beef slowly simmered in red wine with a few choice aromatics: bacon, dried ceps, dried orange peel, bay leaves, sometimes anchovies, sometimes walnuts and cloves. We tend to stick with the first five. Traditionally the cut used for this is mostly chuck steak, but chuck can tend towards dryness, so we go for broke and use ox cheeks. The cheeks emerge from their red wine bath soft and wobbly, slightly sticky but not overly cloying.

Gnocchi is one of the traditional accompaniments to a daube, and does the job of soaking up the rich juices. Sometimes I like to make a purée of cavalo nero, garlic, some cooking water and olive oil – a rich, vibrant green sauce in which to toss your gnocchi, which goes very nicely with peppery new oil.

For this menu we enlisted the help of my friend Max, an itinerant cheesemonger who is at the time of writing currently adding another string to his bow, smoking wild salmon in west Cork. Max helped us make some very fresh cows' milk cheeses, a simple renneted recipe, which, at a few hours old, were delicious with the green oil. I won't recommend that you make your own cheese at home for this, because I'm not an expert, and others have written far more eloquently on the subject. I would, however, recommend that you buy some: either a spanking fresh ricotta, or a very young goats' milk cheese: ask your cheesemonger.

On occasion, the fantastic Mons Cheesemongers, from whom we buy all of our French and Swiss cheeses for the restaurant, have a very young goats' cheese called St. Christophe, like a fresh Charolais. If you can get it when it's only a few days old, it's very special. Otherwise, any fresh, young, moussey goats' cheese works well. Our usual approach to serving cheese is to put it on a plate: no chutney, s'il vous plait. Here, however, a little herb salad, some toasted, crushed hazelnuts, some good honey and the peppery green oil combine to make something a bit more sophisticated.

Lastly, olive oil cake is a delight: spongey, pillowy soft, with an olive oil after kick: delicious with some very slowly cooked quince and some cultured cream.

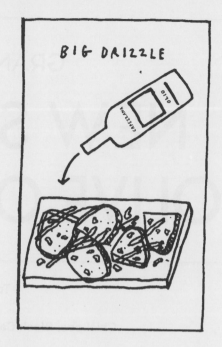

Toast, Salt, Oil

Per person:
1 slice of good, slightly stale sourdough or Pugliese Altamura semolina bread (my Mum uses this and it makes the best toast)
A big pinch of flaky sea salt
Loads of new season's olive oil

Right! Toast the bread, drizzle liberally with the oil, and sprinkle generously with flaky salt.

Chickpea, Black Cabbage & Bread Soup, Olive Oil
Makes too much for 4 in one go, but it's very much like ribollita, so it can be 'reboiled' a couple of times without any harm coming to it

By 'black cabbage' I mean cavolo nero. This soup should be almost thick enough to stand your spoon up in it, but not quite. The bread should be crustless, stale sourdough.

2 tbsp (not new season) olive oil
2 medium white onions, finely diced
½ head celery, finely diced
1 carrot, peeled and finely diced
4 garlic cloves, peeled and finely sliced lengthways
1 bay leaf
1 bunch cavolo nero, leaves picked from stalks and stalks discarded, washed
2 x 400-g/14-oz cans cooked chickpeas (garbanzo beans) in brine, drained
2 plum tomatoes from a can (or posh jar), rinsed of any juice and gunk
4 tbsp stale sourdough, crustless, ripped into large chunks

To serve:
New season's olive oil (loads)
1 tbsp Parmesan cheese (optional)

Fry the onions, celery, carrot, garlic and bay leaf slowly in the olive oil for a very long time – at least 45 minutes. The slow cooking of this soffrito is key to making the soup sweet, deep and delicious. Add a pinch of salt at the start to help things along.

Meanwhile, boil the cavolo nero in boiling salted water for a few minutes, until soft. Drain, cool slightly, then squeeze very well to remove excess water. Chop quite small but not to a mulch. Be thorough. No big strands of floaty cabbage in my soup, thank you.

When the soffrito is very soft, add the chickpeas and stir around for a minute or two so that they absorb some of the oil. Add the cooked, chopped cabbage, the tomatoes, squished into little pieces with your hands, and cover with water. Cook at a slow simmer for around 30 minutes then add the bread. Cook for a further 20 minutes on the same slow heat. Check the seasoning for salt, black pepper is nice too.

Serve hot and drizzle LOADS of new season's olive oil over the top of each bowl. A grating of Parmesan is delicious, but it's worth noting that without the cheese this is one of the most delicious vegan things you can cook.

Daube de Bœuf, Potato Gnocchi & Olive Oil
Serves 4

Take your time when cooking the beef in this way: the ox cheeks should be wobbly and fall apart when pushed with a spoon. A little cavolo nero blitzed into a dark green sauce will coat the gnocchi once they come out of the water. The beef needs to be marinated overnight, so plan ahead.

For the daube:
2 ox cheeks, trimmed of all sinew
½ bottle red wine
1 carrot, roughly chopped
2 celery stalks, roughly chopped
1 onion, roughly chopped
2 bay leaves
A thyme sprig
50g/1¾oz lardons (or pancetta cubes)
1 piece dried orange peel or the zest of ½ unwaxed fresh orange
2 tbsp plain (all-purpose) flour
A pinch of ground cayenne pepper
2 tbsp olive oil
4 salted anchovy fillets
4 tomatoes from a can, rinsed well and squished a bit
1 tbsp dried ceps, soaked in hot water
Sea salt and freshly ground black pepper

To make the daube, put the ox cheeks in a bowl or pan and cover with the red wine. Add the carrot, celery, onion, bay, thyme, lardons and orange peel. Leave in the refrigerator to marinate overnight.

The next day, discard the carrot, celery and onion from the marinade. Take the ox cheeks out of the marinade. Reserve the marinade. Pat the ox cheeks dry with paper towels, then season with salt and pepper.

Mix the flour with the cayenne pepper and dredge the cheeks in the seasoned flour. Shake and pat the cheeks a few times to remove any excess flour.

Preheat the oven to 160°C fan/180°C/350°F/gas mark 4.

In a deep, roomy, heavy pot with a lid, brown the ox cheeks in the olive oil. Add the anchovies, tomatoes, soaked ceps, the cep water and the reserved marinade, including the lardons, orange peel, bay and thyme. If necessary, top up with water to cover the cheeks. Bring the daube to the boil over a high heat, then reduce to a very slow simmer. Cover with a lid and then place in the preheated oven. Cook the beef very slowly in the oven for around 3 hours, or until the ox cheeks are meltingly tender. Season the daube with salt and black pepper to taste.

For the cavolo nero sauce:
1 garlic clove, peeled
2 heads of cavolo nero, leaves picked and washed
1 tbsp olive oil

To make the cavolo nero sauce, bring a pot of lightly salted water to the boil and add the garlic. Boil the garlic for a couple of minutes, then add the cavolo nero. Cook the cavolo nero for around 5 minutes – it will be slightly overcooked but this helps to make a smooth sauce. You want the garlic to be soft too. Transfer the cavolo nero and garlic to a blender and blitz to a smooth sauce, adding a little of the cooking water and the olive oil. The sauce shouldn't be too thick as you want it to coat the gnocchi without it being cloying.

For the gnocchi:
Coarse rock salt
1kg/2lb 4oz large floury potatoes (1 large potato per person)
2 egg yolks
250g/9oz/2 cups plain (all-purpose) flour, plus extra for dusting
Grated nutmeg, to taste
Scatter a thin layer of coarse rock salt over a roasting tray

and nestle the potatoes on top. Bake in the oven alongside the daube for an hour, or until the potatoes are cooked through. Allow the potatoes to cool slightly while you gather the other ingredients.

Split the baked potatoes with a knife and scoop the cooked flesh into a bowl. Take care not to get any grains of salt in the bowl too. Rice the potato flesh using a potato ricer or mouli-legumes.

Add the egg yolks and the flour to the riced potatoes and mix with a wooden spoon to make a smooth dough. Work the mixture for a minute or two until you have a homogenous mass. There should be enough flour in the dough that your finger does not come out (too) sticky when pressed into it, so add a little more if you feel that the mix is too wet. However, adding too much flour will result in gnocchi that are bouncy rather than fluffy. Season the dough lightly with grated nutmeg.

Cut a slice off the dough, keeping the rest covered with a dish towel to keep it warm and prevent it from drying out. At this stage, it's important to work quickly as things work better when the dough stays warm as you shape the gnocchi. On a lightly floured work surface, roll this slice of dough into a rough sausage of 2-cm/¾-inch thickness. From this sausage, cut the individual gnocchi so that they are slightly longer than they are fat.

Either roll the gnocchi with the tines of a fork, or, easier, press the middle with a lightly floured thumb to create a little dip in the middle – this will help the gnocchi to hold more of the sauce. I find a small twist when thumbing the gnocchi helps to make a slightly more pleasing shape, more of a rhombus than a rectangle. Transfer the shaped gnocchi to a tray floured with semolina flour while you shape the rest. These can be stored in the refrigerator covered with a dish towel if not to be cooked immediately.

When ready to serve, keep the daube hot while you cook the gnocchi.

Boil a pan of water, salt lightly (the stew will hold most of the salt for the dish, and you don't want the stodgy element to be too highly seasoned), and poach the gnocchi at a simmer for a minute or two, until the gnocchi float to the surface. Remove with a slotted spoon and toss with the cavolo nero sauce and a small amount of the water from the pot.

Put a couple of pieces of ox cheek on the plate with some of its sauce, and slide the sauced gnocchi on next to it. Drizzle the lot with new season's olive oil.

Fresh Cheese, Herbs, Hazelnuts, Honey & Olive Oil

Assuming you have bought your cheese, this hardly requires a recipe, but here you go…

1 cheese (a fresh, moussey goats' cheese is best)
1 tbsp hazelnuts, roasted lightly and crushed a bit
1 tbsp best possible honey, warmed slightly to make it runny if necessary
1 tbsp new season's olive oil
Flaky sea salt (optional)
Some mixed herbs (tarragon, chervil and marjoram)

Top the cheese with the crushed roasted hazelnuts and drizzle everything with the honey and olive oil. If serving very fresh cheese without salt, sprinkle some flaky sea salt over the cheese.

Carefully wash and dry the herbs – they are delicate. Make a little salad from the herb leaves. Pile them next to the cheese on a serving plate. A fresh baguette or some rye crackers go nicely here.

MORE MORE MORE!

Preheat the oven to 170°C fan/190°C/375°F/gas mark 5. Grease a 20-cm/8-inch round cake tin and line it with parchment paper. Alternatively, you can use a similarly lined enamel baking dish and bake the cake as a rectangle rather than a round.

Separate the 5 eggs and reserve the whites. Beat the 5 yolks with the sugar for a few minutes until pale and well beaten. Add the grated citrus peel. Mix the flour and salt together, then add little by little to the beaten eggs and sugar, whisking until it is incorporated. Add the sweet wine and olive oil and whisk those in too. Beat the 7 egg whites until they form stiff peaks, then fold the through the cake mixture. Pour the batter into the prepared cake tin.

Place the cake in the preheated oven and bake for 20 minutes. After 20 minutes, lower the oven temperature to 140°C fan/160°C/325°F/gas mark 3 and continue to cook the cake for a further 20 minutes.

Turn off the oven, cover the cake with a round of buttered parchment paper and leave the cake in the closed oven for 10 minutes more. The cake will deflate in a pleasing fashion. Remove from the oven and allow to cool.

Serve slices of the cake with pieces of warm quince, some of the cooking liquor and a spoonful of crème fraîche.

Olive Oil Cake, Poached Quince & Crème Fraîche
Makes one cake (enough for 6–8)

This is delicious made with Sauternes, but we use whatever sweet wine or homemade digestif we have to hand. On occasion we have strawberry or peach wine kicking around, a glug of that does the job nicely. (Side note: olive oil cake is delicious for breakfast.)

For the cake:
5 whole eggs, plus 2 egg whites
150g/5¼oz/⅔ cup caster (superfine) sugar
1 tbsp mixed grated unwaxed orange and lemon peel
130g/4½oz/1 cup plain (all-purpose) flour, sifted
½ tsp fine salt
120ml/4⅓fl oz/½ cup sweet wine
120ml/4⅓fl oz/½ cup extra virgin olive oil

For the quince:
50ml/1⅔fl oz/2¾ tbsp dry white wine
450ml/15¼fl oz/1¾ cups water
100g/3½oz caster/½ cup (superfine) sugar
2 quinces, peeled, cored and cut into thick wedges
1 bay leaf

Bring the wine and water to the boil over a high heat and stir in the sugar. Add the quinces and the bay leaf, then bring back to the boil again. Turn the heat down to a slow simmer. Taste for sugar: the quince needs a lot of it, so add more if you think it's too acidic. Cover with parchment paper, and cook for a few hours or until the quince is soft and has turned a shocking deep red colour. Turn off the heat and keep the quinces warm in the liquid.

TIELLE SÈTOISE
(OCTOPUS PIE FROM SÈTE)

Serves 6–8

For the octopus:

1 octopus, cooked with a small pinch of saffron (see page 154) and cooled to room temperature

For the pastry:

400g/14oz/3¼ cups plain (all-purpose) flour

5 tbsp lukewarm water

1 tsp dried yeast or 2 tsp fresh yeast

5 tbsp sweet wine (preferably one from Languedoc)

100ml/3½fl oz/½ cup olive oil

1 egg yolk

½ tsp sweet paprika

1 tsp tomato passata

A pinch of fine salt

A pinch of caster (superfine) sugar

To bake:

1 egg yolk and 1 tsp olive oil, beaten together

I've not yet been to Sète, but I'm told that the ubiquitous *tielle* found there is too often a small, crimped, crumbly dry thing sold to tourists on the promenade, like a sort of sad seafood Cornish pasty. I refuse to believe this, for the concept of an octopus pie is surely a sound one.

As with any pie, the key is is the ratio of pastry to filling, and how wet the filling is. The braised octopus should cook down until it is thickened and intensified, with enough sauce to keep things moist, but not so much that the pastry base goes soggy. Traditionally these are sold as individual pies. For pastry: filling ratio reasons, I have made one larger pie to be sliced.

———————

Preheat the oven to 180°C fan/200°C/400°F/gas mark 6.

Mix 50g/1¾oz/¼ cup of the flour with the lukewarm water and yeast in a bowl. Cover with clingfilm (plastic wrap) and rest in a warm place for 30 minutes.

Put the rest of the flour in a large bowl. Make a hole in the centre and add the yeast mixture, followed by all the other ingredients. Mix well and work the dough for a few minutes until smooth. Depending on the flour, you might need to add a little sprinkle of water if the dough looks a bit dry. Cover and leave in a warm place to rise for 1 hour or longer. The dough should almost triple in size.

On a lightly floured work surface, cut the risen dough in half. Roll out one half of the dough into a round about 2-mm/¹⁄₁₆-inch thick. Drape the rolled-out dough over your tart tin. Use whatever tin you have, but one with a removable base is preferable, so that you can turn out the pie to present it whole. Some kind of fluted quiche tin of around 20cm/8 inches in diameter would do the trick. Trim off the excess dough and neaten it up if necessary. Prick the tart shell all over with a fork, line with baking beans or whatever you have, and blind bake the tart shell for 10 minutes. Remove from the oven and allow to cool.

Spread the blind-baked tart shell with the octopus filling. Roll out another round of dough to 2-mm/¹⁄₁₆-inch thickness and drape over the top of the pie. Trim off the edges, then crimp the pie, however you like. Prick the surface of the pie with a fork. Brush the pie all over with the egg yolk and olive oil. Bake in the hot oven for 25–30 minutes until the pastry is crisp and starting to blacken in places.

Remove from the oven and cool on a wire rack. When cool, remove the tart from the tin. Serve at room temperature, or slightly warm, with a green salad.

MIXED GAME, WILD MUSHROOMS, RICE & CHESTNUT STUFFED CABBAGE LEAVES

Serves 4–6

For the stuffing:

1 pheasant breast

1 whole wood pigeon

1 whole partridge

1 tbsp unsalted butter

1 tbsp olive oil

2 shallots, finely chopped

2 garlic cloves, peeled and finely sliced

1 tsp picked thyme leaves

1 large handful mixed fresh wild
    mushrooms, finely chopped

Small handful risotto rice

A decent glug of brandy

6 cooked chestnuts

1 tsp finely chopped parsley

50g/1¾oz pork mince

A grating of nutmeg

Sea salt and freshly ground black
    pepper

For the stock:

The carcasses from the game birds

1 chicken carcass, or a handful of
    chicken wings

1 carrot

1 celery stalk

1 onion, halved

A pinch of whole black peppercorns

2 juniper berries

2 cloves

1 bay leaf

A few parsley stalks

A glug of Madeira (optional)

Choux farcis. We first made this for a game dinner at the restaurant, but happily it has returned to the menu again and again in the autumn and winter months. There are recipes out there for a large preparation involving layers of cabbage leaves and meat, to be baked whole and sliced like a cake (hoorah!), but here are some little individual cabbage rolls.

In my wife's native Poland they call these *gołąbki* (little pigeons). Traditionally made with just meat, rice and onions inside, her Grandma Wiera makes a vegan version with mixed wild mushrooms. This recipe is somewhere between the Polish and an embellished French version. Push past the long ingredients list and convoluted method – these are worth it.

These flavourful packages are poached in a stock made from the game birds, and served hot, floating in a pool of clear broth spiked with dried ceps. A spoonful of crème fraîche adds a cooling richness, and reinforces the eastern European/sour cream connection. If you can't find all the game, stick with the pheasant and pork only, and use chicken stock.

———————

Preheat the oven to 160°C fan/180°C/350°F/gas mark 4.

Take the meat off the bones of the game birds, and reserve the bones for the stock. Set the meats aside in the refrigerator.

To make the stock, take the carcasses from the game birds, as well as the chicken carcass if using, and roast in the preheated oven for 10 minutes, or until the fat has rendered and the bones are lightly browned – don't overdo it. Pluck the bones from the roasting tray and transfer to a pot. Cover with cold water and add the other ingredients. Bring to the boil, then turn down straight away to a simmer, skim well, and continue to cook at a slow blip blip for a good 45 minutes, skimming frequently and diligently. Strain the stock and set aside.

Next, make the chestnut and mushroom rice for the stuffing. Fry the shallots, garlic and picked thyme in the butter and oil until very soft. Season with salt and pepper towards the start of the process. When the shallots are soft, add the wild mushrooms and another pinch of salt. Cook these until soft, then add the risotto rice. Stir well to coat the grains in the fat, then glug in the brandy, followed by a few ladles of the game stock. Simmer the rice in the stock, adding more liquid if necessary, until the rice is soft but not mushy – don't worry about

To finish:

1 knob cold unsalted butter

1 savoy cabbage

1 tbsp dried ceps

4 tsp crème fraîche

1 tbsp hazelnuts, lightly roasted,
   crushed and lightly salted

keeping it al dente. When the rice is ready, crumble the chestnuts into the pot in small pieces. Assess your mixture: the mixture should be slightly loose, as it will firm up as it cools, but not swimming in liquid. If it's too wet, then continue cooking until it looks better. Stir in the chopped parsley, then transfer the rice mixture to a flat tray or big plate and allow to cool to room temperature.

To finish the stuffing, remove any bones that remain in the game, paying attention to the legs of the game birds, which have lots of fine bones. Remove the skin of the pheasant and chop the game meats into small pieces with a sharp knife: by small I mean the size of a dried chickpea (garbanzo bean) or smaller. Mix with the pork mince. Season the mixed meats with salt, pepper and a grating of nutmeg.

Mix the meats well with the (cooled) stuffing. Fry a little patty of the mixture to test for seasoning. It should be nicely seasoned with salt and pepper, but with only a hint of nutmeg. When you are happy with the seasoning, put the stuffing in the fridge while you prepare the cabbage leaves.

Remove the very outer leaves and keep for another purpose. Separate the leaves from the cabbage one by one. Boil the leaves in salted water until soft, drain well, then allow to cool. Trim the tough bottoms of each stalk off the cabbage leaves, then trim the stalk horizontally to reduce the thickness of the stalk: the aim is to trim the stalks so that when the leaves bend, the stalks bend with them. Your knife should be almost flat to the board, cutting so that the stalks are the same thickness as the rest of the leaf.

Put a tablespoon or so of the stuffing inside each of the leaves. Rolling away from you, roll the bottom of the cabbage leaf over the filling, then fold over the two outside flaps, left and right. Holding everything taut, finish rolling the leaf away from you until the filling is completely enclosed. The cabbage leaf should sit on top of the open fold so that it is sealed by its own weight.

Carefully transfer the rolled cabbage leaves to a pot, placing them with the open fold downwards and fitting them snugly together so that they stay closed. Cover about halfway up the packages with the game stock, and put in the dried ceps. Cover the pot with a lid and simmer the cabbage rolls slowly in the stock for around 10 minutes, or until the filling is cooked through and piping hot. The stock should be enriched from the filling of the cabbage rolls, but will need salt – season it now. Add the butter and swirl around until emulsified.

Transfer the cabbage rolls to a shallow bowl; you need two per person, but this depends on the size of the rolls and what you are serving with them. Pour over the hot, seasoned stock and some of the dried ceps that have cooked in it. Spoon over some crème fraîche and scatter with toasted, crushed hazelnuts.

BEEF SHIN, CHESTNUTS, WET POLENTA & GRUYÈRE

Serves 4

For the beef:

1 piece of beef shin (approximately 1.5kg/3lb 5oz), on the bone (butchers are often tempted to cut beef shin into 'thick' slices of about 5cm/2 inches 'like osso bucco', but resist this and ask for a big piece that is a third of a whole shin)

1 tbsp black peppercorns

1 head garlic

1 bay leaf

1 bottle of red wine

1 x 250-g/9-oz packet cooked chestnuts

Salt

For the polenta:

1.2 litres/2 pints/5 cups water

250g/9oz good-quality coarse polenta

100g/3½oz/½ cup unsalted butter

Parmesan cheese

Salt

To serve:

100g/3½oz Gruyère cheese

Good-quality olive oil

Much simpler than a *daube*, this red wine beef stew is based on the Tuscan *peposo*, which is usually pared down to the bare bones – beef, red wine, garlic, pepper and salt. Sometimes I tuck a bay leaf in too alongside the chestnuts that soften and soak up the broth. Wet polenta or mashed potato provide a bit of buttery ballast. Use a proper Gruyère, aged for eighteen months or more, or else something similar like Maréchal, L'Etivaz or Beaufort. Beef shin is an ideal cut for a stew like this. It requires no browning, just lots of time; simmering gently into submission.

To make the beef stew, put the beef shin in a heavy-based pan with all the other ingredients except the chestnuts. Top up with cold water to cover if necessary. Bring the pan to the boil over a high heat, then turn down to a gentle simmer. Using a slotted spoon, skim any scum that gathers on the surface. Be careful when adding salt at this stage. The beef will cook for a long time and the broth will reduce and intensify the seasoning: aim for seasoned but not salty.

Cook the beef shin for 3½–4 hours, or until falling off the bone. It's important the tendons in the shin become soft and gloopy; these are good eating but not when undercooked. When the beef is almost ready, add the chestnuts – keep them as whole as possible at this stage. Either keep the beef warm until ready to serve, or cool and chill in the refrigerator overnight, which will only improve it.

Meanwhile, make the polenta. The polenta should take about an hour to cook so try to time it to be ready roughly at the same time as the beef. Bring the water to the boil in a pan with a lid, then whisk in the polenta in a steady stream. The polenta will soon bubble in a violent volcanic fashion: turn the heat down so that the polenta blip blips slowly. Put on a tight-fitting lid and leave the polenta on the lowest heat possible for around 1 hour. This method, courtesy of an Italian chef who worked with us, requires no stirring! If you rather like stirring, as meditative as it can be, ignore the lid and stir the polenta every 5–10 minutes or so. Top up the water if you feel it is getting a bit too thick. After around 45 minutes to an hour, taste the polenta. It should be thick and creamy, the coarse grains softer and no longer gritty: it is ready. Whisk in the butter, some salt and Parmesan to taste. Keep the polenta covered and warm.

To serve, put some polenta on a plate. Scoop out a piece or two of the melting beef, as well as some of the marrow from the bone. Spoon on a few chestnuts and some of the thin, tasty broth. Drizzle with olive oil and coarsely grate the Gruyère over the top – no Microplanes here, please.

A WHOLE BAKED CHEESE
WITH ALL THE TRIMMINGS

Serves 4

1 x 500-g/1lb 2-oz French raw milk Vacherin (also called Mont D'Or or Vacherin du Haut Doubs), left whole in the box but plastic removed (I speak from experience)

A splash of white wine (something from the Jura would be appropriate)

½ garlic clove, peeled and sliced thinly lengthways

1 thyme sprig

Some delicious waxy potatoes, such as Ratte or Pink Fir, washed well but unpeeled

Some slices of ham and other charcuterie – choose what you prefer – thinly sliced prosciutto, speck, Jésus de Lyon or Jésus Basque Salami, and/or decent cooked ham in slightly thicker slices

Some pickles – cornichons, small Polish pickled cucumbers (ogórki kiszone), some (raw, still crunchy) choucroute, even some spicy, vinegar-pickled, green Turkish peppers

Leafy green salad – lettuces, domestic rocket, mustard leaves

Fresh black Périgord or white Alba truffle (optional but encouraged)

The equivalent of a Sunday roast in the Swiss or French Alps is a fondue, a wholesome family activity for those cold winter nights. I have never hosted a fondue party (a bit too seventies for my taste), but I have baked a whole cheese for friends: a self-contained party in a box.

Camembert is readily available and will feed two, but Vacherin, in season during the autumn and winter, is the connoisseur's cheese of choice. Vacherin is a raw cows' milk cheese, wrapped in strips of spruce and washed in salted water. At the start of the season the young cheeses are milky and pine-resin sweet, then as the age develops they acquire more than a hint of farmyard funk and a texture as smooth as silk.

A whole 500g/1lb 2oz Vacherin will feed four, but there are larger ones too: stud with garlic and thyme, douse with white wine, then bake in a hot oven and the cheese emerges golden, blistered and bubbling in its box. Any Sunday roast needs its trimmings, and this one requires things to dip into the molten goo – waxy boiled potatoes, hams (both cured and cooked), a leafy green salad dressed with mustard, and sharp pickles to cut thorough the fat. Gild the lily with a grating or slices of black Périgord or white Alba truffle, and this meal becomes rather special indeed.

Preheat the oven to 180°C fan/200°C/400°F/gas mark 6.

Unwrap the Vacherin. Remove the box lid, setting it aside for later, then remove and discard the plastic wrapping. Cut some slits in the cheese and push in the garlic and little bits of thyme. Drizzle a glug of white wine over the top. Put the lid back on the box to cover the cheese, put it on a roasting tray to catch any drips, and bake in the hot oven for around 30–45 minutes, or until the cheese is molten, bubbling and the smell fills the whole house.

Meanwhile, boil the potatoes in salted water, slice the charcuterie if necessary, and dress the salad with a light mustardy vinaigrette. Arrange the charcuterie, pickles and potatoes on a large platter. Lift up the lid and shave over a generous helping of truffles (if using). To eat, scoop out spoons of cheese straight onto the waiting potatoes, and pick away at the vast platter of charcuterie, taking intermittent bites of pickle to see you through.

SLOW-COOKED PORK SHOULDER WITH WINTER SAVORY

Serves 4

¼ pork shoulder (approximate weight 2kg/4lb 6oz), boneless, skin removed, but with all the fat still on

2 heads of garlic, broken into cloves

1 large woody branch of winter savory – no messing around – or bay or sage

1 tbsp fennel seeds

1 dried red chilli (nothing too hot), broken into pieces

8 salted anchovy fillets (optional, but very good)

A couple of (posh) plum tomatoes from a jar

½ bottle dry white wine

1 tsp best-quality red wine vinegar

Salt and freshly ground black pepper

To serve (some ideas):

Swiss chard

Fresh white beans (Coco de Paimpol)

Your best olive oil

Green sauce (see page 217, optional)

And quite a lot of garlic. Choose an old-fashioned rare breed of pork such as Tamworth or Gloucester Old Spot, and a piece of shoulder that still has a nice thick bit of fat on it. The fat will keep the meat moist as it renders slowly into the broth. Winter savory is a punchy herb very typical of the Provençal hillsides, and one of my favourites; it's like a cross between rosemary and thyme, leaning heavily on the woody thyme flavour. If you can't find it, use both of the above, or just (fresh) bay leaves or a branch of myrtle. The anchovies are optional but add a savoury, unfishy depth of flavour.

Season the pork well with salt and pepper. Brown the pork in olive oil in a big pan – do this slowly to avoid scorching and to best render a little of the fat. Remove the pork to a plate.

Scrape up any excess salt that has gathered at the bottom of the pot. Add the garlic, savory or bay or sage, fennel seeds, chilli and anchovies, stir briefly in the leftover fat, then return the pork to the pan. Tear in the tomatoes in small pieces, then pour in the wine. Top up with water if needed: the pork doesn't need to be completely covered, but the liquid should sit about three-quarters of the way up the meat.

Bring to the boil over high heat, then turn down to a very gentle simmer and put a lid on top. Cook the pork for around 3 hours, or until the meat tears into soft pieces when explored with a pair of tongs. The connective tissue needs to be soft and delicious. The pork should be yielding, but take care not to overcook – we're not making a pork sauce for pasta. Add the teaspoon of vinegar, and check the seasoning for salt – both the broth and the meat should be delicious.

To serve, boil the Swiss chard and dress with olive oil and red wine vinegar. Warm the beans and pour in some olive oil, then plate the beans followed by the chard. Using tongs, pick out a few nice pieces of pork – leave the bigger pieces of fat if you want. Spoon over some of the juices. Drizzle the lot with some more good olive oil. A nice green sauce with anchovies, capers and mustard would be delicious here, but isn't strictly necessary.

MIXED GRILL WITH
MUSTARD SAUCE & SHOESTRING FRIES

Per person:

1 whole quail

1 lamb's kidney

1 Toulouse sausage

1 tbsp good chicken stock

1 tsp crème fraîche

1 tarragon sprig, leaves picked

6 or so salted capers (soaked well)

1 tsp Dijon mustard

½ tsp cold unsalted butter,
   cut into small cubes

1 medium starchy potato
   (such as a King Edward)

Sunflower oil, for frying

Sea salt and freshly ground
   black pepper

This recipe isn't quite your 8-oz steak, onion rings, gammon and grilled tomato medley, although any way you cut it, a mixed grill is always a thing of beauty. Don't feel bound to cook too many meats: a mix of two is still a mix. I derive a simple satisfaction from deliberating over what the mix should be: steak, bone marrow and snails; lamb chop, sweetbreads and whole ceps; brochettes of lamb leg, calves' liver, bacon and bread; half a grouse, sausage and chips. There's much fun to be had.

Here's one with a spatchcocked quail, fat, garlicky Toulouse sausage, lamb's kidney, pink in the middle, and a simple mustard cream sauce to tie everything together. A pile of shoestring fries sits in a nest, absorbing the sauce and soaking up the juices from the meat.

To spatchcock a quail, using sturdy kitchen scissors, cut out the backbone. Pushing down on the breast with the palm of your hand, press the bird flat.

Trim any suet from the lamb's kidney and remove the thin membrane. Cut the kidney in half laterally to keep its curved shape. Remove the tough fatty core.

Lightly oil both the quail and kidney, then season with salt and pepper. Lightly oil the sausage. Grill the sausage, quail and kidneys (listed here in order of how long each takes to cook). This would be done preferably over a charcoal and/ or wood fire, but under the oven grill (broiler) will do fine. I don't need to tell you how to cook a sausage, but the quail should be charred a lively golden brown, with a slight bounce when pressed at the breast, remaining a light pink inside. Grill the kidneys quickly and keep them a pink inside too. When the meats are cooked, set aside to rest in a warm place while you make the sauce.

Bring the stock to a simmer in a pan over a low heat. Whisk in the crème fraîche, tarragon, capers and mustard in that order. Bring back to simmering point, but don't let the sauce boil or it will split. Whisk in the cubes of cold butter. Taste the sauce for balance. Add more salt, mustard or crème fraîche as needed.

Peel the potato and cut it into long matchsticks, or julienne. Deep fry in hot (180°C/350°F) sunflower oil for about a minute or until golden brown and crisp. Drain on paper towels and season the fries lightly with salt.

Pour the sauce onto a plate or serving platter and arrange the meats on top, along with any resting juices. Pile up the shoestring fries on the same plate.

ROAST JOHN DORY, CLAMS, POTATOES, ARTICHOKES & ROSEMARY

Serves 4

4–6 Desiree or other red potatoes

2 tbsp olive oil, plus extra for frying

4 stem artichokes, outer leaves removed, tops cut off, choke removed and peeled of any woody green bits – keep in lemony water to stop them discolouring

1 posh peeled tomato from a jar

1 whole John Dory (weighing at least 1kg/2lb 4oz), scaled, gutted, head on, but spiky fins removed

1 woody branch of rosemary

1 tsp fennel seeds

125ml/4fl oz/½ cup dry white wine

500g/1lb 2oz palourde clams, washed well and checked over

1 tbsp chopped parsley

Sea salt and freshly ground black pepper

John Dory is a fine fish and I buy it whenever I can. It suits itself well to roasting whole, and cooking the fish over potatoes supplies some starch to soak up the winey juices. Clams, artichokes, rosemary and fish make for an elegant combination, and you won't need anything else with it.

———————

Preheat the oven to 200°C fan/220°C/425°F/gas mark 7.

First, pre-cook the potatoes: peel them and cut into slices a little thinner than 1cm/½ inch. Bring some salted water to the boil and slide in the slices of potato. Cook at a gentle simmer for around 5 minutes, or until the potatoes are just cooked through but not falling apart. Gently remove the potatoes with a slotted spoon and allow to cool on a tray. When cool, fry the potatoes in some hot olive oil until they are lightly coloured.

Line a roasting tin big enough to fit the fish with parchment paper, and put the potatoes in.

Cut the prepared artichokes in half, then into wedges of around 1cm/½ inch thickness. You'll be roasting them from raw with the fish so take care not to cut them too thick (they will stay raw) or too thin (burnt to a crisp). Season the artichokes with salt, drizzle lightly with olive oil, then mingle them in with the potatoes in the tray. Tear the tomato into small pieces and mix in with the vegetables – you want just enough tomato to provide an extra hit of acidity and add a little colour, but you aren't cooking the fish in tomato sauce.

Season the John Dory on both sides and rub with olive oil. Put the branch of rosemary atop the potatoes and artichokes, followed by the fish. Scatter over the fennel seeds, pour over the white wine (pour the wine around the fish to avoid washing off the seasoning) and drizzle everything liberally with olive oil.

Put the tray into the hot oven and roast for 10 minutes before adding the clams. Cook for a further 5 minutes, or until the clams have all opened (discard any that refuse to) and the fish is cooked. To test the doneness of the fish, insert a skewer into the thickest piece near the head. If the skewer meets any resistance in the flesh, then return to the oven for a couple more minutes.

When it's ready remove the tray from the oven. The fish should be lightly golden, the artichokes cooked through, the clams open and the assembly should be sitting in a delicious pool of intense roasting juices. Scatter the tray with parsley and take it to the table.

ALIGOT (WITH TOULOUSE SAUSAGES & SAFFRON TRIPE STEW)

Serves 4

For the aligot (this makes quite a lot):

1kg/2lb 4oz floury potatoes

500g/1lb 2oz Aligot cheese (Tomme Fraîche de Cantal, de Laguiole or de l'Aubrac, or failing that, some young Cantal or Cheddar)

2 garlic cloves, peeled and crushed with a little salt

250ml/8fl oz/1 cup hot milk

100ml/3½fl oz/½ cup double (heavy) cream

150g/5¼oz/⅔ cup butter

Mooching around the Aveyron, one might spot by the roadside a cheap plastic banner advertisting a mysterious event called an Aligot Géant. Aligot is an Auvergnat speciality of mashed potato with cheese and garlic. An Aligot Géant is a giant version of this dish, but what is actually being advertised here is a royal knees-up fuelled by vast quantities of potatoes, cheese, grilled sausages, tripe and dodgy music. I first encountered aligot at a local village garlic festival near Albi, where a rustic farmhand type with rippling biceps was manoeuvring a large wooden paddle and stirring with great virtuosity a huge pot. In this way the man worked at his task for a good half an hour, sweating in the summer heat, until slowly the crowd moved in when the aligot was ready. Paper plates were passed around, onto which was slopped a stringy mass of hot cheesy mash. Some sizzling grilled sausages were snipped off the links onto the awaiting plates, and the crowd tucked in.

Hot mashed potato with cheese is perhaps not the first thing that springs to mind to eat on a hot Saturday in August, so I usually wait until the colder months. Aligot uses a cheese called Tomme Fraîche de Cantal: very young, unsalted, squeaky curds that, when melted, go really stringy. When the aligot is ready and 'ça file' (it runs), as they say, it's impossible to tell where potato ends and melted cheese begins. Despite the generous amount of garlic, aligot can be bland on it's own and so grilled sausages are a great accompaniment here, but I think it's nice to have something a little wetter too. A traditional accompaniment is a 'tripoux', a bundle of sheep's tripe and feet, which I haven't yet attempted, because it doesn't sound very nice.

When we cooked our own version of an Aligot Géant at the restaurant, which sadly didn't feature any dodgy music and dancing, we made a (cow's) tripe stew with saffron, tomato, bacon and white wine, which went down a treat. Our friend Adam gave us the gift of a giant, engraved, ceremonial spoon, which we used to stir the pot enthusiastically and carried around the restaurant slopping top-ups of aligot both onto people's plates and all over the floor. A success!

For the tripe stew:

500g/1lb 2oz cow's honeycomb tripe

50g/1¾oz pancetta, diced

1 tbsp olive oil

2 medium onions, finely diced

2 celery sticks, finely diced

2 garlic cloves, peeled and finely
  sliced lengthways

1 tsp fennel seeds

2 bay leaves

1 thyme sprig

Small pinch of saffron

1 carrot, peeled and diced

½ x 400-g/14-oz can peeled plum
  tomatoes, drained of any water or
  juice, or 250g/9oz fresh tomatoes,
  blanched and skinned

½ bottle white wine

A glug of brandy

1 tbsp chopped parsley

Sea salt and freshly ground black
  pepper

To serve:

Parmesan cheese

Grilled Toulouse sausages

The best tripe is washed but unbleached, however this is increasingly hard to get hold of. Uncleaned green (i.e. brown) tripe is positively unsanitary, but if you can find it already washed and cleaned then it has a much, much better flavour. Bleaching tripe renders it more palatable and less smelly, but does remove a lot of its charm. If you can get your hands on green tripe then before using wash it well, soak it, and bring it to the boil twice, throwing away the water each time. For me, the honeycomb section is the best bit.

If the tripe is washed but unbleached, bring the tripe, in one big piece, to the boil in unsalted cold water. Drain the tripe, throw away the water, then wash briefly and repeat once. If the tripe is bleached these steps are unnecessary.

To make the tripe stew, chop the tripe into 2-cm/¾-inch squares. Fry the pancetta in the olive oil, then add the onions, celery, garlic, fennel seeds, bay leaves and thyme. Fry the soffrito slowly together for 30 minutes, or until soft and sweet. Add the saffron, stir around, then add the carrot. Stir together and cook for a few minutes, then add the blanched and chopped tripe. Continue cooking for a further few minutes until the tripe has absorbed some of the oil and flavour from the soffrito, then add the tomatoes and a good pinch of salt. Cook for a few minutes until it starts to look like a rough sauce, then add the wine and brandy. Top up with water if necessary, bring to the boil, skim, then turn down to a slow simmer and cook for 2½–3 hours, until the tripe is tender and the stew tasting full, rounded and delicious. Season with salt and pepper, stir in the parsley and serve with grated Parmesan on top.

For the aligot, cut the potatoes into medium-sized chunks and simmer (from cold) in lightly salted water until soft. Drain the potatoes and allow them to release steam for a few minutes. Mash the potatoes well, then return to the empty pot. Add the crushed garlic, milk, butter and cream, and stir well to combine. Over a low heat, stirring the potatoes all the while, add the Aligot cheese, cut up into 1-cm/½-inch pieces, bit by bit. I have found that it is best to stir in only one direction. As all the cheese melts into the potatoes, the cheese will start to go stringy. If your potatoes feel a bit too stiff, add a little extra warm milk. Cook until the aligot is stringy enough to fall in a long, unbroken strand from the spoon held high over the pot. Check the salt, and it is ready.

Serve the hot, stringy aligot with grilled Toulouse sausages and the tripe stew. Don't make the aligot wait for either its accompaniments or the guests as, when kept for too long, it loses its stringiness.

NIÇOISE-STYLE PORCHETTA

Serves 8, hopefully with leftovers
for sandwiches

Note: A Stanley knife is an important
tool for scoring the pork skin, and
you'll need some butcher's string

1 large bunch Swiss chard, leaves only
(reserve the stalks for something
else), washed

1 tbsp risotto rice

2 tbsp chopped offal from the pig –
kidney, heart and liver, whatever
your butcher has – 1 kidney and a
bit of liver will be plenty

1 tbsp fennel seeds, crushed in a
pestle and mortar

1 tsp grated unwaxed orange zest

1 fat garlic clove, peeled and crushed

1 tsp olive oil

3kg/6lb 8oz boneless porchetta joint
(a piece of pork loin with the belly
still attached, skin on, and all bones
removed)

Salt

Porchetta crossed the hills from Piedmont to Nice a long time ago. A true *porchetta Niçoise* differs from the Italian version in that it's made with a whole suckling pig, stuffed with itself: all of the offals and some of the loin meat, chopped up and seasoned with sage and pepper, to be served cold in a thin slice with roast potatoes. I won't propose that you buy a whole suckling pig and stuff it with its innards, so this recipe is a hybrid – a boneless loin and belly cut with a stuffing of Swiss chard, rice, a few wobbly bits. By way of seasoning, I find sage overpowering, so rosemary is my herb of choice. Fennel seeds are a given. A little orange zest adds pep.

Bring some water to the boil, add some salt, then throw in the rice. Boil until it's almost cooked, then put in the chard leaves. Cook until both are soft, then drain well and set aside to cool. Squeeze out all of the excess water and chop the chard finely. Mix the chard with the chopped offal, some salt, the fennel seeds, orange zest, crushed garlic and the olive oil.

Take a look at the pork. The loin is much fatter than the belly, so we're going to even that up a little bit for ease of rolling. Place the pork skin-side down on the work surface. Use a knife to score deeply along the length of the pork loin, pushing down to flatten it out a bit. Don't get carried away. Season the pork flesh with salt, then spread evenly with the stuffing. Roll up the porchetta, starting with the loin end, so that the loin is in the middle of the roasting joint. Tie the porchetta up as tightly as you can with butcher's string.

Score the skin, as deep as you can go without cutting into the fat underneath. Make the scores as wide as you want your slices to be – 5mm/¼ inch is ideal, as you'll want to cut it into thin slices. Season the rolled porchetta well with fine salt. Leave the joint out at room temperature for at least 2 hours, or cover with aluminium foil and put it in the refrigerator overnight, if it fits. This will help to dry out the skin to facilitate crisping. If you do keep it in the refrigerator overnight, make sure you remove it from the refrigerator at least an hour before cooking.

Meanwhile, preheat the oven to 160°C fan/180°C/350°F/gas mark 4.

Roast the porchetta in the hot oven for 3½ hours, or until the internal temperature is around 58°C/135°F. Remove the pork and increase the heat to maximum. When the oven has reached temperature, return the pork to the very hot oven. Roast for a further 20–30 minutes to crisp up the crackling, but watch it like a hawk as it can quickly catch too much colour. Remove from the oven and rest for at least 45 agonising minutes before slicing thinly.

CHOCOLATE, HAZELNUT & PEAR TART

Makes 1 galette, to serve 6–8

For the pastry:

1 quantity of sweet shortcrust pastry
(see Apricot & Brown Butter Tart
on page 76)

For the filling:

65g/2oz dark chocolate
(minimum 70% cocoa solids)

135g/5oz hazelnuts

A pinch of salt

200g/6½oz/¾ cups unsalted butter,
cubed and softened

165g/6oz/¾ cups caster (superfine)
sugar

2 eggs

4 pears

Crème fraîche, to serve

Chocolate and hazelnuts are both excellent partners for pears and are brought together in this tart, which is similar to a hazelnut frangipane but with chocolate added to the mix. Making this tart is an absolutely delicious winter morning's activity.

Preheat the oven to 170°C fan/190°C/375°F/gas mark 5.

Following the instructions on page 76, make the sweet shortcrust pastry and use it to line a 24-cm/9-inch tart tin, then blind bake the pastry case. Remove the tart case from the oven and leave to cool.

Reduce the oven temperature to 160°C fan/180°C/350°F/gas mark 4 for baking the tart.

To make the filling, first pulse-chop the chocolate into small pieces in a food processor. Transfer to a bowl and set aside. Add the hazelnuts to the food processor with the pinch of salt and blitz to a very fine powder, but try not to overwork the mixture as it can become a little greasy as the oils are released from the nuts. Transfer the hazelnuts to another bowl and set aside. Add the softened butter and the sugar to the food processor and blitz until smooth. Return the powdered hazelnuts and blitz briefly, before adding the eggs, one by one, with the motor running. Finally, return the blitzed chocolate and pulse briefly to combine.

Peel the pears, then halve and core them. Place the pears in the blind-baked tart case cut-side down, but arranged however you like. (I usually place the pears in the tart case so that the thin ends point towards the centre.) Pour the filling mixture over the pears. You may not need quite all of it, and bear in mind it will expand during cooking anyway.

Bake the tart for 45 minutes. Allow to cool before cutting.

Serve with crème fraîche.

BUCKWHEAT CRÊPES WITH APPLES COOKED IN CALVADOS

Serves 6–8

For the pancakes:

60g/2oz/¼ cup unsalted butter, plus
    extra for frying

150g/5¼oz/1 cup plain
    (all-purpose) flour

75g/2½oz buckwheat flour

1 tbsp granulated sugar

A pinch of salt

450ml/15fl oz/1¾ cups whole milk

1 tbsp olive oil

125ml/4fl oz/½ cup beer

4 eggs

For the apples:

4 apples, such as Cox's, Russet
    or Granny Smith's

50g/1¾oz/¼ cup cold unsalted butter

A tiny pinch of salt

1 tbsp Calvados or cider brandy

Vanilla ice cream (shop-bought is fine,
    but the best quality you can find),
    to serve

Buckwheat flour pancakes – strictly galettes rather than crêpes – are traditionally savoury. While very nice with ham, cheese and egg, or salmon, asparagus and cream, here we're serving them with apples cooked in butter and Calvados, the apple brandy from the north of France. The buckwheat adds a delicious sour note that stands up well to sweet fruit and a glug of booze. The apples for this should be an eating variety; one that won't fall apart when cooked, such as Cox's, Russet or Granny Smith's.

The day before, to make the crêpes, melt the butter and then leave to cool. Mix the flours, sugar and salt in a food processor. With the motor running, add the milk and oil, then the cooled melted butter and beer, then the eggs, one by one. Leave the batter to rest overnight in the refrigerator.

For the apples, peel, core and cut the apples into wedges. Heat a generous knob of the butter in a pan and cook the apples, with a tiny pinch of salt, until they are quite soft. Add the Calvados or brandy, and cook with the apples until the apples are soft but not falling apart. Add the rest of the butter and a little splash of water to make a sauce. Keep the apples warm but don't reduce the sauce too much as it provides much-needed lubrication for the crêpes.

When it's time to cook the crêpes, melt a small knob of butter in a non-stick pan. Swirl the butter around, then spoon in a ladle of batter. Tip the pan around to form a circular pancake. The batter should form lacy holes as it hits the hot fat. Cook the crêpe for half a minute on each side (the first one, as always with pancakes, will be a disaster). Fold the crêpe into quarters and serve on a plate with the warm apples, some of the juices from the fruit, and a scoop of vanilla ice cream.

RHUBARB GALETTE

Makes a 28-cm/11-inch tart

For the pastry:

250g/9oz/1¾ cups plain
   (all-purpose) flour

175g/6oz/¾ cup cold butter,
   cut into 2-cm/5-inch cubes

2 tbsp caster (superfine) sugar

A pinch of salt

2 tbsp ice-cold water

For the filling:

500g/1lb 2oz forced rhubarb,
   cut into 6-cm/2-inch batons,
   trimmings saved to make a syrup

Finely grated zest of 1 unwaxed
   orange

Juice of ½ orange

200g/7oz/1 cup caster
   (superfine) sugar, plus extra for
   sprinkling

A pinch of salt

1 tbsp sweet dessert wine
   such as Muscat (optional)

25g/1oz/2 tbsp butter, melted

To glaze the galette:

1 egg yolk

A dash of cream

1 tbsp demerera sugar

Vanilla ice cream or crème fraîche, to
   serve

Rhubarb is the galette I turn to in the winter when the forced rhubarb comes into season. This one is particularly nice served warm, with some crème fraîche or a scoop of vanilla ice cream. A nice little touch here is to cook the trimmings from the rhubarb down into a sticky syrup, which can be used to glaze the fruit straight after it comes out of the hot oven.

Sift the flour into a bowl. Add half the butter and work it into the flour with your hands until the mixture resembles fine breadcrumbs. Add the remaining butter, but this time keep the butter in pieces the size of chickpeas (garbanzo beans). When the pastry is rolled out, those pieces of butter will make your pastry puffed and flaky. Drizzle in the ice-cold water, little by little, until the pastry dough is about to come together. Pick up the dough lightly with your hands and drop it back into the bowl to encourage the pastry to come together, but don't work or knead it.

Once the pastry comes together, wrap it in clingfilm (plastic wrap) and chill it in the refrigerator for an hour or so. Roll out the pastry between two sheets of parchment paper to a 3-mm/¼-inch thickness. Peel back the parchment and flip the pastry over to avoid sticking. Chill the rolled pastry again before filling.

Preheat the oven to 220°C fan/240°C/475°F/gas mark 9. Take the rolled pastry out of the refrigerator and remove the top layer of parchment.

Toss the rhubarb with the orange zest, orange juice, sugar, salt and wine. Mix well, then arrange the rhubarb on the rolled out pastry, leaving a 5-cm/2-inch border on all sides. Fold the pastry around the rhubarb, overlapping slightly to form a rough crimp. Brush the fruit with the melted butter, then sprinkle with some extra sugar. Repeat with more butter and sugar. Mix the egg yolk with the cream and brush the edges of pastry, then sprinkle them with demerara sugar.

Return the galette to the refrigerator while you preheat a heavy baking tray. Once hot, slide the galette on its parchment paper onto the tray and bake in the oven for 15 minutes (this helps to cook the pastry base). Reduce the heat to 180°C fan/200°C/400°F/gas mark 6 and cook for a further 30 minutes, or until the pastry is crisp and golden brown and the fruit is soft, juicy and bubbling.

Meanwhile, make the glaze: cook the rhubarb trimmings (about 50g/1¾oz) with just enough water to cover and 2 tbsp sugar. The rhubarb will be soft after 5–10 minutes of simmering. Strain the rhubarb and reduce this liquid slightly. Once out of the oven, brush the fruit with the rhubarb glaze. Allow to cool, but perhaps not all the way, and serve with vanilla ice cream or crème fraîche.

INDEX

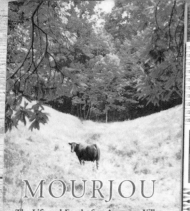

MOURJOU

The Life and Food of an Auvergne Village

PETER GRAHAM

PROSPECT BOOKS

THE ALICE B. TOKLAS COOKBOOK

Summer Cooking

Elizabeth David

Recipes from CORSICA

ROLLI LUCAROTTI

RICHARD OLNEY
foreword by Alice Waters

LULU'S PROVENÇAL TABLE

The Food and Wine from Domaine Tempier Vineyard

Armand Arnal

BRUT DE CAMARGUE
CUISINE SOUS INFLUENCE LOCALE

Photographies de Martin Bruno

Keribus éditions   ACTES SUD

A CATALAN COOKERY BOOK

IRVING DAVIS

CHEZ PANISSE MENU COOKBOOK

ALICE WATERS

A Table in PROVENCE

Classic Recipes from the South of France

Collected & Illustrated by Leslie Forbes

LE CUISINIER PROVENÇAL

ÉDOUARD LOUBET

LES 100 RECETTES INCONTOURNABLES

SKIRA

Elizabeth
David
French Provincial
Cooking

Madame Prunier's
FISH COOKERY BOOK

1,000 Famous Recipes
Edited by Ambrose Heath
Illustrated
HUTCHINSON

J.-B. REBOUL

LA
CUISINIÈRE PROVENÇALE

P. TACUSSEL ÉDITEUR
MARSEILLE

ELIZABETH
DAVID

A Book of
Mediterranean Food

HONEY FROM A WEED
PATIENCE GRAY

FASTING AND FEASTING
IN TUSCANY, CATALONIA,
THE CYCLADES AND APULIA

When French
Women Cook
A GASTRONOMIC MEMOIR WITH OVER 250 RECIPES

Madeleine Kamman
Foreword by Shirley Corriher

Sardegna in Bocca

GULLIVER

The Cooking of
South-West France

Paula Wolfert

TOULOUSE-LAUTREC MAURICE JOYANT
THE ART OF CUISINE

LA MÈRE
BRAZIER

THE MOTHER OF
MODERN FRENCH COOKING

MÈRE
BRAZIER

'Three-hundred recipes from the small
restaurant that opened in 1921 and came to embody
the heart and soul of Lyonnais cooking.'
THE NEW YORK TIMES

EUGÉNIE BRAZIER
Foreword by Paul Bocuse Translation by Drew Smith

AUTHOR'S ACKNOWLEDGEMENTS

This book is dedicated to my little family, Pat and Zofia, and also to Peg, who might have been proud.

Thank you:

To the rest of my family, for being as into food as I am.

To the whole team at Pavilion Books, and in particular Steph, Helen, Katie, Michelle and Polly, as well as Lisa and Jane.

To Caz and the rest of the team at Here Design.

To Rebecca and Nat (@whatwashad) for their fantastic illustrations.

To Matt for his excellent photography and cheap laughs, and to Aya for holding it all together.

To my agent Emily, for her support and words of wisdom.

To my friend Max, and to his flat in Invalides, a fridge full of French cheeses, and Claude the Mouse, buried next to Napoleon.

To the entire staff, past and present, of Sardine, and in particular Alex Vines, not just for several of the recipes in this book but also some brilliant off-the-cuff cooking on the nights in question. Baldo and Marina for many years long and faithful service, Louisa for steering the ship in my absence, Clo for her eclectic bar stock legacy, Kosta for keeping it all running smoothly and giving me excellent wine to drink. Adam for making the restaurant busier. Liam for his unseen efforts behind the scenes. Pierre for all his support.

To all our loyal customers at Sardine, without whom none of this would have happened.

To Stevie, for many years of light-hearted bullying/mentoring, many great recipes (I stole it first!), and for teaching me a sensibility that's hard to teach.

PUBLISHER'S ACKNOWLEDGEMENTS

The Publishers would like to thank Matt Russell for photography and @whatwashad for illustration. Book design concept by Here Design, www.heredesign.co.uk.

First published in the United Kingdom in 2019 by Pavilion, 43 Great Ormond Street, London WC1N 3HZ

Copyright © Pavilion Books Company Ltd 2019
Text copyright © Alex Jackson 2019

All rights reserved. No part of this publication may be copied, displayed, extracted, reproduced, utilised, stored in a retrieval system or transmitted in any form or by any means, electronic, mechanical or otherwise including but not limited to photocopying, recording, or scanning without the prior written permission of the publishers.

ISBN 978-1-91162-438-7 (*Sardine*)
ISBN 978-1-91164-112-4 (*Provençal*)

A CIP catalogue record for this book is available from the British Library.

10 9 8 7 6 5 4 3 2 1

Printer is 1010 Printing International Ltd, China
Reproduction by Mission, Hong Kong

www.pavilionbooks.com

FSC
MIX
Paper from responsible sources
FSC® C016973